WRITING TO THE MOMENT

Tom Paulin was born in Leeds in 1949 and grew up in Belfast. He was educated at the universities of Hull and Oxford. His most recent collection of poetry, *Walking a Line*, was published in 1994 and was shortlisted for the T. S. Eliot Prize. Well known for his appearances on the BBC's *Late Review*, he is the G. M. Young lecturer in English Literature at Hertford College, Oxford University, and is writing a book on William Hazlitt.

by the same author

poetry
A STATE OF JUSTICE
THE STRANGE MUSEUM
LIBERTY TREE
FIVEMILETOWN
SELECTED POEMS 1972–1990
WALKING A LINE

adaptations
THE RIOT ACT: a version of Sophocles' *Antigone*
SEIZE THE FIRE: a version of Aeschylus' *Prometheus Bound*

play
THE HILLSBOROUGH SCRIPT: a dramatic satire

anthologies
THE FABER BOOK OF POLITICAL VERSE
THE FABER BOOK OF VERNACULAR VERSE

criticism
THOMAS HARDY: THE POETRY OF PERCEPTION
IRELAND AND THE ENGLISH CRISIS
MINOTAUR: POETRY AND THE NATION STATE

Writing to the Moment

SELECTED CRITICAL ESSAYS

1980–1996

Tom Paulin

faber and faber

First published in 1996
by Faber and Faber Limited
3 Queen Square London WC1N 3AU
This paperback edition first published in 1998

Photoset by Wilmaset Ltd, Wirral
Printed and bound in Great Britain by
Mackays of Chatham PLC, Chatham, Kent

A CIP record for this book
is available from the British Library

ISBN 0–571–17582–1

2 4 6 8 10 9 7 5 3 1

for Karl Miller

I am grateful to the editors who commissioned these essays and reviews for: *Encounter*, *Field Day Anthology of Irish Writing*, *Honest Ulsterman*, *John Clare: A Bicentenary Celebration*, *Independent on Sunday*, *London Review of Books*, *New Statesman*, *Observer*, *Quarto*, *Sewanee Review*.

'The Tender Voice: Thomas Hardy', 'Political Verse', and 'Vernacular Verse' were originally introductions to *Thomas Hardy: The Poetry of Perception*, *The Faber Book of Political Verse* and *The Faber Book of Vernacular Verse*. 'A New Look at the Language Question' was originally published as a Field Day pamphlet.

T.P.

Contents

Introduction

At some point in the 1980s, a graduate student showed me a copy of the literary magazine *Stand* and opened it at a review of some recent volumes of poetry. The reviewer was Terry Eagleton. Would this be the same Terry Eagleton who writes literary theory? the student asked. It would, I said. He looked confused and disappointed. Eagleton's accessible, even blokeish, reviewing style contrasted with the highly technical vocabulary and uninflected, rather flymo mode of his theoretical writings. The gap between literary journalism and theory has never appeared wider to me than it did in that conversation.

Ideally, journalism and theory should support or challenge each other, but instead they go their separate ways and don't communicate. Even so, it's clear to most contemporary critics that literary theory has effected a huge sea change in the way criticism is now written. I know it has changed my own critical practice, though I still find it impossible to offer theoretical readings of literary texts. Brushed — scratched even — by theory, I'm unable to theorize or apply many of the highly sophisticated concepts and technical terms that have evolved from this type of critical practice. For a long time, I also found it impossible to sit down and devote several years to writing what publishers in rejection letters now term a 'single-author study'. Introduction, chapters developing an argument, conclusion, bibliography, index. I've read many such studies and have a reverential admiration for some of them. In the early 1970s, I spent four years writing a critical study of Thomas Hardy's poetry, then doubted the enterprise shortly after the book was published, and as an alternative began writing essays and reviewing. All the time, there nagged at me the sense that I should be writing a proper book – one that was coherent and centred on a single subject that had first been densely researched.

Though I've always believed that the wellspring of literary criticism is the essay – a difficult form, like the short story – I nevertheless held the view that a collection of essays and reviews wasn't enough. As I gathered various pieces into two collections – *Ireland and the English Crisis* and *Minotaur* – I came to see that these couldn't be completely random gatherings. Some pieces didn't fit and had to be excluded, others demanded to be written so they could be added. Nevertheless, both collections are haphazard, full of gaps, loose ends, hits and misses. As an occasional subscriber to the loose-cannon school of literary criticism, I don't at all mind the roller-coaster, even at times loopy, effect of this kind of uncontrolled searching for an idea. Partly this is because collections of critical essays cannot, and should not, aim to be definitive and unified. They are random – the term I want is 'decentred' – gatherings in which each essay or review should support or strike sparks off the others. Where a book-length critical study is a series of consecutive chapters moving to a conclusion, a collection of essays is less a linear progress than a framed group of animated particles in complex relation with one another – quick, sudden, paired, then all spread out, now bunched together or marking time. Rather like a team playing fast and furious in a match, each member of the group has a dynamic relation to the player running with the ball, the essay we're currently reading. There can be a lucky quality, a winning streak, to this kind of critical writing.

However, selections of essays aren't so lucky. So why select?

The reason is that most of the essays gathered here have either been out of print for a long time or were published only in weekly or fortnightly papers many days before yesterday. I wanted to call back the occasions they represent and to chuck a few stones back in the pond.

From my early teens, I've been fascinated by journalism, particularly by those journalists who run counter to social orthodoxies. My first journalistic hero – I'm talking of the early 1960s, when I was just adolescent – was Ralph Bossence, the political correspondent of

The Newsletter, Belfast's Unionist morning paper. Bossence was, I believe – he could never say so – a supporter of the Northern Ireland Labour Party, and his articles were coded critiques of the criminally narrow-minded politicians who ran the state before disaster struck it later that decade. I never knew him, though I once glimpsed his tubby figure ambling from the newspaper offices in the centre of Belfast to the Duke of York near by, the bar where he met up with his cronies and where, I learnt much later, Gerry Adams was the curate who listened to their stories while he served drinks. Bud Bossence's powerless decency and exasperation shone through his writing. As the Troubles in Ulster deepened he became almost a talismanic figure for me – I could catch a Joycean Bloomabloom leitmotif whenever I thought of him.

Recalling this lonely working journalist is only to try and fix a local emotion and a beginning. At school, I studied Orwell and Swift, and caught the naked gritty direct plainness of their prose styles. More recently I've been fascinated by the swelling cadences of Hazlitt's essays, and have discovered that he sought to embody the practice of critical and political journalism in a series of images which express its ephemeral kinetic force.

Historically, this eager, volatile, intense form of consciousness would appear to be one of the legacies of the Reformation. The free individual conscience and the accompanying concept of free speech shape the critical essay – in Hazlitt's phrase, proper expressions rise to the surface from the heat of the essayist's mind 'like bubbles on an agitated stream'. This is consciousness in process, like an American poem.

In his sketch of the famous editor of the *Edinburgh Review*, Francis Jeffrey, Hazlitt says that that journal's style of 'philosophical criticism' began around 1796 in a series of articles by the Unitarian scholar William Taylor which appeared in a now-forgotten periodical called the *Monthly Review*. Anyone who examines dissenting culture is bound to notice how many magazines and journals it produced. From *The Review*, which Defoe started in 1704, to the *London Review of Books* there is a cultural line which may one day find its historian.

In calling this selection – selection rather than collection – *Writing to the Moment*, I'm trying to pay tribute to the neglected culture which is British and Irish dissent. The phrase originates with Samuel Richardson, who speaks in the preface to *Sir Charles Grandison* of the 'nature of familiar letters, written, as it were to the *moment*, while the heart is agitated by hopes and fears'. Lovelace in *Clarissa* similarly remarks, 'I love to write to the moment' – a self-reflexive, throwaway line which describes Richardson's epistolary technique.

Journalism, too, is written to the moment. It aims to be instant, excited, spontaneous, concentrated – like theatre, or like a letter dashed off quickly before breakfast. To write like this is to reject what Yeats terms the 'ghostly paradigm of things' in favour of the social and subjective spume which blows across the notional platonic pattern that underlies them. There is something provisional, off-hand, spontaneous, risky in this volatile mindset – it seeks but never finds absolutely definitive judgements. It is in dialogue or argument with the world, and is closely related to the diary entry and the familiar letter.

Describing Francis Jeffrey's written style, Hazlitt says that he weaves words into any shape he pleases 'as the glass-blower moulds the vitreous fluid with his breath'. This image of the glassblower as a figure for the literary journalist is also developed in an essay 'On Application to Study', where Hazlitt confronts the fact that all journalism is written rapidly to a deadline, and then argues that this is its strength, its unique identity:

I do not conceive rapidity of execution necessarily implies slovenliness or crudeness. On the contrary, I believe it is often productive both of sharpness and freedom. The eagerness of composition strikes out sparkles of fancy, and runs the thoughts more naturally and closely into one another. There may be less formal method, but is more life, and spirit, and truth. In the play and agitation of the mind, it turns over, and we dally with the subject, as the glass-blower rapidly shapes the vitreous fluid. A number of new thoughts rise up spontaneously, and they come in the proper places, because they arise from the occasion. They are also sure to partake of the warmth and vividness of the ebullition of mind, from which they spring. *Spiritus precipitandus est*. In these sort of voluntaries in composition, the thoughts are worked up to a state of projection: the grasp of the subject, the presence of mind, the flow of expression must be something akin to *extempore* speaking; or perhaps such bold but finished draughts may be compared to *fresco* paintings, which imply a life of study and great previous preparation, but of which the execution is momentary and irrevocable.

What this image catches is the sudden concentrated social moment – the beautiful extemporized bulging precipitate sense of emergency which such occasional pieces of writing carry and express. For Hazlitt, they're like glowing pictures – frescoes or transparencies in lantern shows – while nowadays they may aim at the huge presence of the movies or the unpredictable drama of live television.

Another image for the *engagé* nature of journalism is Hazlitt's dramatic portrait of Cobbett:

We see his ideas in their first concoction, fermenting and overflowing with the ebullitions of a lively conception . . . This is one cause of the clearness and force of his writings. An argument does not stop to stagnate and muddle in his brain, but passes at once to his paper. His ideas are served up, like pancakes, hot and hot.

That image of pancakes as simultaneously rushed copy and freshly published text is brilliantly concentrated – Cobbett's writings represent cheap popular instant nourishment as well as a shimmeringly permanent but apparently ephemeral form of the Good which, like an inspired showman, he has risen up out of the crowd to communicate.

What interests me about this type of writing is its meltfresh, newpainted, all-in-the-moment living quality. Whitman, Lawrence, Ted Hughes are masters of this apparently formless, often iconoclastic mode of composition – writing whose active, bristling openness to sensations and new ideas breaks down the barriers between prose and poetry. In a note to *Moortown Diary*, Hughes offers a heroic image for its extemporized nature when he celebrates his father-in-law, the farmer Jack Orchard, and says that he was 'equal to any job, any crisis, using the most primitive means, adapting and improvising with any old bit of metal'.

Like someone repairing a tractor engine in a hurry, or like an artist making a cento, a collage, a sculpture out of bits and pieces – a few quotations, scraps of paper, some nuts, bolts, lengths of piping –

these writers work very fast, very intensely. They adapt and recycle what's given or lies to hand. Hence the adrenalin, all-in-a-rush excitement of the process. And all to produce something that's gone the next day, like a Navaho sand painting.

More than that, it seems impossible to express what the practice of writing a commissioned piece to a deadline actually feels like. The stress, the hurry, the excitement, the rapid research and background reading – if there's time – the hit-and-miss quality, furious checking, worry about mistakes – all that helterskelter wildness running with the sense of social connectedness and communication now – they're all part of the fun of this kind of writing. It begins with the search for an opening sentence, an invocation, a muttered *here goes*. Take a hazel rod, strip its bark and flex the lithe slippery sappiness – there you have the wand. Now wave it.

The Making of a Loyalist

If there is a centre to Conor Cruise O'Brien's writing, it must lie in the belief that politics and art are mutually absorbed in the production of historical fictions. Like Burke, he habitually views politics as theatre, and this habit has inspired him to write a number of plays which deal with political issues. His dramatic writings issue from a sub-Shavian rationalism, and although this prevents them from being convincingly imaginative they do express his sense of the inseparability of politics and imagination. Recently, however, he has decided that they can be separated after all. In the last of the lectures in *Neighbours* he recommends that politics in the North of Ireland should be abolished. Those who talk of 'fresh political initiatives' are, he says, 'barking up the wrong tree'. They should instead offer prayers to a force called 'international attention'. That force will then establish an institution which as yet exists solely in O'Brien's imagination. This supreme fiction is called 'the Northern Ireland Fund', and in a revealing statement its author promises to pursue it 'as a private citizen with some international contacts and communications'.

This promise resembles that moment in Joyce's 'The Dead' when Gabriel Conroy tells his audience that the tradition of Irish hospitality is 'unique as far as my experience goes (and I have visited not a few places abroad)'. As he says this, Gabriel is thinking of the nationalist, Miss Ivors, who has earlier embarrassed him by calling him a West Briton because he writes a literary column for the *Daily Express* and refuses to visit the Aran Islands. His speech is an act of revenge against her and reveals him as falsely cosmopolitan, a timid, servile and self-conscious figure. Pitilessly, Joyce places him in relation to an influential strand of Irish culture, and in doing so

Review of Conor Cruise O'Brien, *Neighbours: The Ewart-Biggs Memorial Lectures,*
1978–1979.

explores the dilemma of the Irish intellectual. Curiously, Joyce based the character of Gabriel's mocker, Miss Ivors, on a young woman called Kathleen Sheehy who later married a Dublin journalist and gave birth to a well-known figure called Conor Cruise O'Brien.

In O'Brien's writing, fact and fiction – or politics and imagination – often appear to merge in that ironical manner which is so characteristic of Dublin culture. And among the many ironies of this particular blurring is the spectacle of O'Brien respectfully addressing 'my friend Lord Goodman, and . . . the Fellows of University College, Oxford' in tones which relish their attention, as well as savouring the more international attentiveness which stretches beyond High Table. Part of that attention O'Brien promises to divert to the North of Ireland, and yet the student of his *Observer* column will search in vain for any evidence of his efforts.

In *Neighbours*, O'Brien supports an essentially loyalist position. In order to understand how he has reached it, we must place this work in the context of his other writings. The act of placing raises complex questions of history, identity and intellectual freedom.

In the opening autobiographical section of *States of Ireland* (1972) O'Brien remarks that although historians normally write as if they are free of all conditioning factors, what they offer is mostly *'tribal* history'. Mixing anecdote with brisk name-dropping, he then recounts his own family history and pays an affectionate tribute to his father, Francis Cruise O'Brien, whom he describes as intellectual, agnostic, anticlerical and gifted with 'the power to say wounding things in a memorable manner'. O'Brien senior emerges as the living image of his son, and this is perhaps the most original quality of the memoir (most autobiographers try to establish that they differ from their fathers). However, Francis Cruise O'Brien died when his son was ten, and this filial piety must be to a memory which O'Brien has at least in part invented. He has both submitted to the conditioning factors of the past and made an existential leap of the imagination which frees him from them. Put another way, he has combined Irish piety with European freedom.

Francis Cruise O'Brien ensured that his son received a Protestant education, and this tempered his inherited Catholic allegiances. In

O'Brien's self-portrait we can see how the two traditions balance each other and allow that rare figure, the 'objective' historian, to emerge. This transcendental historian is able to voice and confirm Protestant fears of domination by a Catholic state. Reaching back into history, O'Brien seeks to corroborate those fears by emphasizing the sectarian divisions within the 1798 rebellion (and here he is echoed by the loyalist historian A. T. Q. Stewart in his study *The Narrow Ground*). Throughout *States of Ireland* O'Brien presents himself as the concerned but non-partisan commentator, and rebuts accusations that he is 'hyper-sensitive' about Protestants and indifferent to Catholics:

It is to the Irish Catholic community that I belong. That is my 'little platoon', to love which, according to Edmund Burke (whose family were in the same platoon), 'is the first, the germ, as it were, of publick affections'.

It is a mark of O'Brien's continuing uncertainty about his identity that he must compare himself to, among others, Burke, Griboyedov, Milovan Djilas and 'Tolstoy's Prince Andrey on the field of Austerlitz'.

This last exalted comparison occurs in *To Katanga and Back* (1962), which opens with a question: ' "Who," Mr Macmillan was moved to ask one autumn day in 1961, "is Conor O'Brien?" ' The answer might well have been 'An Irishman who is delighted to be noticed by the British Prime Minister.' The gratifying attention of Harold Macmillan helped to create O'Brien's image, and this was an important stage in the promotion of a public personality which became a personal identity.

O'Brien would have the audience of *States of Ireland* believe that his identity is rooted in the Irish Catholic community, but the grouping is too wide to be helpful. In fact, he inadvertently reveals that there are really two Catholic communities when he admits that he writes 'specifically' from the point of view of the Southern Catholics. Nowhere does he point to the deep hostility which much of that community feels towards both communities in the North. Many Southerners – Catholic, Protestant and agnostic – are quite capable of believing in a United Ireland while at the same time regarding Northerners as members of what are sometimes scathingly referred to as 'hill tribes'. To the Southerner these tribes belong to an imaginative territory very similar to that symbolized by Galway and the West in 'The Dead'. They are beyond the pale and threaten the ironical civilities of Dublin.

Something of this is apparent in O'Brien's accounts in *States of Ireland* of a lecture which he gave to a Civil Rights meeting at Queen's University, Belfast, in October 1968. The main point of the lecture was 'that civil disobedience, in Northern Ireland, was likely to prove an effective lever for social change'. In the discussion which followed, the students criticized him 'quite heatedly' for mentioning 'the existence of two separate communities, Catholics and Protestants'. The student activists believed in working-class solidarity and they dismissed religion as 'irrelevant'. O'Brien's aim in his account of this meeting is to present himself as the objective historian, the *engagé* intellectual who is also disengaged by virtue of his superior wisdom. He presents the students as ignorant, idealistic and sloppy, and then reprints as part of his account an article which he published in the *Listener* that same October, where he compared the events in the North of Ireland to *Antigone*:

Antigone's action was one of non-violent civil disobedience, the breaking of a law which she considered to be contrary to a higher law. The consequences of her non-violent action emerge in acts of violence: Antigone's own violent death; Haemon's turning of his sword first against his father Creon and then fatally against himself; the suicide of Eurydice, Creon's wife and Haemon's mother. A stiff price for that handful of dust on Polyneices. Nor is it possible to put all the blame on Creon. Certainly his decision to forbid the burial of Polyneices was rash, but it was also rash to disobey his decision . . . Ismene, who was Polyneices' sister just as much as Antigone was, would not risk her life for the sake of her brother's dead body. It was Antigone's free decision, and that alone, which precipitated the tragedy. Creon's responsibility was the more remote one of having placed this tragic power in the hands of a headstrong child of Oedipus.

O'Brien published this interpretation of *Antigone* on 24 October 1968, and he lectured the students on the likely effectiveness of civil disobedience in 'late October'. He has never been slow to publish his lectures – why then did he not publish the lecture on civil disobedience? This is a most pertinent question because O'Brien informed the readers of the *Listener* that

The disabilities of Catholics in Northern Ireland are real, but not over-whelmingly oppressive: is their removal really worth attaining at the risk of precipitating riots, explosions, pogroms, murder? Thus Ismene. But Anti-gone will not heed such calculations: she is an ethical and religious force, an uncompromising element in our being, as dangerous in her way as Creon, whom she perpetually challenges and provokes.

If O'Brien recommended civil disobedience in his lecture then he can hardly have told his audience that the injustices they were protesting against were 'not overwhelmingly oppressive'. Of course, this bland statement is attributed to Ismene, but it is plain from his description of Creon's responsibility as 'more remote' and his description of Antigone as 'headstrong' that his sympathies – at least when not lecturing in Belfast – lay with the status quo.

There is yet another revealing omission from *States of Ireland*. It is the statement, 'Without Antigone, we could attain a quieter, more realistic world. The Creons might respect one another's spheres of influence if the instability of idealism were to cease to present, inside their own dominions, a threat to law and order.' These two sentences appeared in the article which O'Brien published in the *Listener*, but they were silently dropped when he reprinted it.

Possibly this was because a year after O'Brien suggested that Creon might have a change of heart, members of the RUC fired machine-guns indiscriminately at Divis Flats near the centre of Belfast, killing a nine-year-old boy and a young British soldier who was home on leave. The status quo was discredited and the British army arrived. From the perspective of 1971, the statement appeared both wrong and vulnerably naïve, and so it disappeared from the text.

Reflecting on the *Listener* article in *States of Ireland*, O'Brien says that he is no longer in sympathy with its conclusion. That conclusion suggested that Antigone may express 'the essence of what man's dignity actually is', but now O'Brien rejects this:

. . . after four years of Antigone and her under-studies and all those funerals – more than a hundred dead at the time of writing – you begin to feel that

Ismene's common-sense and feeling for the living may make the more needful, if less spectacular element in 'human dignity'.

Here Antigone (i.e. Bernadette Devlin and the Civil Rights movement) becomes responsible for 'all those funerals'. This means that the Unionist state is virtually absolved of all responsibility and Creon's hands appear to be clean.

O'Brien's political analysis is inspired and supported by his interpretation of Sophocles' great tragedy, so it is crucial to recognize how badly he misinterprets the play. According to Hegel, for whom *Antigone* was 'the perfect exemplar' of tragedy, the sacred laws which Antigone revered are 'the instinctive Powers of Feeling, Love and Kinship, not the daylight gods of free and self-conscious, social and political life'. As Hegel shows, in the play 'neither the right of family, nor that of the state is denied; what is denied is the absoluteness of the claim of each'. It is in the clash of these opposing 'rights' that the tragedy resides. Antigone represents the absolute assertion of family against the state, and if O'Brien had truly felt that he and Bernadette Devlin belonged to the same 'little platoon' then he would have been unable to turn against a member of that extended family and assert the virtues of what Creon terms 'simple obedience'. But as Bernadette Devlin is a Northern Catholic he cannot feel any natural bond with her.

O'Brien's loyalties are to the 'daylight gods', and he sees the political conflict in the play as one of unequal values and unequal personal responsibilities. Creon, therefore, is both individual and institution, yet he appears to be more an institution, while Antigone, like St Joan, appears as an individual ahead of her supporters. She is 'headstrong' and therefore more responsible because she can supposedly exercise choice. So Creon is rendered almost innocent by his immobile precedence, his simply being there. This is a severe distortion of the tragic conflict and it provoked Hugh Lloyd-Jones to rebuke O'Brien in the next issue of the *Listener*: 'Tiresias makes it clear that Creon has offended against the laws of the gods.'

O'Brien ignored Lloyd-Jones's rebuke and also omitted to notice that Ismene eventually sides with Antigone. He has always attempted to occupy a middle position, and his omission suggests that such a position is tenable here. But in recommending Ismene's common sense he is really supporting Creon's rule of law. It is as though a future member of Creon's think-tank can be discerned hiding behind the unfortunate Ismene. Tragedy teaches no moral, but the analogy between the play and events in the North of Ireland shows us a terrible truth – neither Ismene, nor even Conor Cruise O'Brien, can prevent a civil war happening. O'Brien has often warned that such a war is imminent and he no doubt believes that so far he has helped to prevent it. But if it breaks out he will be able to say, 'I told you so.' That is the advantage of being pure.

Essentially, the thrust of O'Brien's argument is towards a position where he can be both politically influential and absolutely pure. Having once recommended a campaign of civil disobedience, and now believing that the campaign in the North of Ireland was responsible for political violence, he must prove that there is no blood on his hands. Throughout his published writings he returns obsessively to Yeats's famous question: 'Did that play of mine send out / Certain men the English shot?' The question preys on O'Brien's mind, because as an international communicator and moulder of opinion he must believe in his power to influence history.

Yet, as he observes in his first and best book, *Maria Cross* (1954), the relationship between 'the imagination and moral guilt' is by no means simple. This is an observation which issues from his sense of 'the oppressive domination of the rational faculties over the passions', and from his dislike of the 'levelling rational men' who set puritan reason against the imagination. In an earlier period, the puritan imagination created two great epics – *Paradise Lost* and *Clarissa* – but O'Brien rightly points to its subsequent lassitude. 'Modern Protestantism,' he remarks in *Maria Cross*, is 'dead from the waist down' and has nothing to offer the Catholic imaginations he is exploring. What is important, he argues, is that 'community of feeling' which enables Catholic writers to transform a private and incommunicable suffering 'into public utterance and communion with others'. Here, he writes in a manner that is passionately and warmly intelligent, and his prose is utterly unlike his later style. Where the mature style is rational, self-conscious and broguishly ironic, the early prose is lavish, ornate, agonized and often febrile. It sets the author's personality aside in order to explore a higher and more mysterious knowledge, and it swirls with cries of 'pain' and references to 'historical change', 'solidarity' and 'this revolutionary urge'. It is the intuitive pressure of the prose which guarantees O'Brien's assertion here that Sartre and Camus 'lack just that irrational instinctive force whose explosion made the greatness of Mauriac's prime'.

O'Brien has never written in this manner again. His work since *Maria Cross* has increasingly turned away from the instinctive and the intuitive towards the 'rational'. Possibly he was disturbed by his use of that metaphor of an explosion and wished to repudiate it by embracing an ideal of eighteenth-century reason. Another answer would be that the dazzling light of 'international attention' transformed him into a personality. Hammarskjöld read *Maria Cross* and admired it, and it was partly because of this that he selected O'Brien in 1961 as the United Nations Special Representative in Katanga. In an article in the *Observer* at the end of that year O'Brien dwelt on this 'somewhat eccentric element' in Hammarskjöld's choice. A journalist writing for an Arizona newspaper drew on this article in order to attack O'Brien and his criticisms provoked a vulnerable footnote in *To Katanga and Back* (1962):

The emphasis, in the *Observer* article . . . was due, not so much to any real modesty on my part, as to the strategy of self-depreciation which one almost instinctively adopts when writing for a certain kind of English audience. I now realise that it is foolish for a foreigner to attempt this technique. Only a true-born Englishman knows the trick of being self-depreciatory without actually doing himself any damage – I only succeeded in making people as far away as Arizona think I was 'boasting'.

The Arizonans were right, but this is unimportant beside the hypersensitivity to other people's opinions which the statement reveals. O'Brien admits that his authorial personality owes much to his sense of his audience's expectations. It is little wonder that Macmillan asked who this shifting, 'almost instinctive' person was. He may have mistaken him for Brendan Bracken.

O'Brien offers the following self-portrait in the words of an attentive UN aide in *Murderous Angels* (1969), his play about the Congo affair: 'He's a trouble-maker . . . Clever. Bumptious. Talks too much. The British say he's a Communist, but they just mean that he's Irish.' It's as though his identity is a figment of public opinion, and since there are many opinions there must be many identities.

All the same, the anti-imperialism evident in the play also helped to inspire a lucid and brilliant study of Camus which was published in 1970. In it he demonstrates that Camus was far from being an exemplar of the truly independent intellectual and that his conception of 'Mediterranean culture' served to legitimize France's possession of Algeria. The court scene in *L'Étranger* similarly endorses this myth of French Algeria:

What appears to the casual reader as a contemptuous attack on the court is not in fact an attack at all: on the contrary, by suggesting that the court is impartial between Arab and Frenchman, it implicitly denies the colonial reality and sustains the colonial fiction.

O'Brien's prose has a sweet rigour as he first explores Camus's sense of estrangement and unreality, and then places his work within a social context. This brief study displays O'Brien's cultivated intelligence at its most joyous pitch, and like *Maria Cross* it demonstrates his unique critical talent, but in the context of his other work it is remarkably inconsistent. Camus, he shows, criticized revolutionary violence but did not consider 'the question of violence used to defend the status quo'. Yet in his last book, *Herod: Reflections on Political Violence* (1978), O'Brien scorns the phrase 'institutionalised violence' and defends the status quo.

But two years before he published *Camus* he had suggested that the world would be quieter and 'more realistic' without Antigone. This idea is the reactionary equivalent of radical utopianism. It is a kind of negative idealism which argues that life would be better if only we could abolish part of human nature – in this case radical protest. Here, O'Brien emerges well to the right of Camus, who criticized revolutionary violence while O'Brien criticizes non-violence by suggesting that it is responsible for political terrorism. And, as we have seen, that missing 1968 lecture on the effectiveness of civil disobedience adds a further inconsistency.

There is a yet deeper contradiction. It appears in the introduction to a collection of essays which O'Brien co-edited, entitled *Power and Consciousness* (1969). There he considers why 'sympathy with other people's revolutions is so deceptive' and shows how the sympathizer's retreat

> may become a rout, his disenchantment apostasy. Thus we may find that the man who has refused to make the decisive intellectual and moral sacrifices for the revolution will go on to make them for the status quo and in that cause proclaim: 'This sham is true, these injustices are just, these oppressed have all the opportunities of the free world.' These sacrifices, whether made for the revolution or for the counter-revolution, constitute, of course, the abdication of the intellectual.

The introductory essay in which this statement occurs was published in New York in 1969 and must have been written soon after his *Antigone* article. The reason for this contradiction must be that his warning against 'the abdication of the intellectual' was directed chiefly at an American audience. Here, he speaks in the persona of a New York intellectual, while in the *Listener* he adopts a Burkean mask and speaks of 'the instability of idealism'. The Burkean mask is many-layered – as O'Brien points out in his introduction to *Reflections on the Revolution in France* (1968), Burke wrote 'in the persona of an Englishman', but was 'Irish to the marrow of his bone'. And in 1969 O'Brien discovered that Burke's education and origins were 'very similar to my own'. It seems that either O'Brien writes in the persona of a persona or that the Burkean mask looks almost exactly like his own face. This leaves no room for his other identities of New York intellectual, anti-imperialist, lecturer on civil disobedience and critic of Camus. Unless, that is, we adopt a Yeatsian theory of anti-types and regard his portrait of Camus as a self-portrait and its author as a shadowy opposite who is friendly with the New York intellectual.

Connected with the question of identity is that ideal of complete intellectual freedom which O'Brien appears to uphold in his writings. In arguing, for example, that Camus was not truly independent he implies that he himself is. And this is the theme of his introduction to *Power and Consciousness*, where at one point he mischievously suggests that it is 'perhaps' time to attempt a balanced consideration of Stalin's literary talent and then offers this striking comment: 'But of course it remains true that the exercise of power is incompatible with absolutely free intellectual activity, however powerful the intellect of the man in power may be.' What is remarkable about this deeply ingenuous statement is O'Brien's apparent belief that intellectual activity *can* be 'absolutely free'.

It was in 1969, as a New York intellectual, that O'Brien professed his belief in this absolute freedom. That same year he delivered the T. S. Eliot Memorial Lectures at Eliot College in the University of Kent. These were published as *The Suspecting Glance* (1972), and in his introduction O'Brien says that they are the product of what he experienced in New York. The students he taught there were intelligent, serious and left-wing, but he was 'disconcerted . . . by the lack of suspicion in those bright, young eyes'. He therefore told them about Burke, rather than Marcuse or Shelley. Again, he approaches a Yeatsian struggle of opposites here – he writes as a radical in *Power and Consciousness*, yet he redresses radical ideals in student seminars. Far from New York, in Eliot College, Canterbury, he catches the charred fragrance of Eliot's Anglican pessimism and begins to forge a new identity.

As always, the impression is one of balance. On the one hand he addresses the important subject of how certain reactionary intuitions work against 'the optimism of the Enlightenment'; on the other he criticizes Burke for calling for a long counter-revolutionary war. His ambition is to provoke traditional left-wing thought into examining 'what man is actually like'. It is a salutary ambition, but as with that missing 1968 lecture on civil disobedience it appears to be tailored to the occasion.

The static and unfruitful contradictions in his thought are apparent in *Herod* (1978), an undistinguished gathering of reviews, lectures and short plays which looks queasy beside *Writers and Politics*, that melodious work of the mid-1960s. In one play, *Salome the Wild Man*, Salome tells the Sophist, Philo, that they are both 'lonely for the wild man'. O'Brien has discerned loneliness in Burke and we must assume that he is pointing to his own sense of isolation.

The wild man believes in 'the politics of the impossible', and the drama in which he figures represents 'the high water-mark of the tendency to idealize the student revolution'. O'Brien admits to having once had this tendency, but he had it in New York, not in Britain or Ireland. The wild man is clearly related to Antigone, except that he has an American student base. However, as 'wild' is a word with a distinctive usage in Ireland, he may be Irish-American. Where Yeats remembers the pre-revolutionary Constance Gore-Booth 'With all youth's lonely wildness stirred', O'Brien makes a division between loneliness and wildness and founds an idea of civilization on that split. And Philo, the lonely Sophist, represents civilization, which is mistakenly identified with the status quo.

Philo is O'Brien in a toga and at the end of the play he confuses the wild man with Antigone's brother: 'We kill him, we bury him, we even *honour* him. And yet he always comes up again under a new name.' As the tragic action of *Antigone* springs from Creon's refusal to allow Polyneices an honourable burial, this again demonstrates O'Brien's inability to understand the play. As with that phrase 'the politics of the impossible' which he puts into the wild man's mouth, O'Brien's cynical pragmatism rigs the entire analysis. The issues are always prejudged in Creon's favour, like votes in a one-party state.

Yet O'Brien admits to being lonely for the wild man, and this loneliness is apparent in a statement he includes in *Herod*: 'My liberal image, I am told by those who can tell such things, is in bits.' He then suggests that he is 'not too worried' about this, 'not being much of a one for images, having indeed some inclination to iconoclasm'. Here we can sense the loneliness of a performer: instead of honestly admitting that he has changed his convictions, he turns to contemplate his shattered liberal image. The image should be nothing, the conviction everything – unless you are a politician of the most opportunistic kind. As it happens, O'Brien was Minister for Posts and Telegraphs in the Irish government at this time, but it would be unfair to accuse him of political opportunism. He was not a successful politician, and this was due partly to his iconoclastic habits and partly to his neglect of his constituency. Yet he regrets the disappearance of his liberal image because for him image is identity.

However, he now has a new image-identity, and this personality can be understood as a kind of negative definition which has become a positive commitment. The free spirit, like the pure lovers in Donne's poem 'The Extasy', must eventually descend to 'affections and to faculties', and in O'Brien's latest work that commitment – or that descent – is made.

Neighbours consists of four lectures which O'Brien gave in memory of Christopher Ewart-Biggs. As these were public lectures and not private messages of condolence to the family of the dead ambassador, it is only with their public function that the reader can be concerned. The function of the lectures is partly a diplomatic one – to improve relations between Britain and Ireland – and in pursuit of that aim O'Brien insists on the links between the two countries. As an iconoclastic critic of Irish nationalism he also attacks the 'anglophobia' which some Irish people profess, and again this is part of a diplomatic stress on common interests.

It is here that we can see the free critical spirit making and revealing its commitment to an external structure. For all O'Brien's apparent diplomacy that structure is not finally the political system of the Irish Republic; nor is it some noble structure of ideas to which he has at last submitted his personality. It is a shaky edifice called 'the Union of Great Britain and Northern Ireland', and O'Brien has dedicated himself to its maintenance. He speaks in the persona of an Official Unionist, and like that fugitive and visionary politician Enoch Powell, he has offered his services to a political party demoralized by its absence of talent and by the political skills of John Hume and Ian Paisley. Just as Camus believed that Algeria was actually part of France, so O'Brien believes that the North of Ireland is permanently wedded to Britain.

His Unionism has a nineteenth-century flavour, and at times he writes as though the whole of Ireland is really incorporated within the British system: 'The sea which we think of as separating the two islands actually joins them.' This is the mental equivalent of walking on water, and it issues from O'Brien's fatuous statement, ' "Break the connection," wrote Wolfe Tone. "Only connect," wrote E. M. Forster.' The fact that Forster was referring to a completely different issue — the relationship of the spiritual to the public life — is not mentioned by O'Brien. This is another significant omission.

O'Brien's intellectual method in these lectures is a kind of grisly comedy which revolves around an obsession with an opinion survey which was carried out in Dublin in 1972. Rather like Winnie addressing her toothbrush in Beckett's *Happy Days*, he directs his monologues at a brittle mass of statistics and quantified opinions. This is the terminal phase of political rationalism, and it is bitter with a sense of intellectual dereliction. In the first lecture on Irish-British relations (delivered at Trinity College, Dublin), O'Brien considers how Dubliners responded to the statement 'I would be happy if Britain were brought to her knees.' A solid 79.3 per cent disagreed while 17.1 per cent of responders agreed. It is the small percentage which concerns O'Brien, because it represents what he terms a 'pathological element in our life'. It is a figure which is 'startlingly and frighteningly high'. Yet it is a statistic which must be located in a specific period — 1972. This was the year when the survey was conducted, and it was also the year of Bloody Sunday, when British paratroopers shot dead thirteen civilians in Derry. From another point of view the 17.1 per cent of anglophobic Dubliners could be described as curiously low.

When O'Brien does mention Bloody Sunday it is to further an essentially Unionist argument. Faced with the statement, 'British soldiers are generally cruel and brutal', 28 per cent of Dubliners agreed and 57 per cent disagreed. Here, O'Brien blithely remarks: 'considering that the interviewing was carried out within a year of Bloody Sunday, the majority disagreeing seems more significant than the 28 per cent minority agreeing.' But of what is that 'majority' significant? It depends on the point of view of the interpreter, and it is likely that the 'majority' of the citizens of Derry would attach a different significance to these figures from the one which O'Brien implies.

There are many more statistics and percentages in his first lecture, and at one point he considers whether it is worth plodding on. Contemplating the 30 per cent who agreed with the proposition that 'the world owes a lot to Britain', he remarks:

Granted that Britain's contributions to the world have been enormous, so also the world's contributions to Britain have been enormous, and not always voluntary. Is it the world that is the net debtor, or Britain? How much does Shakespeare weigh against the slave-trade? How much does Britain's leading part in abolishing the slave-trade weigh against Britain's earlier part in carrying on the slave-trade? Who is to say, who owes who what – and what is the use of saying it anyway?

As with O'Brien's question in *Herod*, 'How many children is it worthwhile to kill to get rid of Derry Corporation?', or his association of Wolfe Tone and E. M. Forster, the Shakespearian slave-trade is an impossible linkage. Bentham remarked, 'quantity of pleasure being equal, push-pin is as good as poetry.' The scales in O'Brien's non-argument are those of the hedonic calculus, and it is unfortunate that he avoids his Beckettian question, 'and what is the use of saying it anyway?'

When he turns to consider the contribution of Irishmen to 'the building of the British Empire', he makes a very revealing mistake. He asserts that the 'most execrated figure in the eyes of Indian nationalists in the twentieth century was General O'Dwyer, who gave the order that brought about the massacre at Amritsar'. It is characteristic of his sloppy method of argument that he should mistake the English general called Dyer, who gave the order, for the Irish colonial administrator O'Dwyer, who ratified it. O'Brien has an obsessively analogical imagination and the motive for this mistake becomes apparent when we remember that he referred to Bloody Sunday in order to further an anti-nationalist argument. For 'Amritsar' we should read 'Derry'. O'Brien wishes to exculpate the British Army of all responsibility for the shooting of the thirteen men there, and he does so by, as it were, blaming a nationalist called General O'Somebody who was actually Irish. This is a version of the argument that the army was replying to terrorist gunfire and so was justified in shooting non-violent demonstrators. Again, it shows how O'Brien's concept of personal responsibility enables him to blame such demonstrators for political violence.

It is only in the second of these lectures, 'The Northern Connection in Irish-British Relations', that O'Brien displays any real uneasiness. This is because, ten years after that lecture on civil disobedience, he is again addressing an audience in Queen's University, Belfast. He remarks that his audience is 'likely to agree' with his admission that he knows 'relatively little about Northern Ireland'. He then offers an Empsonian political analysis which involves 'six possible dual inter-relationships among the four entities'. He speaks of triangles, dualities, 'twelve sets of attitudes', invokes further opinion polls, and eventually emerges from this numbers game by declaring: 'Give direct rule a chance.' The essential frivolity of his historical aestheticism is revealed when he compares the political differences in the North of Ireland to a game of football between 'Micks' and 'Prods'.

His intention – and this is clear in the relaxed third lecture in New York – is to demolish the idea that Britain is preventing the formation of a United Ireland: 'This fantasy, proceeding from a brain oppressed by the Irish Republican version of history, is of course one that legitimizes the IRA campaign in Northern Ireland.' Here, O'Brien's tactics work to lay responsibility for the IRA campaign at the door of everyone who believes that terrorist violence is the result of partition.

Does O'Brien's support of the Union mean that he condones the actions of terrorist groups which also support the link with Britain? Might those groups not receive succour and encouragement from a Ewart-Biggs lecture? Did O'Brien's lecture at Queen's University in 1978 send out certain men? Or his 1968 lecture? The relation between the imagination and moral guilt is not as simple as this.

Among the many percentages he cites there is one figure that particularly angers O'Brien – 75 per cent of the British people seem to be Irish republicans. At least, this is one way of reading the fact that only 25 per cent of the population of Britain believe that the North of Ireland should remain part of the United Kingdom. O'Brien calls this percentage 'miserable' and he believes that it would be much increased if only people listened to the 'reasonable policies' he is advocating. Elsewhere he warns of the dangers of losing through compassion 'the power to think'. It is not compassion which has destroyed his much-vaunted intellectual ability, but an abiding affection for Creon and a mistaken identification of civilization with the status quo. His defence of the free spirit now appears as a rearguard action fought in support of a permanent Unionist state, and these eccentric and self-regarding lectures are an attempt to persuade the British government to maintain that state. It is to be hoped that Creon's daylight gods ignore the advice he offers them.

The British Presence in *Ulysses*

The first book of *Ulysses*, Telemachus, is saturated with a sense of oppression and lack of freedom. Stephen is staying in a government watchtower – one of many that ring the coast of Ireland and which were built in 1804 to guard against a French invasion. When Buck Mulligan explains to his English friend, Haines, that William Pitt had the towers built 'when the French were on the sea', he ironically implies his attitude to them by echoing the famous song from the 1798 rebellion which celebrates the French landing at Killala:

> 'Oh the French are on the sea,' says the Sean Bean Boct,
> 'Yes the French are on the sea,' says the Sean Bean Boct.
> 'The French are in the bay, they'll be here without delay,
> 'And the English will decay,' says the Sean Bean Boct.
> 'Yes the English will decay,' says the Sean Bean Boct.*

The rent of the martello tower is paid to the Secretary of State for War, and this underlines the way in which Stephen's existence in Dublin is trammelled by the British connection. He sees himself as someone who is humiliated by a double service: 'I am the servant of two masters . . . The imperial British state . . . and the holy Roman catholic and apostolic church.' Both ignoble services fuse as Stephen lifts Mulligan's shaving-bowl and is reminded of the boat of incense he carried at mass at school: 'I am another now and yet the same. A servant too. A server of a servant.'

The bowl also becomes like a loyal address presented to the king –

---

* In *Ireland Sings* Dominic Behan explains: 'Sean Bean Boct, Poor Old Woman – a code name for Ireland, Shan Van Vocht.'

Mulligan has just been mockingly singing a song about the coronation of Edward VII, and in the previous year Dublin Corporation had decided by a narrow majority against presenting a loyal address to the king when he visited Ireland. Yeats affirms a similar anti-colonial attitude in the title-poem of *In the Seven Woods*, which was published in 1904, the year in which *Ulysses* is set. He cunningly pretends to have grown quiet and apolitical:

> I have forgot awhile
> Tara uprooted, and new commonness
> Upon the throne and crying about the streets
> And hanging its paper flowers from post to post,
> Because it is alone of all things happy.

Although Buck Mulligan appears to share this scornful attitude, Stephen regards him as a servile figure, and as Stephen is momentarily Mulligan's servant he, too, is 'a server of a servant'. Also, the Roman Catholic Church is presented here as a servant of Britain – so Stephen is doubly the server of a servant. Almost comically, he considers the action of refusing to take Mulligan's shaving-bowl down as a revolutionary act – a *non serviam*. The shaving-mirror, too, assumes a colonial significance as Stephen regards it as a 'symbol of Irish art. The cracked looking-glass of a servant.'

This insistence on the national indignity of service is provoked by the presence of Haines in the tower – he is a symbolic usurper and is the butt of petty revenges. The atmosphere is nervous, edgy and highly self-conscious. Haines attempts to be sympathetic when he says, 'We feel in England that we have treated you rather unfairly. It seems history is to blame.' Here, Haines sounds lofty and patronizing, and Stephen later transforms him into a symbol of naval supremacy: 'The seas' ruler. His seacold eyes looked on the empty bay.' As he visualizes Haines in this Nelson-like manner, Stephen is listening to Mr Deasy – an authority figure who has a portrait of Prince Albert in his room. Deasy is a Unionist and his loyalist remarks spark a series of images for Stephen: the phrase 'Glorious, pious and immortal memory' evokes the loyalist culture of Orange banners and gable-ends (it refers to William of Orange), while the phrase 'Croppies lie down' is the refrain from a sadistic loyalist song of 1798:

> In Dublin, the traitors were ready to rise
> And murder was seen in their lowering eyes.
> With poison, the cowards, they aimed to succeed,
> And thousands were doomed by Assassins to bleed,
> But the Yeomen advanced, of Rebels the dread,
> And each Croppy soon hid his dastardly head.
>   Down, down, Croppies lie down.

Stephen is shown in reaction against the Unionist atmosphere of the school, and his history lesson inevitably assumes a political significance. Asked to define a pier, one of the pupils replies, 'A kind of bridge. Kingstown pier, sir.' Stephen answers wryly, 'Yes, a disappointed bridge.' Because Kingstown (now Dun Laoghaire) is a port near Dublin, the idea of a connecting link with Britain is suggested. Yet a pier is not a bridge, and the boy's mistake seems natural for one who cannot think outside the connection between the two countries.

Like many present-day Unionists, Deasy is anti-English – he tells Stephen that he has 'rebel blood in me too' – and Joyce emphasizes the essentially racist nature of this attitude by giving him anti-Semitic views (Haines is similarly anti-Semitic). Deasy also anticipates the nationalistic racism and anti-Semitism of the Citizen who will abuse Bloom in the Cyclops section. Deasy's conversation is another history lesson, and Stephen reacts against its tedium by saying, 'History . . . is a nightmare from which I am trying to awake'. This effort to 'wake' is essential to Joyce's inspiration, because the epic imagination – which the heroic Stephen possesses – draws on history in order to free itself from the past, to make the leap into imaginative freedom.

In the Proteus section, Joyce implies a parallel between the epic modernist artist and the revolutionary activist in Stephen's memories of his stay in Paris. The fashion for cropped hair began in Paris during the French Revolution and was imitated by Irish revolutionaries – hence the pejorative term 'Croppies'. And for many generations Paris was regarded as both the symbol and centre of imaginative freedom – Wolfe Tone went there to organize the invasion of Ireland and Parnell often met his colleagues there. Stephen associates Kevin Egan, the old Fenian whom he visits, with the explosion at Clerkenwell Prison in 1859 and with these lines from 'The Wearing of the Green':

> I met with Napper Tandy and he took me by the hand,
> Said he, 'How is old Ireland and how does she stand?'
> 'She's the most distressful country that ever could be seen,
> For they're hanging men and women for the wearing of the
> green.'

Napper Tandy was one of the leaders of the 1798 rebellion, and like Wolfe Tone he sailed to Ireland in a French warship. The Irish, Stephen reflects, have forgotten Egan, 'not he them. Remembering thee, O Sion.' Here Joyce introduces one of the first biblical parallels *Ireland/* between the Irish and the Jews – the Promised Land is Irish freedom, *chosen* Egypt is the bondage of British imperialism. Stephen's visit to Egan *people* is an act of piety, and Egan's taking of him 'by the hand' is like a paternal blessing in an epic – old Anchises encouraging his pious son, Aeneas. Thus Stephen, the artist-hero, is the inheritor of a long tradition of political rebellion, and Joyce saw Parnell's stern, cold, 'formidable' nature as a paradigm of the true artist's integrity. Indeed, the epic inspiration of Joyce's art resembles that which informs Parnell's famous statement: 'No man has a right to fix the boundary of the march of a nation; no man has a right to say to his country – thus far shalt thou go and no further.'

If Stephen is the future epic artist – the uncrowned king – it is Bloom who carries the historical consciousness in *Ulysses*. As he moves through the streets of Dublin, personal and historical memories are triggered by buildings, statues and casual passers-by. Bloom associates the sun with the sun of Home Rule (his son, Rudy, is dead) and with Arthur Griffith, the editor of the radical paper *The United Irishman*, and a friend of Joyce's. Griffith was the inventor of the famous 'Hungarian Policy' – i.e. 'the policy successfully pursued by the Hungarian patriot, Franz Déak, who organized a massive abstention of Hungarian representatives from the Imperial Diet at Vienna in order to secure the establishment of a separate Hungarian parliament at Budapest'. Significantly, Joyce makes Bloom's father Hungarian and credits Bloom with giving Griffith the idea for Sinn Fein. Here, the personal and the political are identified, as they are again in Bloom's fantasies of orange groves in Jaffa, where an ideal sexual fulfilment and the promised land of Irish freedom are fused. Both frustrations are present when the mourners wander round Glasnevin Cemetery after the funeral of Paddy Dignam and agree that Parnell will 'never come again'. And Bloom's sexual impotence reflects the political impotence of sentimental Parnellites like Joe Hynes.

Both Daniel O'Connell, the 'breedy man', and Parnell are presented as potent liberators, and Joyce associated Parnell with Christ, whom he imagined, in Blakean terms, as a revolutionary saviour. The parallel is implied in the Cave of Aeolus section when a minor character called Brayden passes through. Brayden has a 'solemn beardframed face', and one character asks, 'Don't you think his face is like Our Saviour?' Here, the bearded face of Parnell is superimposed on Christ's. Joyce hints at parallels between Moses and Bloom and between Stephen, Christ and Parnell. Biblical scholars see Moses as a precursor of Christ, and imaginatively Stephen is Bloom's son, the substitute for Rudy, who has sunk out of sight like the sun of Home Rule. The parallels cross and melt because Parnell is also associated with Moses.

In the newspaper offices Bloom reads some type backwards, and his mingled personal and political obsessions are again triggered: 'papa with his hagadah book, reading backwards. Next year in Jerusalem . . . All that long business about that brought us out of the land of Egypt and into the house of bondage.' And the advertisement Bloom designs itself has a mild and virtually invisible political implication – the two crossed keys symbolize both the grocer called Keyes and 'the Manx parliament. Innuendo of home rule.' Passing a squad of constables, Bloom immediately recalls the day he took part in a demonstration against Joseph Chamberlain (Parnell called him 'the man who killed Home Rule'). Bloom's Parnellism is then ironically subverted when he almost immediately passes someone who is in a sense Parnell's ghost – his brother, Joseph Howard Parnell. The brother was a kindly, harmless, rather stupid man, and Bloom remembers Simon Dedalus saying earlier that when they put him in parliament Parnell would come back and lead him out of the House of Commons. The effect of this is to stress the mock-heroic, anti-epic world which is Ireland after Parnell's death.

At the end of the Lestrygonians section Bloom passes a placard which includes the phrase, 'His excellency the lord lieutenant', and this is immediately followed by the startled, 'Straw hat in sunlight. Tan shoes. Turnedup trousers. It is. It is.' Bloom has glimpsed Blazes Boylan and grown fearful – in the lovely phrase Joyce uses, his heart 'quopped softly'. This establishes the first association between the Lord Lieutenant – the chief representative of British rule in Ireland – and Blazes Boylan, the usurper of Bloom's marriage bed. The association is developed two pages later in Scylla and Charybdis, where Stephen's thoughts chime with Bloom's: 'Cranley's eleven true Wicklowmen to free their sireland. Gap-toothed Kathleen, her four beautiful green fields, the stranger in her house.' Boylan is the stranger in Bloom's house.

The Kildare Street Library, where Stephen reflects on these nationalist images, is the centre of Dublin literary culture, and it's presented as a mixture of the cosmopolitan and the provincial. It is gossipy, sometimes silly, and yet there is a firm sense of an emergent literary culture. 'Our national epic', we hear, 'is still to be written', and with a curious kind of simultaneous hindsight we see its author-hero inside this epic as Stephen adds to the rambling, self-conscious, precious conversation. At one point, he politicizes Shakespeare: 'His pageants, the histories, sail fullbellied on a tide of Mafeking enthusiasm.' Like Bloom, who shouted 'Up the Boers!' at Joseph Chamberlain, Stephen momentarily identifies with the Afrikaaner cause and transforms Shakespeare's mystic English patriotism into British jingoism.

The two masters in whose service Stephen writhes jostle through the Wandering Rocks section in the shape of Father Conmee and the vice-regal cavalcade – both are greeted by 'obsequious policemen'.

Father Conmee – the rector of Stephen's old school, Clongowes – has a hollow and polite conversation with Mrs David Sheehy and this is, implicitly, a moment when the forces of reaction preen and consolidate themselves. David Sheehy was an Irish MP who adopted what his grandson, Conor Cruise O'Brien, describes as 'the Catholic and clericalist position' and voted against Parnell. Joyce was a frequent visitor to the Sheehy household, and in the Wandering Rocks the Sheehys represent that pious respectable tyranny which he, as a politicized aesthete, hated.

The vice-regal cavalcade is a moment of arid and tyrannical dullness. It is 4 p.m. and there is a slack, neap feeling of demoralization or defeat. Tom Kernan muses:

Down there Emmet was hanged, drawn and quartered. Greasy black rope. Dogs licking the blood off the street when the lord lieutenant's wife drove by in her noddy.

The sense of squalor and defeat is increased as the prose describing the vice-regal cavalcade takes on the 'toady' style of the *Irish Times*, and as Blazes Boylan moves in counterpoint towards his assignation with Molly: 'jogjaunty jingled Blazes Boylan'. Meanwhile Ben Dollard is singing a rebel song of 1798, 'The Croppy Boy', to a bar-room audience that is lost in sentimental pity. Ironically, Ben Dollard is metamorphosed into 'Big Benaben Dollard, Big Benben' – far from being a rebel, he becomes the symbol of imperial authority.

By leaving the hotel at this point Bloom refuses to serve that symbol, and his reaction to the portrait of Robert Emmet which he sees in a shop window is a rejection, less of Emmet's example, than of sentimental nationalism and martyrology. Joyce had an intense dislike of Patrick Pearse, the leader of the 1916 uprising, and Bloom's flatulent 'I have done' echoes Pearse's echo of Emmet's last words.* Like the *pok-pok* of the corks in 'Ivy Day in the Committee Room', Bloom's fart belongs to a beery mock-heroic world.

In his famous speech from the dock, Emmet said:

I have but one request to make at my departure from this world. It is the charity of silence. Let no man write my epitaph. When my country shall

* See Dominic Manganiello's invaluable study, *Joyce's Politics*.

have taken her place among the nations of the earth, then, and not till then, let my epitaph be written.

In a very important sense, *Ulysses* is that epitaph, because its epic scope and classic perfection gave Ireland a national and international identity. To insist on this is not to make a narrowly nationalistic point, partly because the identity Joyce forges is in advance of Irish political reality (it absolutely has to be in advance of *that*) and partly because of his manner of presenting the Citizen. The Citizen sees a wholly green Ireland through his bigoted Cyclopean vision, and the effect of this is to make Bloom an alien in his own country. Bloom symbolizes the Irish as the Jews enduring Egyptian bondage, so it is ironic that there is no place for the Irish in the Citizen's patriotic Ireland.

During a long servile curse against the English, the Citizen asks, 'Where are the Greek merchants that came through the pillars of Hercules, the Gibraltar now grabbed by the foe of mankind?' Gibraltar, we remember, is Molly Bloom's birthplace, and so we recognize that Joyce chose it not just for the Homeric reference but because it symbolizes imperial occupation. In her great sleepy monologue Molly scorns all Bloom's 'blather' about Home Rule and bathes in a collusive admiration for the Union Jack, redcoat soldiers and gallant English officers. She finds Britishness erotic.

In the Oxen of the Sun episode there is a drunken definition of British imperialism: 'Beer, beef, business, bibles, bulldogs, battleships, buggery and bishops', and past uprisings are re-enacted in Circe when a navvy shouts 'Come on, you British army!' and sings a snatch of patriotic song. In this wonderfully neo-colonial phantasmagoria Bloom becomes a castle Catholic, and a voice calls him a 'turncoat' and reminds him that he once shouted 'Up the Boers!' Bloom replies stuffily, 'My old dad too was a J.P. I'm as staunch a Britisher as you are, sir.' And he claims to have fought for King and Country in the Boer War. Frightened by the street violence, Bloom abases and humiliates himself before the fantasy jury of his conscience. He has, however, an alternative fantasy of himself as a Parnellite liberator, though he is only able to express this in a borrowed literary style which comically subverts it. Joyce offers a hilarious parody of Shakespeare's histories, where John Howard Parnell appears, raises a royal standard and declaims, 'Illustrious Bloom! Successor to my famous brother!' Bloom's habitually Fabian and utilitarian attitudes are set aside and he begins to speak in a melodiously patriotic English accent: 'We thank you from our heart, John, for this right royal welcome to green Erin, the promised land of our common ancestors.' Bloom becomes God and announces that the 'new Bloomusalem' is at hand. In a recapitulation of Parnell's downfall, the mob threatens to lynch Bloom, and a parallel is suggested with *The Playboy of the Western World*. Synge's play is a symbolic version of Parnell's career and its first audiences reacted in a predictably vengeful manner that reflected the villagers' treachery towards Christy Mahon, the liberating 'Christ Man'.

In Circe, history becomes farce as innumerable atavistic images circle round a brawl on a Dublin street. Stephen taps his brow and says, 'But in here it is I must kill the priest and the king', and this provokes a riot which is the parodic equivalent of Emmet's failed uprising, or 'scuffle on a Dublin street' as it is often referred to.

As in the Oxen of the Sun episode, Joyce is fascinated by the trapped and servile consciousness which is doomed to a hell of brilliant parody (in Hegel's commentary on Diderot this protean imitative brilliance is embodied in Rameau's nephew). And as the language of *Ulysses* tires, he pays an extended, ironic, loving and exasperated tribute to Defoe by reducing 'reality' to a gigantic inventory. Joyce deeply admired Defoe's work (he owned his complete works), but he also saw Robinson Crusoe as the 'true symbol of the British conquest . . . the prototype of the British colonist'. In this inventorial sentence we see Bloom's idealistic vision of Home Rule trapped in a plain factual colonial reality:

a butt of red partly liquefied sealing wax, obtained from the stores department of Messrs Hely's Ltd., 89, 90 and 91 Dame street: a box containing the remainder of a gross of gilt 'J' pennibs, obtained from the same department of the same firm: a sealed prophecy (never unsealed) written by Leopold Bloom in 1886 concerning the consequences of the passing into law of William Ewart Gladstone's Home Rule bill of 1886 (never passed into law): a bazaar ticket No. 2004, of S. Kevin's Charity Fair, price 6d. . . .

For Matthew Arnold – he appears in *Ulysses* as a gardener mowing a college lawn – the Irish imagination is always in revolt against 'the despotism of fact', and that positivist tyranny is given an enormously detailed elaboration here. Molly Bloom's monologue breaks that factual boredom and Poldy's prophecy is finally unsealed in her breathless closing affirmation

and then he asked me would I yes to say yes my mountain flower and first I put my arms around him yes and drew him down to me so he could feel my breasts all perfume yes and his heart was going like mad and yes I said yes I will Yes.

Paisley's Progress

In 1969, while he was serving a prison sentence for unlawful assembly, Ian Paisley sent this message to his congregation:

I rejoice with you in the rich blessings of last weekend. I knew that our faithful God would pour out His bounty. In prayer in this cell I touched the Eternal Throne and had the gracious assurance of answered prayer. What a joy to hear from Mr Beggs of a £1000 gift for the pulpit. Hallelujah! May that pulpit be the storm centre of the great hurricane of revival. Oh for a tempest of power, a veritable cyclone of blessing. Lord, let it come!

Eight years later, the preacher rose up in that enormous pulpit and waved a copy of a historical study which had just been published. 'Brethren and sisters in Christ,' he shouted, 'here is a great book that tells the Truth about Ulster. Go home, friend, and read it.'

The book was *The Narrow Ground* by A. T. Q. Stewart, and until I heard of that Sabbath review I'd believed that historians were a type of Brahmin – pure vegetarians who existed at a level of consciousness far above that of politicians and other carnivores. I'd believed in their disinterestedness, their objectivity, their lack of axes to grind. Now I began to understand what F. H. Bradley meant when he said that we reflect 'in general not to find the facts, but to prove our theories at the expense of them'. In that moment of discovery historiography appeared like an ascent towards the Supreme Fiction, and among the mountaineers were Daniel Defoe, Wallace Stevens, Edward Gibbon and A. T. Q. Stewart – all imaginative writers with a style and vision of their own, but none with a style that was any 'truer' than another's.

Historians may be disinterested – some of them certainly like to congratulate each other on their disinterestedness – but they are doomed to be read by an *interested* audience. And many people must recall the comic sequel to the two televised accounts of Irish history in which an earnest Ludovic Kennedy asked Paisley what he'd learnt from the programmes and a group of Irish historians back in the studio held their noses at the whole enterprise. Inevitably, historians are drawn into politics – E. P. Thompson, for example, has an audience which supports both the Campaign for Nuclear Disarmament and the Labour Party, while historians in the North of Ireland have power-bases or followings on the Republican side or in the Democratic Unionist Party. How far historians are able to free themselves from the simplifications which their readers visit on them is problematic, but as far as the writing of Irish history is concerned I'm convinced that it is now, and will be for the foreseeable future, inescapably *political*. Those historians who are bored or embarrassed by the version of history offered in the schools and elsewhere in the Irish Republic may believe that it is possible to escape from that version into a sophisticated objectivity, but as far as I can see, they simply become trapped in a rival simplification – the Unionist version of history. In either case, the embarrassment of, in that well-worn phrase, 'legitimizing' a particular cause is bound to result.

The question that concerns me initially is this: where does the imaginative inspiration for a historical argument come from? Did *The Narrow Ground* inspire Paisley, or did the voice of Old Ravenhill inspire *The Narrow Ground*? Accompanying this question is the problem of the relation of middle-class Unionism to working-class Unionism, or – to put it in cultural terms – the relation of establishment and anti-establishment ideas within Unionism. As Unionism cracks and splinters, a form of class politics begins to emerge – a populism in the case of Paisleyism and a form of socialism in the Ulster Defence Association.

For the UDA the problem is essentially one of identity: 'The prods have been brainwashed into believing that they were strictly a British Community, have no Irish or Ulster traditions and therefore didn't need to learn Irish dancing, Gaelic, or folk music.' Thus Andy Tyrie, the leader of the UDA. Tyrie supports this view with a historical argument to the effect that there was an ancient British people ('British' in the non-imperial sense) called the Cruthin and who existed in Ulster long before the seventeenth-century settlement. He also emphasizes his Ulsterness by having a photograph of the statue of Cuchulain in the GPO above his desk. Cuchulain is therefore an authentically *Ulster* hero in a way that Carson – a Dubliner who privately despised the province – can never be. Where James Joyce offers a definition of Irish identity which is non-sectarian and truly republican, and which exists somewhere in the future, the UDA looks back to a dreamtime occupied by aboriginal ancestors in order to affirm an identity which is both epic and provincial. At the moment the UDA has stepped aside from the conflict and is insisting that it is a socialist and non-sectarian organization composed of forward-looking people who are 'tired of being classed as Neanderthal bigots'. They may draw their inspiration from a form of atavistic energy, but they are also modern in their outlook and they are opposed to the link with Britain. They have parted company with what is now termed 'Official Unionism'.

Although the UDA has now distanced itself from Ian Paisley, he more than any other Unionist politician appears to belong to a dreamtime of Presbyterian aborigines – giant preachers who strode the Antrim coast long before the birth of Christ. He is a complex and protean personality who imagines cyclones of blessings, compares himself to the diminutive figure of a famous Brahmin called Mahatma Gandhi, and probably nurses a secret admiration for Parnell, on whose parliamentary tactics some of his own appear to be modelled.

Ian Paisley was born in Armagh in 1926. His father, James Paisley, came of a Church of Ireland family who had lived in Co. Tyrone for many generations. In 1908 his father was 'saved' by an evangelical preacher and became a Baptist. In a memorial sermon, the son describes how his father went down to a frozen River Strule one Easter Sunday morning with a pastor who first broke the ice and then put him under the water:

My father tells when he went under the waters of that river he identified himself with his Lord in death, in burial and in resurrection. When he came out that day he had lost many of his friends, he had lost many of the people that once associated themselves with him in the gospel. He realised that there was a reproach with the gospel. My father as I told you, was uncompromising in his character. He did not care. The more he was opposed the more he preached and the more he was persecuted the more he excelled in evangelism. God blessed him and eventually he went to Armagh to business.

This is a characteristically Protestant piece of writing: there is the assertion of uncompromising principle, a strong self-justifying theme which runs throughout the sermon, an affirmation of the work ethic (that brutal verb 'to business' echoing the anti-Home Rule slogan 'Ulster Means Business'), and finally there is the idea of being born again. In a very fundamental sense it is a description of revolutionary commitment because this is, imaginatively, a seventeenth-century world where religion and politics are synonymous. And so on Easter Sunday 1908 the puritan revolutionary rises out of the deep, having rejected friends, family, leisure and the private life. The old life of compromise, scepticism and individual personality is set aside in the moment of commitment. And that commitment is made out in the open air, as compared with, say, T. S. Eliot's Anglican and institutional commitment which is a 'moment in a draughty church at smokefall'.

Paisley senior later broke with the Baptists because of their ecumenism and set up his own Independent Fundamentalist Church. The son has inherited this characteristic of breaking with established institutions and he has a Cromwellian scorn of formalism, an instinctive libertarianism which conceals, or creates, a monumentally dictatorial personality. It appears that the alternative to compromised institutions could be a series of pyramids dedicated to his version of the egotistical sublime, to his relentless monomania.

One of the strongest features of puritanism is its autobiographical tendency, its passionate self-regard. Paisley likes talking about himself, and in one of his published sermons he describes his 'apprenticeship in preaching in the open air'. During the Second World War he was a student at the Barry School of Evangelism in South Wales, and his tutor in open-air preaching was an ex-boxer:

He had his prize gold belt always at the gospel meetings. He used to swing that great gold belt, which he won as the welter-weight for the South of

England, around his head and shout as only Ted Sherwood could shout. He had a voice like a trumpet. People had to heed and listen to him. When he got tired and husky, he used to say, 'Go on Ian, you have a go.' So he drew the crowd, and so I served my apprenticeship, preaching when his voice was gone, his throat husky and his powerful frame exhausted.

It's like a scene from Ben Jonson: a fairground world where that ex-boxer swinging his gold belt is a Herculean showman with a voice so powerful it might bring walls crashing down. The charismatic mountebank – or sincere preacher – must draw and play the crowd, amuse it, hector it and put down hecklers. He is like a politician on a platform as well as being a flashy Autolycus-figure. That ex-boxer with the greenwood name stands as an archetype of inspiration, an entertainer and fighter, a displaced version of Cuchulain.

In 1949 Paisley began a mission in Belfast's dockland and he also joined the anti-Roman Catholic National Union of Protestants. Somewhere about this time there is a moment outside the printed record where he appears to have been snubbed by a member of the Unionist establishment. That establishment regarded him as a working-class rabble-rouser, and his outspoken unrestrained bigotry threatened and parodied its defter sectarianism. The rebuff demanded vengeance and Paisley began the long march which was to bring him to the walls of the Unionist establishment, to the barrier around the demesne.

The Paisley of this period is partly modelled on the Reverend Henry Cooke, a reactionary and highly influential nineteenth-century preacher who did much to counter Presbyterian radicalism. This Paisley is an autochthonous bigot who once organized a mock mass on the platform of the Ulster Hall. Patrick Marrinan, his biographer, describes the sinister shabbiness of this occasion, the nervous fascination of the audience laughing at a renegade Spanish priest reciting unfamiliar Latin words, the canny showmanship, the plastic buckets brimming with money.

Paisley's particular kind of puritan egotism is voracious in its subjectivity, and for all its insistence on sincerity is in practice highly theatrical. He is a compulsive role-player and is fond of dressing up in other people's personalities. After the Almighty, after St Paul – for whom he confesses 'a strange liking' – his most influential model, or imaginative icon, is John Bunyan, whose life and work obsess him. He calls Bunyan a 'poor unschooled tinker' who became 'the most prominent man of letters as far as English literature is concerned'. Bunyan is this 'dreamer and penman' who had 'the tinker's power of reaching the heart' – there is a hint of rural superstition and natural magic here. He admires Bunyan for his 'strong doctrinal preaching', his opposition to the civil and ecclesiastical authorities, the enormous crowds he drew, and for his prose-style. Bunyan's appeal is theological, social and aesthetic – he *is* culture and tradition. It's here that we enter a time-warp and see that world of Ranters, Fifth Monarchy Men, Levellers and millenarian preachers which E. P. Thompson and Christopher Hill describe in their work. For Thompson, *Pilgrim's Progress* is one of the two 'founding texts of the English working-class movement' (the other is Paine's *Rights of Man*). And so to admire Bunyan is by definition to be a dissenting radical, a nonconformist and a republican – Bunyan was a soldier in the Parliamentary Army.

Bunyan was also imprisoned for twelve years for preaching without a licence, and in 1966 Paisley was imprisoned for three months for demonstrating outside the General Assembly of the Presbyterian Church. In a statement he said, 'it will take more than Captain O'Neill's nasal twang to defy us' – the class grudge is clear, even though class politics was an impossible concept then. O'Neill warned of the dangers of alienating 'our British friends' and with an unconscious dismissiveness referred to Northern Ireland as 'this small corner of the British Commonwealth'. Angered by this diminution, Paisley retorted: 'To Our Lord, puppet politicians are but grasshoppers with portfolios.' Like any republican he refused, in one of his favourite phrases, to 'bow the knee' to the colonial authority and its deputies. And so, in a small corner of the British Commonwealth, Ulster's Bunyan was imprisoned by a grasshopper with a portfolio.

While he was in prison Paisley wrote the most substantial of his four books. It is an exposition of Paul's Epistle to the Romans cast in the form of a puritan journal. Each section is dated, and the

33

exposition ends with this dramatic, deadpan postscript: 'This section completed in the dawn of the eighty-third day of imprisonment: Tuesday, 11 October 1966.' It is the dawn of righteousness, conviction and inspiration, and it looks forward to Paisley's second prison term three years later, when he sent this letter to his congregation:

Beloved in the Lord,

The day which we have prayed for and longed for has dawned. Captain O'Neill the tyrant is no longer the ruler of our country. We, who have suffered under his tyranny and wrath, can surely sing Psalm 124. The Lord has wrought for us a great deliverance, and to His great Name we ascribe the glory. Let us be careful to return our heartfelt thanks.

I heard the news here in my cell, No. 20 (B2), as prisoner 636, at approximately 4.30 on Monday afternoon. Immediately I sang the doxology and fell upon my knees to give God thanks. We have had a long and bitter struggle. As a people we have suffered. As your minister I have been maligned and persecuted, and you have all shared the maligning and persecuting. We have been in the depths together. Every effort has been made to smash the testimony of the Church and the credibility of me, the minister of the church. THEY HAVE FAILED, FOR GOD WAS OUR HELPER. We are just a lot of nobodies, and the enemy thought he could trample us out, BUT GOD DELIVERED US.

Like some Luddite pamphlet, this message rises up from the very depths of popular culture, and that phrase 'We are just a lot of nobodies' concentrates much of the emotion which Paisleyism draws on and expresses. The plain, strenuous, autodidactic atmosphere that clings to Paisley's published works – a combination of earnest assertive pride and a deep lack of confidence – tells of a disadvantaged population which feeds its persecution complex by reading the Psalms and which dreams of emerging from the underground status of subculture into the light of power and society.

It is impossible to nourish such an ambitious dream and to see yourself as a grateful inhabitant of a small corner of the British Commonwealth, and Paisley's rejection of that dependent status is formulated in a theological argument. Commenting on Romans 1.1 – 'Paul, a servant of Jesus Christ, called to be an apostle, separated unto the gospel of God' – Paisley notes, 'Paul was a separatist.' This idea of separation is one of his major themes, and in his commentary on Romans he is forming an idea of Ulster nationalism which entails separation from both the United Kingdom and the Republic of Ireland.

He is also fascinated by the phrase 'for a little season' which occurs in Revelation 6.11, and he cites a similar phrase from Hebrews: 'By faith Moses, when he was come to years, refused to be called the son of Pharaoh's daughter; choosing rather to suffer affliction with the people of God, than to enjoy the pleasures of sin for a season (11.25–6).' For Paisley, Ulster under O'Neill is like Egypt under Pharoah, a sinful bondage which is to be endured for a season. He draws this analogy in his commentary and it appears to be a puritan favourite. In Richardson's *Pamela*, for example, Pamela confides to her journal:

I think I was loth to leave the house. Can you believe it? – what could be the matter with me, I wonder? . . . Surely I cannot be like the old murmuring Israelites, to long after the onions and garlic of Egypt, when they had suffered there such heavy bondage?

In its restless search for liberty the puritan spirit sometimes welcomes suffering, sometimes looks back over its shoulder to a warm and muddied slavery, to the old temporizing life of compromise and subjection.

There is an epic moment in one of Paisley's published sermons where he insists obsessively that *'the sea speaks of separation'*:

I stand at the edge of the sea. I look over its waves, and my loved ones are across in another continent. Between me and them stretches the waves of the briny depths. I know what it is to be separated from them. Nothing separates like the sea. What a barrier the sea makes. What a terrible barrier the sea makes. Separation.

The word obsesses him, and in a cassette recording entitled *Separation*, which was released in 1980, he explains that Moses 'chose the affliction of the people of God' and rejected 'the beggarly elements of Egypt'. Here, Egypt is the United Kingdom – Ulster under direct rule from Westminster – and Paisley is offering a Pauline separatist argument: 'May God make us a separated people.' By 'us' he means the Protestants – there is a tribal exclusiveness central to this definition – and he sees himself as Moses leading his people out of bondage to the Promised Land. This parallel is employed more elaborately by Joyce in *Ulysses*, where Bloom is Moses, the precursor of Christ, the liberator; Parnell is both Moses and Christ, and Stephen is Christ the Hero. However, Joyce's idea of the Irish nation is inclusive rather than exclusive – it is a definition beyond tribalism, beyond religious creed. And those Irish historians who congratulate themselves on their freedom from tribal simplicities might reflect on whom exactly they mean by 'we' – what audience do they speak for and address? A long time ago Yeats asked himself this question in 'The Fisherman' and answered it by praying for an ideal reader, a 'man who is but a dream'.

Paisley's political ambition and his motivating fire – a fire he has stolen from the Unionist establishment – are sometimes transparently evident in his scriptural exegesis. Commenting on the phrase, 'for it is the power of God' (Romans 1.16), he remarks:

Gospel preaching is charged with the dynamic of heaven. Dynamite to be displayed in all its mighty potency must have the fuse and the fire. When the fuse of true prayer is set alight with the fire of the Holy Ghost and thus the gospel dynamite is exploded, what tremendous results occur. Then do the strongholds of Satan topple. Then do the bulwarks of idolatry collapse. Then do the towering walls of sin suddenly fall. Then is the enemy dislodged. Then is all opposition blasted and the power of truth is proved to be more than a conqueror. Oh for a day of real gospel preaching and gospel power! Lord let me witness such a day.

This prayer for power was offered in the prison cell in 1966 and three years later, in April 1969, there was a series of explosions which were blamed on the IRA, and which helped to bring about O'Neill's resignation. Though no one had accused them, the Ulster Volunteer Force denied responsibility for the explosions and it's generally accepted that they, or freelance Protestant terrorists, were responsible. Puritan metaphor is a form of irony which has a habit of becoming literal: a dynamic millenarian rhetoric can inspire men to place actual dynamite under the status quo.

Paisley's theological argument is that 'righteousness without the law' must be received by faith, and he explains that the seed of Abraham are not heirs of the law but heirs by the righteousness of faith without the law. According to the Anglican *New Commentary on Holy Scripture* Paul argues that an 'act of faith' procured Abraham's acquittal, and by 'faith' Paul means 'the whole act, or attitude, of surrender to Christ, intellectual, moral, and emotional'.

This idea of an act of faith is fundamental to Paisley's thought, and from time to time it is given calculated existential expression – as, for example, in his demonstration in the House of Commons after the assassination of the Reverend Robert Bradford and his subsequent call for a campaign of passive disobedience to force the British out. Of necessity, the leap of faith is intensely subjective and assertive, and it is informed or sustained by an idea of martyrdom. Paisley comments that Christ makes frequent references to his death as 'the culminating act of his ministry on earth', and this inspires his projection of himself as an exemplary figure, ready to stake all and do or die for his faith and his people ('sell our lives dearly', as he put it outside the House of Commons).

Although Paisley resembles De Valera in the theological cast of his mind, the religion he subscribes to is an apparently unstructured, intensely emotional experience. 'Justification,' he argues, 'is heart work as opposed to head work.' This assertion of emotion over intellect is both authoritarian and romantic, and Paisley finds its dogmatic justification in Romans 10.10: 'For with the heart man believeth unto righteousness; and with the mouth confession is made unto salvation.' This is what he terms 'heart belief', though according to the meek and wily Anglican commentary 'heart' is a word which designates 'the inner self, with special reference to the intellect'. Essentially, this is a version of that dull old eighteenth-century dichotomy between the heart and the head: the Anglican hegemony is for Reason, the puritan evangelical opposition is for Feeling. Reason is a form of social control, Feeling a type of subversion – as Henry Fielding implies in his criticisms of Whitfield.

Paisley's argument in his exposition is that when 'the Spirit comes, the curse of the law is removed and its hideous tyranny broken and he [Paul] is freed from the law of sin and death'. Although this does appear to have connections with antinomianism, Paisley rejects 'the pernicious doctrines of the antinomians' in his introduction to chapter seven, where he discusses the concepts of 'law' and 'grace'. Although he later states that a Christian 'must also give due and proper respect to those above him in society', it's impossible not to perceive that 'law' and 'grace' are essentially irreconcilable.

In his commentary on Romans, C. K. Barrett remarks:

Jesus had been condemned by the law. He had been tried and found guilty of blasphemy (Mark 14.64) by the supreme court of his people; moreover, he had died a death which exposed him to the curse declared in the law (Deuteronomy 21.23; Galatians 3.13). Yet God had not cursed him; on the contrary, he had ratified his claims and declared his approval of him by raising him from the dead. On this crucial issue, therefore, the law – or, at least, Israel's understanding of the law – had been wrong. This did not mean that the law was to be rejected out of hand. Jesus himself had reaffirmed its validity as the word of God, and, rightly understood, it bore witness to him. But it must be rightly understood, and not understood in the old way. It could no longer be regarded as the mediator between God and man; this function had been assumed by Jesus Christ.

Barrett further states that Paul's theological development consists 'in the adjustment of old convictions based upon the Old Testament and formulated within Judaism to the new Christian conviction that Jesus is Lord'. Ironically and paradoxically, therefore, Paisley here appears to be on the side of what is new, rather than being a simple Mosaic fundamentalist. Inevitably, his exposition is both political and theological, and his assertion that 'Election' is an act of God 'governed only and solely by His good pleasure' looks forward to his two election victories in 1970.

At this pitch of imaginative extremity, metaphor and irony take on a superreal brightness, and the conventional line between fact and fiction melts in a manner that is characteristic of puritan journalism. This is apparent in one of Paisley's prison messages:

We are not the servants of men, nor the servants of the rulers of men. We are the servants of the Lord. This, of course, does not appear to the world. They think of us as devils, as troublemakers, as servants of hell, and as disturbers of the peace. *They do not recognise our imperial loyalty* as they did not recognise the imperial royalty of our Master. For if the princes of this world had known they would not have crucified the Lord of Glory. Some day however, our imperial royalty will be manifested before heaven, earth and hell.

He was in prison for abusing the Governor of Northern Ireland, who was the representative of 'imperial royalty'. However, the royal glow which it was his function to impart appears not to have warmed the unofficial side of Unionism, and Paisley's statement is an assertion of his and his followers' sense of their own worth, their own 'imperial royalty'. It is a gesture of defiance and independence, and if the attitude which informs it is characteristically raw, edgy, brutal, dangerous, it is at least the beginning of an idea and so is far in advance of Official Unionism. That dismal political philosophy has never shown any talent for, or interest in, forming ideas.

Terence O'Neill dismissed Ian Paisley's chiliastic rhetoric and his political demonstrations as 'mindless', and the establishment view of him is expressed in two later remarks of Brian Faulkner's. When the British Government suspended Stormont, Faulkner accused it of reducing Northern Ireland to 'a coconut colony'. Later, when the power-sharing Executive fell, Faulkner called Paisley 'this demon doctor'. This habit of drawing analogies – whether with Hungary or Algeria – is a deep-seated Irish characteristic, and the parallel here must be familiar to anyone who has read the novels of V. S. Naipaul. It invites us to imagine a West Indian island, drums beating, the governor's mansion, a messianic revolutionary leader, riots, carnival and independence. Indeed, Paisleyism is curiously similar to reggae music – both are assertions of post-colonial identity, though reggae is much more advanced, sophisticated and culturally eclectic.

In 1970 Paisley became a Stormont MP, then a Westminster MP. In the following year Brian Faulkner introduced internment, and towards the end of 1971 Paisley emerged as a kind of republican statesman. With the SDLP, he opposed the introduction of internment 'in principle', though he had favoured it at first. At the end of November he suggested that if the Constitution of the Irish Republic were amended then 'good neighbourliness in the highest possible sense' might prevail between the Republic and Northern Ireland. He said:

I would like to see anything done that would be for the good of all the people of Northern Ireland and all the people of Ireland. I believe it could deal with the cancer and the cancer is not the 1920 Act and not the partition of the country but the cancer is the 1937 Constitution and the domination of the Catholic Church through it. I would like to see the whole thing thrown out.

When asked if he would favour a united Ireland if the Republic were to remove Protestant fears by amending its Constitution, he replied:

If you ask me whether I can see at some time some way, somewhere in the future a united Ireland, that is a question I cannot answer because I cannot now say what will happen in the future and, anyway, I cannot answer the question because I am too much of a realist and such a question is really not even worthy of consideration now.

The establishment Unionists were quick to exploit this apparent rejection of the old anti-Home Rule slogan 'We won't have it', and they accused Paisley of being prepared to sell out to Republicanism. He quickly drew back and claimed he'd been misquoted.

Three months later he emerged as a total integrationist in a pamphlet called *The Ulster Problem, Spring 1972: A Discussion of the True Situation in Northern Ireland*. This pamphlet contains a section called 'A brief history of Ireland' which is an interesting example of Unionist historiography. All mention of the 1798 rebellion is carefully avoided and we are moved briskly from the plantation of Ulster to the year 1800:

... the Irish Parliament decided for legislative union or parliamentary union with Great Britain; and there was passed the Act of Union. The Irish Parliament was abolished, and from 1800 the members of Parliament from Ireland had their seats in the mother of Parliaments – the British House of Commons at Westminster.

Later in the pamphlet Paisley insists on the necessity of 'the complete union of Northern Ireland and the United Kingdom'. He wants 'full legislative union'. This appears straightforward – it was for a long time the policy of Enoch Powell and the Official Unionists – except that that favourite word 'separated' appears three times in his brief history of Ireland. He describes Daniel O'Connell and Parnell as separatist leaders, and the wish to equal them in stature is not beyond his ambition – he is a natural overreacher who has no regard for the ideas of balance, decorum and limitation which are such strong features of English culture.

In order to 'separate' he has had to appear to be leading his people back into Egypt, and it is now clear that Britain has absolutely no intention of granting Northern Ireland full, permanent legislative union. Paisley therefore understands Austen Chamberlain's remark that Northern Ireland is 'an illogical and indefensible compromise', and his policy can be interpreted as an ironic double bluff which invites both Britain and the Republic to lay their cards on the table. British policy may now be defined as 'Get out' – the phrase hurled at Paisley, McQuade and Robinson by angry Westminster MPs – while the policy of the Irish Republic has recently become clear in the New Ireland Forum Report.

If total integration is a dead duck (and everyone recognizes that it is), and if a united Ireland is an impossibility, then the only alternative is for Northern Ireland to secede and go independent – to 'separate'. Ultimately – and tragically – there never is any choice between this, that, and a something else which is neither this nor that. However, the idea of Ulster independence does express a conflict which is other than the Unionist/Republican conflict. Southerners appear to regard Northerners as incomprehensible savages, while Northerners look South and see, in the words of Henry Joy McCracken, 'a set of gasconaders'. At a deep level there is a shared perception, a common bond, between the minority and majority populations in the North, and this bond is altogether other than the sentimental concept of 'ould dacency' purveyed by writers like Benedict Kiely.

It emerges, for example, in a speech which Paisley made in 1973, the year the House of Commons approved a White Paper for a Northern Ireland Assembly. During the Commons debate, Paisley said this:

For too long the representatives of Northern Ireland have been asked: 'Who do you speak for?' It is important at this juncture that the people be given the opportunity to speak by the ballot box. In many senses we have been caught up in a struggle that goes far beyond the basic differences between two sections of the community. There are other elements in the situation that do not want a settlement of any kind, that are purely and utterly destructive, that want to see the destruction of Northern Ireland not merely as an entity in the UK, but as part of the Western democratic system. This House must face up to the fact that these forces in Northern Ireland care not about any Government White Paper or the democratic vote. They believe that violence in the end shall pay. It is sad but in many degrees violence has paid off in Ulster. Throughout this debate there has been the dangerous suggestion that if the elections throw up a group in Northern Ireland which this house does not like, then, with a stroke of the pen, they can say on 31 March next year: 'fare thee well'. When we say this makes us feel like second-class citizens, we are telling the truth. I would not like to see Northern Ireland ever going outside the Union, but there is a section there who are feeling restless with the attitudes of the members of this House and the Government.

Perhaps this was the first time that a Unionist had stated in public that he felt like a 'second-class citizen'. It marks a significant movement of the spirit and helps to define the difference between official and unofficial Unionism. The majority of the constituents of Fermanagh and South Tyrone will hardly have needed to recall the phrase when the House of Commons simply ignored their wishes in a dangerous display of near-unanimity, or 'me-tooism' as one dissenting Labour MP courageously defined it.

Here we arrive at something hard and fast – a principle which unites Paisleyism with Republicanism. We come up against the collision between that principle and the sort of eyes-averted Burkean shuffle which characterizes British policy towards Ireland. The principle of one-man-one-vote is a great leveller, and it has even prompted one Burkean commentator to suggest that Fermanagh-South Tyrone should become United Nations territory.

The complication in Paisley's attitude to this principle lies in his perception of himself as British. It is an intermittent and fluctuating perception (for the *Sunday Times* he is a 'defiler of the British way of life'), and it was expressed forcibly during a meeting Paisley had with Bernadette Devlin in 1968. She suggested that the Unionist state had been unjust and unfair, and although he conceded that there might have been injustices Paisley insisted, 'I would rather be British than fair.' In Ulster, the condition of being British is that you somehow believe in one-man-one-vote but are selective about its implementation. And so it is possible to have a situation where a group of demonstrators waves a placard saying ONE MAN ONE VOTE and a rival group waves either the Union Jack or a placard saying BETTER BRITISH THAN FAIR.

Paisley would appear to have discarded the idea of Britishness now, though his response to Bernadette Devlin's question shows his wish to reduce every question to fundamental principles. And here John Hume's remark the day after Bloody Sunday – 'it's a united Ireland now or nothing' – defined another fundamental principle for the first time.

Because he possesses a theological temperament, Paisley is as opposed to liberalism as any Marxist. In one sermon, for example, he attacks the 'sinking sands of an easy believism' – he means ecumenism, liberal theology and politics. In another sermon he begins by stating, 'Ours is a Laodicean age,' and in another he says, 'Make sure of this, there will be no neutrals in this service. There will not be a man or a woman go down the stairs today out onto the streets of Ballymena who will not have made a vital and a terrible decision.' This is the Baptist doctrine of total immersion or complete commitment, and anyone familiar with the ideological temperament will recognize it here in an earlier, theological form. It's a temperament dipped in icy, not lukewarm, water, an urgent single-minded attitude which says that the 'only minute you can be sure of is this minute' and which states that it's 'now or never'.

This tremendous leap of faith is directed both at personal political power and at an idea of God, and Paisley's God resembles a cross between Judge Jeffreys and Albert Pierrepoint. This 'God of inflexible justice' is described in a sermon called 'After This Judgement' in which Paisley gives a relished description of a court 'in the old days' where the chaplain comes and gives the judge 'the black cap.' He then states, 'Some day Jesus will put on the black cap,' and this idea of God as a hanging judge is developed in his study of George Whitefield where he quotes a contemporary witness:

'I have known him . . . avail himself of the formality of the judge putting on his black cap to pronounce sentence. With his eyes full of tears, and his heart almost too big to admit of speech, he would say after a momentary pause, "I am now going to put on my condemning cap. Sinner, I MUST do it! I MUST do it. I MUST pronounce sentence." Then in a burst of tremendous eloquence he would repeat our Lord's words, "Depart ye cursed!" and not without a powerful description of the nature of that curse.'

Paisley admires this obscene, righteous and murderous egotism – an egotism which violently overthrows formalities and social bonds. Somewhere deep in his personality lies a fascination with judicial murder which involves a contradictory identification with both the victim and his executioner.

In a published sermon, 'Richard Cameron: The Lion of the Covenant', there is a stark and savoured quotation from the sentence of hanging and disembowelling which the 'Council of Blood' passed on one of the Covenanters. Here Paisley appears as a Scottish Nationalist laying the 'tribute wreath' of his sermon on the memorial to a Protestant martyr (his mother was 'born into a Scots Covenanting home' and he makes much of his Scottish inheritance). This is apparent in two cassette sermons on the Covenanters which are awash with cries of 'Blood' and whose delivery at times resembles the intonation necessary to a reading of the closing lines of Yeats's 'Easter 1916'. Although Paisley doesn't write the sacred names out in a verse, he does recite them in a rolling, drawn-out, ululating intonation which elevates the 'Covenanting martyrs' and affirms their holiness. These almost forgotten historical figures are invested with a vocal halo by the preacher and so are changed into transcendent heroes. This is a Protestantism which is pushing deep into the territory of mystery and mythology; it is a celebration of chthonic forces and a rejection of secular and utilitarian values.

In particular, Paisley singles out one young Covenanter, Hugh McKail, who was 'only 27 years old' when he was led to the scaffold. His description of McKail's execution is ironically similar to Patrick Pearse's account of Robert Emmet's execution, where the body of the 'comely' young man is desecrated on the scaffold. Paisley thanks God that there is 'in my heart a wonderful affinity with Richard Cameron', and here he again identifies with the martyred victim rather than the hanging judge. The Covenanters, he states, were 'bold, courageous, strong men . . . these were not the putty paper men of the twentieth century – these were the rugged men of the Reformation'. Quoting a 'great master of English literature' – someone he calls 'Jupiter Carlyle' – he terms them 'real heroes', and he refers to this passage from *Heroes and Hero Worship*:

. . . many men in the van do always, like Russian soldiers, march into the ditch at Schweidnitz, and fill it up with their dead bodies, that the rear may pass over them dry shod, and gain the honour . . . How many earnest rugged Cromwells, Knoxes, poor Peasant Covenanters, wrestling, battling for very life, in rough miry places, have to struggle, and suffer, and fall, greatly censured, *bemired*, – before a beautiful Revolution of Eighty-eight can step over them in official pumps and silk-stockings, with universal three-times-three!

This is a burning and rebarbative evocation of that buried unrecorded level of anonymous historical experience from which Paisley draws much of his inspiration, and it could be that other Irish historians are also fired by this subterranean energy.

When heaven was opened, Paisley says, the Covenanters hoped to see Christ 'on his white horse coming forth to put every enemy underneath his feet'. Here, Christ and William of Orange, the Second Coming and the Glorious Revolution, melt into each other. The Day of Judgement is a gable-end in Sandy Row and the white horse becomes the pale horse of Revelation. Paisley is an amateur and obsessive numerologist and he has a particular fascination for the apocalyptic vision of Revelation. In another Covenanting sermon he explains the symbolism of the fifth seal in terms which echo his discussion of grace and law in the exposition. Five is the 'number of grace' and this is the 'mighty sovereign free grace of God' which enabled the Covenanters to 'stand true and uncompromisingly'.

In this sermon, metaphor and substance become confused: blood is both symbol and reality. The preacher shouts out:

. . . all the attributes of God flow in the bloodstream of Calvary . . . we're under the blood-stained banner of the Cross . . . must sail through bloody seas . . . blood . . . blood . . . blood . . .

The sermon lurches towards a Churchillian rhetoric – 'there's a storm coming that will try all our foundations' – and it also has moments of bloody and paranoid dementia. At times it sounds a note of bitter failure, at others it is fired with a notion of glorious martyrdom. It looks beyond this world to the resurrection, yet it is also directed towards this world in its imagination of a radically new, radically changed society. It is part Protestant triumphalism careering off into heaven, part an attempt to heal the puritan split in consciousness by summoning a millenarian vision of a new heaven and a new earth. The sermon offers an essentially Lawrentian ethic – blood consciousness and the healing rainbow at the end.

This apocalyptic vision is given an antiquarian treatment in Paisley's book *The 'Fifty Nine' Revival*, which is an account of the revolutionary 'flood time of revival' which swept parts of Ulster in 1859. F. S. L. Lyons discusses this movement briefly in *Culture and Anarchy in Ireland*, though he sees it – wrongly I think – as an almost exclusively emotional and psychological phenomenon. His understanding of Presbyterianism is limited and inadequate, and this is because historiography – at least in the North – is still at the polemical stage. Future historians will have a mass of pamphlets, tracts, sermons and journalism to draw on. Lyons has failed to commence this excavation, and this may explain why his discussion of Northern culture is so unsatisfactory.

In his conclusion, Lyons states that between the fall of Parnell and the death of Yeats there was an anarchy

. . . in the mind and in the heart, an anarchy which forbade not just unity of territories, but also 'unity of being', an anarchy that sprang from the collision within a small and intimate island of seemingly irreconcilable cultures, unable to live together or to live apart, caught inextricably in the web of their tragic history.

Despite the counterbalancing quotation from Yeats with which he caps this, Lyons's Arnoldian terminology is unhelpful, and it could be argued – indeed it *was* argued long ago by George Birmingham in *The Red Hand of Ulster* – that Irish culture is really unified at its extremes. An example of this can be found in Paisley's historical study *The Massacre of St Bartholomew*, where he explores the doctrine of martyrdom. He believes that 'true faith is a martyred faith' and gives the traditional argument that the blood of the martyrs is the 'seed' of the Church. This is close to the phrase 'elect seed' which he employs in his exposition, and it resembles Pearse's notion of martyrdom.

Does this mean, then, that it is Paisley's ambition to take over the GPO in Belfast and give his life for Ulster? Will there be a generation of Democratic Unionist hunger-strikers? Will there be a civil war of the kind Paisley describes in his history of the Huguenots? Will a shrunken, independent Northern Ireland barricade itself against an enlarged Republic? And will an ambitious group of Ulster Nationalists demand the return of Cavan, Monaghan and Donegal, as well as the counties lost from the six? Or will there be negotiation, argument, compromise, a new Constitution, a parliament in Armagh and the beginnings of a way of writing history that is neither Orange nor Green, but is instead as white as the middle band of the Irish tricolour?

History, by its very nature, has no answers.

The Earnest Puppet: Edward Carson

Early in 1981 Ian Paisley mounted a midnight demonstration on an Antrim hillside where 500 men gathered to threaten the British government with firearm certificates. When a puzzled journalist asked him exactly what he was playing at, Paisley told his interviewer to go away and acquaint himself with the life and times of Sir Edward Carson. Here, then, is the book which political journalists and their uninformed public may have been waiting for – a life of that grim and righteous figure whose ghost stalks through the North of Ireland now.

Carson was born in Dublin in 1854 and was descended from 'Honest John' Lambert, one of Cromwell's major-generals. A tall, ungainly, dyspeptic figure whose schoolfellows called him 'Rawbones', his personality suggests many of the darker aspects of puritanism – he was a joyless barrister, a canny hypochondriac, a brooding philistine, a savagely destructive politician. He knew Oscar Wilde at Trinity, and appeared a dull and conscientious plodder beside his brilliant contemporary (many years later he vengefully destroyed Wilde in a famous cross-examination). He was a histrionic advocate who loved to simulate a stony integrity, and his favourite ploy – both in the court-room and in the Commons – was to lose his temper and walk out. Without irony, without subtlety, he possessed a peculiarly harsh and negative will, which was stoked by huge bunkers of moral self-righteousness.

In 1910 he gave up the chance of leading the Tory Party and became the parliamentary leader of the anti-Home Rule Irish Unionists. Soon this distinguished KC and former Solicitor-General was supporting loyalist gunrunners and doing his fanatic best to undermine the legal and political institutions he claimed to revere.

Review of A. T. Q. Stewart, *Edward Carson*.

According to George Dangerfield – a compelling authority who is oddly absent from this study – Carson possessed a nature which 'ought never to be allowed within the walls of a Parliament'. He was one of the rough beasts who assisted at the death of liberal England, a case-hardened lawyer who was so passionately and uncompromisingly lawless in his utterances that his seditious rhetoric won the admiration of Patrick Pearse and Sir Roger Casement. It was the Loyalist rebellion of 1912 which Carson led that helped to inspire the 1916 Easter Rising, and this paradox finds contemporary expression in the admiration which David O'Connell, one of the Provisional IRA leaders, feels for the most extreme loyalist leaders.

Carson's public life was a long and relentless success story, and yet he felt he had been a failure. His maiden speech in the House of Lords is a spectacular example of the contradictory, self-pitying, childish and festering sense of grievance which is at the centre of the Loyalist mentality. Addressing the Lords in 1921, he first attacked the government for negotiating the Treaty with Michael Collins and then turned to lambast his colleagues in the Tory Party. He complained bitterly that the Tories had merely used the Unionists during the previous thirty years: 'I was in earnest. What a fool I was! I was only a puppet, and so was Ulster, and so was Ireland, in the political game that was to get the Conservative Party into power.' It's a naïve and anguished political testament which never arrives at the perception that Unionist MPs at Westminster must always have the status of political whores. Lord Randolph Churchill, Austen Chamberlain and Lord Birkenhead all used the Unionists ruthlessly, and when Edward Heath betrayed them many years later they glumly sold their votes to the Labour Party – a party which will never repeal the Unionists' constitutional veto, despite its vague and contradictory gestures towards Irish unity.

Although Stewart's biography is a useful addition to Gill and Macmillan's welcome series, it is a sometimes sentimental piece of loyalist hagiography whose style is well below his characteristic standard. Stewart assumes the integrity of the Ulster Unionists' quarrel, and although he quotes A. J. P. Taylor's verdict that Carson was dangerous in opposition but ineffective in office, he fails to explore the glaring and obvious limitations of Carson's Loyalist credo. He does, however, comment on the incompatible nature of Carson's cultural allegiances, and on the manner in which he became the prisoner of the Ulster Unionists. Carson's costive self-importance was founded on the belief that the Tory Party was 'earnest' about the Union with Britain. He came to believe his own theatrical gestures and so failed to notice the element of fantasy and games-playing in public life which was so clear to the ironic intelligence of his old enemy, Wilde.

A New Look at the Language Question

The history of a language is often a story of possession and dispossession, territorial struggle and the establishment or imposition of a culture. Arguments about the 'evolution' or the 'purity' of a language can be based on a simplistic notion of progress or on a doctrine of racial stereotypes. Thus a Spenserian phrase which Samuel Johnson employs in the famous preface to his dictionary – 'the wells of English undefiled' – is instinct with a mystic and exclusive idea of nationhood. It defines a language and a culture in terms of a chimerical idea of racial purity. But Johnson doesn't profess this idea either visibly or aggressively, and in the less well-known essay which follows his preface he comments on the historical sources of the English language. Reflecting on the extinction of the ancient British language, he remarks:

. . . it is scarcely possible that a nation, however depressed, should have been mixed in considerable numbers with the Saxons without some communication of their tongue, and therefore it may, with great reason, be imagined, that those, who were not sheltered in the mountains, perished by the sword.

Anglo-Saxon society was among the very first European societies to establish a tradition of vernacular prose. However, for several centuries after the Norman conquest English was regarded as a rude and uncultivated tongue. At the beginning of the fourteenth century, the chronicler Robert of Gloucester notes with concern that English is spoken only by 'lowe men'. He remarks that England is the only country in the world that doesn't 'hold' to its own speech, and implies that such a situation is unnatural. Here he is clearly influenced by the English nationalism which developed after the crown lost Normandy early in the thirteenth century. French, however, continued to be the official language of England until a parliamentary statute of 1362 stated that all lawsuits must be conducted in English. French was displaced and the English language returned from a form of internal exile.

The English language was first brought to Ireland by the followers of Strongbow's Norman invaders in the twelfth century. Norman French and English became established as vernacular languages, though their speakers gradually crossed over to Irish. Attempts were made to resist this process – for example in the statutes of Kilkenny (1366) – but the Irishing of the settlers was completed by the Reformation which united the 'Old English' with the native Irish against the Protestant 'New English'. And as Alan Bliss has shown, the Cromwellian settlement of the 1650s was to be crucial to the history of the English language in Ireland. With the exception of Ulster, the English spoken in most parts of Ireland today is descended from the language of Cromwell's planters. The result, according to Diarmuid Ó Muirithe, is 'a distinctive Irish speech – Anglo-Irish or Hiberno-English, call it what you will'.

In England, the English language reached a peak of creative power during the Elizabethan and Jacobean periods, when writers formed sentences by instinct or guesswork rather than by stated rule. In time it was felt that the language was overseeded and in need of more careful cultivation. Writers began to argue that the absence of a standard of 'correct' English created an ugly and uncivilized linguistic climate, and Dryden remarked that he sometimes had to translate an idea into Latin before he could decide on the proper way of expressing it in English. In a *Discourse Concerning Satire* he noted, 'we have yet no prosodia, not so much as a tolerable dictionary, or a grammar, so that our language is in a manner barbarous'. Dryden's neoclassicism had an epic scope and power, and like Virgil's Aeneas he wished to found a new *civitas* in a country damaged by violence and conflict. He argued that in order to regulate and refine the language properly England must have an academy modelled on the Académie Française. His criticism of the state of the language was developed by Swift in *A Proposal for Correcting, Improving, and Ascertaining the English Tongue*, which was addressed to Robert

Harley, the Lord High Treasurer of England, and published in 1712. Although Swift strategically avoided mentioning the idea of an academy, it is clear that he intended his readers to make that deduction. Only an academy would be capable of 'ascertaining and fixing our language for ever, after such alterations are made in it as shall be thought requisite'.

Swift's proposal appears to be innocent of political interest, but a Whig paper, the *Medley*, detected Jacobitism in his preference for the Romance languages over the Saxon on the grounds that he was opposed to any 'new addition of Saxon words by bringing over the Hanover family'. According to his Whig critic, Swift wished to hasten 'a new invasion by the Pretender and the French, because that language has more Latin words than the Saxon'. Partly as a result, the idea of an academy came to be regarded as essentially unpatriotic, and it was on these grounds that Johnson took issue with Swift's 'petty treatise'. In the preface to his dictionary he remarks that he does not wish 'to see dependence multiplied' and hopes that 'the spirit of English liberty' will hinder or destroy any attempt to set up an academy in England. Although Matthew Arnold revived Swift's proposal in a provocative essay entitled 'The Literary Influence of Academies', the idea of an academic legislature for the language was effectively extinguished by Johnson's preface.

Johnson's argument is insular, aggressive and somewhat sentimental, yet there can be no doubt that he is expressing an ingrained cultural hostility to state intervention in the language. Johnson believed that a dictionary could perform the function of correcting English better than an academy could, and he argued that the organic nature of language ought to be respected. It was both misguided and tyrannical to attempt to freeze the English language artificially as Swift had suggested.

Johnson's English patriotism and his anarchistic conservatism inform his view of the language, and in accordance with his libertarian principles he avoids imposing any guide to pronunciation in his dictionary. Swift, however, advocated a standard English pronunciation, and in an essay 'On Barbarous Denominations in Ireland' he criticized the Scottish accent and most English regional accents as 'offensive'. He also observed that an Irish accent made 'the deliverer . . . ridiculous and despised', and remarked that 'from such a mouth, an Englishman expects nothing but bulls, blunders, and follies'. For Swift, a standard English accent is a platonic ideal which will give dignity and self-respect to anyone who acquires it. He is therefore rejecting a concept of 'Hiberno-English' or 'Anglo-Irish' and is advocating a unified culture which embraces both Britain and Ireland. This ideal of complete integration still has its supporters, but it must now be apparent that a Unionist who retains a marked Irish accent is either an unconscious contradiction or a subversive ironist.

Dictionaries generally do legislate for pronunciation, and towards the end of the eighteenth century a 'war of the dictionaries' took place in England. The argument was between supporters of Thomas Sheridan's 'pronouncing dictionary' and those who preferred John Walker's rival dictionary. Sheridan had what Johnson termed 'the disadvantage of being an Irishman', and so was not allowed to fix the pronunciations of English. On patriotic grounds the controversy was therefore decided in Walker's favour.

If sentiments about the English language can at times be informed by an idea of ethnicity, attempts to refine and ascertain the language almost instinctively relate it to the Houses of Parliament, to those institutions where speech exercises power. In his *Dictionary of Modern English Usage* H. W. Fowler frequently draws examples from parliamentary debates, and in this entry he reveals the simple patriotism which fires his concept of correct usage:

England, English(man). The incorrect use of these words as equivalents of *Great Britain* or *The United Kingdom, British, Briton*, is often resented by other nationals of the U.K., like the book-reviewer who writes of Lord Cherwell's 'dedication to the service of Britain, which, in the annoying way foreigners have, he persisted in calling "England" '. Their susceptibilities are natural, but are not necessarily always to be deferred to. For many purposes the wider words are the natural ones. We speak of the *British Commonwealth*, the *British Navy, Army*, and *Air Force* and *British trade*; we boast that *Britons* never never never shall be slaves; we know that Sir John Moore sleeps in a grave where a *Briton* has laid him, and there is no alternative to *British* English if we want to distinguish our idiom from the American. But it must be remembered that no Englishman, or perhaps no Scotsman even, calls himself a Briton without a sneaking sense of the ludicrous, or hears himself referred to as a BRITISHER without squirming. How should an Englishman utter the words *Great Britain* with the glow of emotion that for him goes with *England*? His sovereign may be Her *Britannic* Majesty to outsiders, but to him is Queen of *England*; he talks the *English* language; he has been taught *English* history as one continuous tale from Alfred to his own day; he has heard of the word of an *Englishman* and aspires to be an *English* gentleman; and he knows that *England* expects every man to do his duty. 'Speak for *England*' was the challenge flung across the floor of the House of Commons by Leo Amery to the Leader of the Opposition on 2 September 1939. In the word *England*, not in *Britain*, all those things are implicit. It is unreasonable to ask forty millions of people to refrain from the use of the only names that are in tune with patriotic emotion, or to make them stop and think whether they mean their country in a narrower or wider sense each time they name it.

More recently, a Conservative MP praised Michael Foot for 'speaking for England' during the comic and hysterical debate which followed Argentina's invasion of the Malvinas Islands. It would appear that at moments of crisis in the United Kingdom a ruling Englishness overcomes the less satisfying concept, British.

Englishness is an instinctual, ethnic identification, while the relatively recent concept, British, lacks its inspirational power. Indeed, as Fowler demonstrates, some English people feel a form of cultural cringe in relation to the imperial label, and in the 1980s terms like 'British car', 'British justice' or 'British industry' have increasingly either a less confident or a downright pejorative usage within England. In many ways this new usage is connected with a movement of consciousness which Tom Nairn has termed 'the break-up of Britain'. On the other hand, Great Britain is a society composed of many different ethnic cultures, and those who identify with it would argue that the term 'British' can be seen as inclusive, positive and multiracial, where 'English' may be construed in an exclusive and negative manner. Again, many West Indians and Asians would reject this idea and argue that racist attitudes are on the increase in Britain.

Fundamentally, the language question is a question about nationhood and government, and some lexicographers perceive an occult connection between the English language and the English constitution. Johnson appears to have initiated the analogy when he concluded his attack on the idea of an academy by saying, 'we have long preserved our constitution, let us make some struggles for our language'. James Murray, the editor-in-chief of the *New English Dictionary*, developed this analogy when he observed that 'the English Dictionary, like the English Constitution, is the creation of no one man, and of no one age; it is a growth that has slowly developed itself down the ages'. Murray also compared Johnson's work to a 'lexicographic cairn' and so added a sense of primitive magic to the idea of anonymous tradition which he was asserting. Murray's two comparisons to cairn and constitution help to infuse a magisterial, legislative authority with a form of natural piety that is partly the expression of his Scottishness. For Swift's platonic or rational ideal of complete integration and classic standardization, Murray substitutes a slightly lichened idea of the dictionary as the equivalent of Wordsworth's leech-gatherer. It is both book and sacred natural object, one of the guardians of the nation's soul. And because the *New English Dictionary* was dedicated to Queen Victoria, the imaginative power of the crown was joined to the natural magic of the cairn and the reverential power of the unwritten constitution. Thus the *NED*, or *Oxford English Dictionary* as it became, stands as one of the cornerstones of the culture which created it. It is a monumental work of scholarship and possesses a quasi-divine authority.

The *Oxford English Dictionary* is the chief lexicon of a language which can be more accurately described as 'British English'. In a sense, its compilers worked in the shadow of Noah Webster's *An American Dictionary of the English Language**. Something of the rivalry which Murray's team felt with American culture is reflected in the single example of a 'typical' reader's quotation-slip which is given in the preface to the *NED*:

Britisher

1883 Freeman Impressions U.S. iv. 29 I always told my American friends

* Published in 1828. The change in title from *A Dictionary of the American Language* (1800) reflects Webster's growing conservatism.

that I had rather be called a Britisher than an Englishman, if by calling me an Englishman they meant to imply that they were not Englishmen themselves.

The disinterested scholar, laboriously and often thanklessly at work on a dictionary, cannot fail to have first asked himself this fundamental question: for what nation am I compiling this lexicon? Murray's identification with Victorian Britain and his sense of the importance of the Scottish scholarly tradition to that cultural hegemony clearly inspired his labours.

The career of Noah Webster, like that of James Murray, was partly fired by an inherited Calvinism, but it was a career dedicated to overthrowing, not consolidating, an imperial hegemony. Webster had to challenge the dominating force of Johnson's dictionary and personality. And the challenge he mounted was so effective that Webster's *Dictionary of American English* became a great originating work, the scholarly equivalent of an epic poem or a prose epic like *Ulysses*.

Webster was born in 1758 and served briefly in the American Revolution. While working as a schoolteacher he became dissatisfied with textbooks which ignored American culture. He was convinced that America needed a uniform language, its own school books and its own intellectual life. In 1783 he published his famous 'Blue-Backed Speller' or *American Spelling Book*, and this initiated his concept of linguistic separation. The social and political totality of that concept is expressed in an influential pamphlet of 1778 in which he advocated the adoption of the Federal Constitution. Two years later, in his *Dissertations on the English Language*, Webster offered a powerful argument for linguistic and cultural independence.

In the *Dissertations* Webster attacks Johnson's lumpy neoclassicism, criticizing him for the 'intolerable' Latinity of his style and for a pedantry which has 'corrupted the purity of our language'. He argues that it is essential for America to grow away from the concept of language and nationality which Johnson's dictionary enforces:

As an independent nation, our honor requires us to have a system of our own, in language as well as government. Great Britain, whose children we are, and whose language we speak, should no longer be *our* standard; for the taste of her writers is already corrupted, and her language is on the decline.

Webster argues that 'uniformity of speech' helps to form 'national attachments', while local accents hinder a sense of national identity. Here his argument resembles Dante's in *De Vulgari Eloquentia*, for like Dante he is advocating a language that is common to every region without being tied to any particular locality.

In a concluding appeal, Webster states:

Let us then seize the present moment, and establish a *national language*, as well as a national government. Let us remember that there is a certain respect due to the opinions of other nations. As an independent people, our reputation abroad demands that, in all things, we should be federal; be *national*; for if we do not respect *ourselves*, we may be assured that *other nations* will not respect us. In short, let it be impressed upon the mind of every American, that to neglect the means of commanding respect abroad, is treason against the character and dignity of a brave independent people.

Like Swift, whose Gulliver he echoes,* Webster argues for linguistic self-respect, but he does so as a separatist, not an integrationist. His classicism is national and federal, and does not aspire to a platonic norm which transcends the nationalities inhabiting different countries. This separatist idea has been influential, and there now exist a *Scottish National Dictionary*, a *Dictionary of Canadianisms on Historical Principles*, and a *Dictionary of Jamaican English*.

Webster's dictionary and the concept of American English which it embodies succeeded in making that language appear to be a native growth. In Ireland, the English language has traditionally been regarded as an imposed colonial tongue, and Irish as the autochthonous language of the island. British policy was hostile to Irish and in 1904, for example, a Commissioner of National Education wrote to Douglas Hyde: 'I will use all my influence, as in the past, to ensure that Irish as a spoken language shall die out as quickly as possible.' However, as Sean De Fréine has argued, the movement away from Irish in the nineteenth century was not the product of

* In 'A Voyage to Lilliput' Gulliver protests that he 'would never be an instrument of bringing a free and brave people into slavery'.

'any law or official regulation'. Instead it was the result of a 'social self-generated movement of collective behaviour among the people themselves'. English was the language of power, commerce and social acceptance, and the Irish people largely accepted Daniel O'Connell's view that Gaelic monolingualism was an obstacle to freedom. Particularly after the Famine, parents encouraged their children to learn English as this would help them make new lives in America.

Although the conflict between English and Irish can be compared to the struggle between Anglo-Saxon and Old British, such an analogy conceals the ironies and complexities of the problem. This is because the English language in Ireland, like English in America, became so naturalized that it appeared to be indigenous. The Irish language, however, was not completely suppressed or rejected, and it became central to the new national consciousness which formed late in the nineteenth century. As a result of the struggle for independence it was reinstated as the national language of a country which comprised three provinces and three counties of the four ancient provinces of Ireland. It forms an important part of the school syllabus in the Irish Republic, is on the syllabus of schools administered by the Roman Catholic Church in Northern Ireland, and is absent from the curricula of Northern Irish state schools.

Traditionally, a majority of Unionist Protestants have regarded the Irish language as belonging exclusively to Irish Catholic culture. Although this is a misapprehension, it helps to confirm the essentially racist ethic which influences some sections of Unionist opinion and which is also present in the old-fashioned nationalist concept of the 'pure Gael'. As a result, Unionist schools are monolingual while non-Unionist schools offer some counterbalance to English monolingualism. Put another way, state education in Northern Ireland is based on a pragmatic view of the English language and a short-sighted assumption of colonial status, while education in the Irish Republic is based on an idealistic view of Irish which aims to conserve the language and assert the cultural difference of the country.

Although there are scholarly studies of 'Hiberno-English' and

'Ulster English',* the language appears at present to be in a state of near anarchy. Spoken Irish English exists in a number of provincial and local forms, but because no scholar has as yet compiled a *Dictionary of Irish English* many words are literally homeless. They live in the careless richness of speech, but they rarely appear in print. When they do, many readers are unable to understand them and have no dictionary where they can discover their meaning. The language therefore lives freely and spontaneously as speech, but it lacks any institutional existence and so is impoverished as a literary medium. It is a language without a lexicon, a language without form. Like some strange creature of the open air, it exists simply as *Geist* or spirit.

Here, a fundamental problem is the absence of a classic style of discursive prose. Although Yeats argues for a tradition of cold, sinewy and passionate Anglo-Irish prose, this style is almost defunct now. Where it still exists it appears both bottled and self-conscious, and no distinctive new style has replaced it. Contributors to the *Irish Times* – Owen Dudley Edwards, for example – tend to write in a slack and blathery manner, while the *Belfast Newsletter* offers only a form of rasping businessman's prose. The *Irish Press* differs from the *Irish Times* in having an exemplary literary editor, but its copy-editing is not of a high standard.† And although Irish historians often like to congratulate themselves on their disinterested purity, a glance at the prose of F. S. L. Lyons reveals a style drawn from the claggy fringes of local journalism.‡

* Notably by Alan Bliss and John Braidwood. Professor Braidwood is at present compiling an Ulster dialect dictionary. A dictionary of Hiberno-English, which was begun under the auspices of the Royal Irish Academy, has been abandoned due to lack of funds.

† E.g. 'Born in Rathdrum, Co. Wicklow, where her father was a flour miller, she was educated privately and later at a convent school but, when her father died, when she was 14, she was told that she would have to learn to earn her own living.' Obituary of Maire Comerford in the *Irish Press*, 16 December 1982.

‡ E.g. 'Nevertheless, the university remained the objective and as Charles settled into harness his work and even, apparently, his manners, improved and we learn of village cricket (he was that valuable commodity, a good wicket-keeper-batsman) and of frequent invitations to dances. And at last Cambridge materialized.' F. S. L. Lyons, *Charles Stewart Parnell*, Chapter 1.

Perhaps the alternative to a style based on assorted Deasyisms* is a form of ideal, international English. Samuel Beckett's prose is a repudiation of the provincial nature of Hiberno-English in favour of a stateless language which is an English passed through the Cartesian rigours of the French language. In its purity, elegance and simplicity, Beckett's language is a version of the platonic standard which Swift recommended nearly three centuries ago in his *Proposal*. Paradoxically, though, Beckett's language is both purer than Swift's and yet inhabited by faint, wistful presences which emanate from Hiberno-English.

Most people, however, demand that the language which they speak have a much closer contact with their native or habitual climate. Here, dialect is notable for its intimacy and for the bonds which it creates among speakers. Standard speech frequently gives way to dialect when people soothe or talk to small children, and sexual love, too, is often expressed through dialect words. Such words are local and 'warm', while their standard alternatives can be regarded as coldly public and extra-familial. Often a clash is felt between the intimacy of dialect – from which a non-standard accent is inseparable – and the demands of a wider professional world where standard speech and accent are the norm. For English people such tensions are invariably a product of the class system, but in Ireland they spring from more complex loyalties (listeners to the 1982 Reith Lectures will have noticed how Denis Donoghue's accent oscillates between educated Southern speech and a slight Ulster ululation).

If Donoghue speaks for a partitioned island, G. B. Thompson speaks for a divided culture:

As to the content of the book I must confess to being ill-equipped to comment on it. I am not a serious student of dialect, and any knowledge I have of the subject comes from the fact that as a native of County Antrim my first 'language' was the Ulster-Scots dialect of the area, described elsewhere in this book by G. B. Adams and by my fellow townsman Robert Gregg.

---

* See Mr Deasy's letter about foot-and-mouth disease in the Nestor section of *Ulysses*.

Eventually, like so many others before and since, I was 'educated' to the point where I looked upon dialect as merely a low-class, ungrammatical way of speaking. The essays in this book, therefore, have been a revelation to me, and I find myself hoping that my experience will be shared by others who have not as yet come to realise the full significance of Ulster dialect, but who may still see it as merely a source of humour and the language of Ulster's folk plays – the kitchen comedies. That it can be, and often is, incomparably humorous is undeniable, but it also makes for eloquence of power and beauty, and if this book were to do no more than help raise the popular conception of our dialect above the level of the after-dinner story it would serve a useful purpose.

This statement was made in 1964, and with hindsight we can see in it a slight movement of consciousness towards the separatist idea which is now held by a significant section of 'loyalist' opinion. Nearly twenty years later, Ian Adamson has offered an account of language which is wholly separatist in intention. It is a response to the homeless or displaced feeling which is now such a significant part of the loyalist imagination, and its historical teleology points to an independent Ulster where socialist politics have replaced the sectarian divisions of the past.

Adamson is in some ways the most interesting of recent loyalist historians because he writes from the dangerous and intelligent edges of that consciousness. In 'The Language of Ulster' Adamson argues that the province's indigenous language – Old British – was displaced by Irish, just as Irish was later displaced by English. In this way he denies an absolute territorial claim to either community in Northern Ireland, and this allows him to argue for a concept of 'our homeland' which includes both communities. His account of an ancient British, or Cruthin, people is a significant influence on the UDA's Ulster nationalism and has helped shape that organization's hostility to the British state.

Where the IRA seeks to make a nation out of four provinces, the UDA aspires to make six counties of one province into an independent nation. Official Unionism, on the other hand, tries to conserve what remains of the Act of Union and clings to a concept of nationality which no longer satisfies many of the British people whom the Unionists wish to identify with. This can now be observed in England, where the movement of opinion against Cruise missiles and the continuing demonstration at Greenham Common exemplify that alternative English nationalism which is expressed in Blake's vision of Albion and reflected in the writings of E. P. Thompson. Despite the recent election, this visionary commitment is still a powerful force within English society, and it is connected with the shift in public opinion in favour of withdrawal from Northern Ireland.

Adamson's historical myth necessarily involves the concept of a national language, and he is deeply conscious of the need to prove that he speaks a language which is as indigenous – or as nearly indigenous – as Irish. He argues:

Neither Ulster Lallans nor Ulster English are 'foreign' since the original dialects were modified in the mouths of the local Gaelic speakers who acquired them and eventually, after a bilingual period, lost their native tongue. These modified dialects were then gradually adopted by the Scottish and English settlers themselves, since the Irish constituted the majority population. The dialect of Belfast is a variety of Ulster English, so that the people of the Shankill Road speak English which is almost a literal translation of Gaelic.

Adamson's argument is obviously vulnerable, yet it forms part of a worthwhile attempt to offer a historical vision which goes beyond traditional barriers. The inclusive and egalitarian nature of his vision also ensures that it lacks the viciousness of the historical myth which was purveyed by the notorious Tara organization, blessed by the Reverend Martin Smyth and other leading Unionists, and which figured so prominently in the still unresolved Kincora scandal.*

---

* 'On 28 June 1970 Ireland's Heritage Orange Lodge was founded. This was largely a reflection of McGrath's ideas although the Lodge had originally been associated with St Mary's Church of Ireland on Belfast's Crumlin Road and many members shared an obscure sense of Irish identity. It seems to me that many Ulster Protestants have an identity crisis. They don't really like to think of themselves as British, and the Irish Republic has become a foreign nation, with strange ways, to most Protestants. The Lodge did however seem to awaken in many a sense of Irishness which was not uncomfortable. It seems that the objective in having an 'Irish' Orange Lodge was to provide a legitimate means of promoting McGrath's ideas.

'Rev. Martin Smyth and Rev. John Bryans, who was also known as a British Israelite though a non-militant one and was Grand Master of the Orange Order at

In *The Identity of Ulster* Adamson reveals that the loyalist community he speaks for is conscious of itself as a 'minority people'. Like the Irish language, Lallans – or Ulster Scots – is threatened by the English language, and Adamson calls for the preservation of both languages within an independent Ulster. However, a hostile critic would argue that Adamson's work springs from a sentimental and evasive concept of 'ould dacency'. Although the leaders of the main political parties in the Irish Republic have paid at least lip service to the idea of a 'pluralist' state with safeguards for minorities, it is clear that most loyalists distrust them almost as much as they distrust British politicians. Adamson therefore offers an alternative to both the Irish Republic and the United Kingdom. But one of the weaknesses in his argument is an uncertainty about the status and the nature of the English language in Ireland. He sees Ulster Scots as oppressed by educated 'Ulster English' – the provincial language of Official Unionism, for example – but he lacks a concept of Irish English. This is because Adamson, like G. B. Thompson, is unwilling to contemplate the all-Ireland context which a federal concept of Irish English would necessarily express. Such a concept would redeem many words from that too-exclusive, too-local usage which amounts to a kind of introverted neglect. Many words which now appear simply gnarled, or which 'make strange' or seem opaque to most readers, would be released into the shaped flow of a new public language. Thus in Ireland there would exist three fully-fledged languages – Irish, Ulster Scots and Irish English. Irish and Ulster Scots would be preserved and nourished, while Irish English would be a form of modern English which draws on Irish, the Yola and Fingallian dialects, Ulster Scots, Elizabethan

---

the time, took part in the inauguration of the Lodge. We sang a hymn from McGrath's hymn book, "Let me carry your cross for Ireland Lord" which had been written by Thomas Ashe, an IRA hunger-striker who died in a Dublin jail in 1917. Dr Hillery, the Irish Minister for External Affairs at the time, corresponded with the Lodge soon after it was founded and two Irish Government Bulletins were produced depicting the Lodge Banner and carrying the correspondence. McGrath earlier proposed that the flags of the four Irish provinces be carried but rejected any suggestion that the six county Ulster flag be carried.' Roy Garland in the *Irish Times*, 15 April 1982.

English, Hiberno-English, British English and American English. A confident concept of Irish English would substantially increase the vocabulary and this would invigorate the written language. A language that lives lithely on the tongue ought to be capable of becoming the flexible written instrument of a complete cultural idea.

Until recently, few Irish writers appear to have felt frustrated by the absence of a dictionary which might define those words which are in common usage in Ireland, but which do not appear in the *OED*. This is probably because most writers have instinctively moulded their language to the expectations of the larger audience outside Ireland. The result is a language which lives a type of romantic, unfettered existence – no dictionary accommodates it, no academy regulates it, no common legislative body speaks it, and no national newspaper guards it. Thus the writer who professes this language must either explain dialect words tediously in a glossary or restrict his audience at each particular 'dialectical' moment. A writer who employs a word like 'geg' or 'gulder' or Kavanagh's lovely 'gobshite' will create a form of closed, secret communication with readers who come from the same region. This will express something very near to a familial relationship, because every family has its hoard of relished words which express its members' sense of kinship. These words act as a kind of secret sign and serve to exclude the outside world. They constitute a dialect of endearment within the wider dialect.

In the case of some Northern Irish writers – John Morrow, for example – dialect words can be over-used, while southern Irish writers sometimes appear to have been infected by Frank Delaney's saccharine gabbiness. However, the Irish writer who excludes dialect words altogether runs the risk of wilfully impoverishing a rich linguistic resource. Although there might be, somewhere, a platonic Unionist author who believes that good prose should always be as close as possible to standard British English, such an aspiration must always be impossible for any Irish writer. This is because the platonic standard has an actual location – it isn't simply free and transcendental – and that location is the British House of Commons. There, in moments of profound crisis, people speak exclusively 'for England'. On such occasions, all dialect words are the subject of an invisible exclusion order and archaic Anglo-Norman words like 'treason' and 'vouch' are suddenly dunted into a kind of life.

There may exist, however, a type of modern English which offers an alternative to Webster's patriotic argument (Imagist poetry, for example, is written in a form of minimal international English). Beckett's language is obviously a form of this cosmopolitan English, and some Irish writers would argue that this is the best available language. By such an argument, it is perfectly possible to draw on, say, French and Irish without being aligned with a particular concept of society. For creative writers this can adumbrate a pure civility which should not be pressed into the service of history or politics.

This is not the case with discursive writers who must start from a concept of civil duty and a definite cultural affiliation. Discursive prose is always committed in some sense or other and it is dishonest to pretend that it isn't. Historiography and literary criticism are related to journalism, however much historians of the new brahmin school resist such an 'impure' relation. Indeed, a language can live both gracefully and intensely in its literary and political journalism. Unfortunately, the establishment of a tradition of good critical prose, like the publication of *A Dictionary of Irish English* or the rewriting of the Irish Constitution, appears to be impossible in the present climate of confused opinions and violent politics. One of the results of this enormous cultural impoverishment is a living but fragmented speech, untold numbers of homeless words, and an uncertain or a derelict prose.

BIBLIOGRAPHY

G. B. Adams, ed., *Ulster Dialects: An Introductory Symposium* (1964)
Ian Adamson, *The Identity of Ulster* (1982)
A. C. Baugh, *A History of the English Language* (1965)
Alan Bliss, *Spoken English in Ireland: 1600–1740* (1979)
John Braidwood, 'Ulster and Elizabethan English' in *Ulster Dialects*
    The Ulster Dialect Lexicon (1969)

H. W. Fowler, *A Dictionary of Modern English Usage* (1965)

James Root Hulbert, *Dictionaries British and American* (1955)

Samuel Johnson, Preface and 'The History of the English Language' in *A Dictionary of the English Language* (1755)

H. L. Mencken, *The American Language* (1937)

James Milroy, *Regional Accents of English: Belfast* (1981)

James A. H. Murray, *The Evolution of English Lexicography* (1900)

K. M. Elisabeth Murray, *Caught in the Web of Words: James Murray and the Oxford English Dictionary* (1977)

Diarmuid Ó Miurithe, ed., *The English Language in Ireland* (1977)

John Pepper, *What a Thing to Say* (1977)

Jonathan Swift, *A Proposal for Correcting, Improving, and Ascertaining the English Tongue* (1712)

G. B. Thompson, Preface to *Ulster Dialects*

Noah Webster, *The American Spelling Book* (1783)
Dissertations on the English Language (1789)

The Man from No Part: Louis MacNeice

On a cold morning some years ago I was sitting on a bench outside an Oxford college. An Irish tramp came and sat beside me, asked for the price of a drink and then began to talk. He asked me where I was from, and I told him. And then, stupidly, I asked him what part of Ireland he came from. His answer was sad, evasive and very honest. 'I'm that long out of Ireland,' he sighed, 'you could say I come from no part.'

In all kinds of ways – except that of social dereliction – Louis MacNeice's life was like that. His ancestors came from the West of Ireland, he was born in Belfast and educated in England, where he lived for the rest of his life. As he says in 'Carrick Revisited', he was

> Torn before birth from where my fathers dwelt,
> Schooled from the age of ten to a foreign voice,

and in his childhood 'interlude' he lived in Carrickfergus, on the shores of Belfast Lough. He is buried in Carrowdore churchyard, Co. Down.

MacNeice visited many countries, taught for some months in America at the outbreak of war and spent a year in Athens in the early 1950s, and there is a sense in which he was a visitor everywhere, the man from no part. For the English reader he appears to be Irish, while for certain Irish readers he doesn't really belong to Ireland (he is given a cold and grudging welcome in John Montague's *Faber Book of Irish Verse* – four pages of MacNeice, against six of Montague). And in a clever and perverse essay Derek Mahon has argued that the English public school system processed MacNeice into an Englishman. He was 'a fully paid-up member of the British academic, artistic and administrative establishment' who

Review of *Louis MacNeice: Collected Poems*, edited by E. R. Dodds.

'had no place in the intellectual history of modern Ireland'. The Irish sense of place is very exacting and intransigent, and many people can never forgive the man who goes, in that tantalizing phrase, 'across the water'.

MacNeice is always crossing the water, and the feeling of unease and displacement, of moving between different cultures and nationalisms, which he paradoxically returns to in his poetry, means that his imagination is essentially fluid, maritime and elusively free. He cannot identify himself exclusively with one or other part of the island: the North of Ireland is 'devout and profane and hard', while the South is 'a gallery of false tapestries'. And in *Autumn Journal* he asks

> Why should I want to go back
>   To you, Ireland, my Ireland?
> The blots on the page are so black
>   That they cannot be covered with shamrock.
> I hate your grandiose airs,
>   Your sob-stuff, your laugh and your swagger,
> Your assumption that everyone cares
>   Who is the king of your castle.

Ireland, he concludes, is 'both a bore and a bitch'. Her children 'slouch around the world with a gesture and a brogue / And a faggot of useless memories'. His dismissive celebration is wild and melancholy, gay and sober – a series of passionate Irish contradictions.

Of course the lines are deliberately journalistic, and MacNeice's technique of setting clichés dancing to a hurdy-gurdy rhythm can be tedious. This throwaway lyricism – 'the beer-brown spring / Guzzling between thé heather, the green gush of Irish spring' – often resembles a commercial jingle, and the images are frequently stale or received, like the contemporary surfaces he was so fascinated by and on which they are partly modelled. In 'When We Were Children' he compares laburnum blossom to scrambled eggs, and his witty copywriter's eye often pins down such slick gimmicky images. The urban rootless world of rootless urban clichés, consumer durables and advertising hoardings is an essential part of his imagination, and while he sometimes recycles images of the Irish landscape like a tourist board official eager to woo 'the sentimental English', few Irish writers have totally resisted the temptation to export their Irishness. And in any case Irishness is a sometimes clownish commodity which depends on being transported elsewhere.

It's wrong to condemn MacNeice for his deracinated, even at times ersatz quality because it's something which is implicit in the Irish landscape – the West of Ireland, for example, is strewn with derelict cottages abandoned by emigrant families and it's also covered with breezeblock suburban bungalows built with money brought back from abroad. Landscape and journeys fray against each other, and it is a shore and a seascape crossed by a journey which is at the centre of MacNeice's imaginative vision. From his first mature poem, 'Belfast', to his last poem, the stoic 'Thalassa', his imagination is caught by ships and 'the salt carrion water':

> Down there at the end of the melancholy lough
> Against the lurid sky over the stained water
> Where hammers clang murderously on the girders
> Like crucifixes the gantries stand.

Here the eye crosses Belfast Lough to the gantries in Harland and Wolff's shipyard which stand over the quays where the passenger ferries and cargo boats dock. The image catches the provincial introversion, the puritan work ethic, the cruelty and injustice of the stagnant society MacNeice only peripherally belonged to. The unfinished ships, he implies, stand in their scaffolds, and this fuses birth and death in a manner that is distinctively Irish (like Joyce's puns in his title, *Finnegans Wake*, or like Beckett's gravedigger's forceps). Although the view here is down the lough towards the city, because ships are launched there and other boats leave from the quays, the image also looks out towards the open sea and England.

MacNeice responds to an idea of doomed freedom, the emigrant's ship leaving 'the husk of home' as he says in 'The Left-Behind', one of a sequence of poems which investigate the dilemma of the displaced exile who is condemned to be a tourist in the land of his birth. With a characteristic mixture of freedom and fatalism he says in this poem that his youth is a 'tall ship that chose to run on a rock', and in 'Death of an Old Lady' he makes a most complex image from this:

> At five in the morning there were grey voices
> Calling three times through the dank fields;
> The ground fell away beyond the voices
> Forty long years to the wrinkled lough
> That had given a child one shining glimpse
> Of a boat so big it was named Titanic.

The *Titanic* was built in Belfast and in this marvellous elegy for his stepmother MacNeice returns to the shores of Belfast Lough, the estuary of birth and death where 'shipyard voices' travel over the wet fields:

> They called and ceased. Later the night nurse
> Handed over, the day went down
> To the sea in a ship, it was grey April,
> The daffodils in her garden waited
> To make her a wreath, the iceberg waited;
> At eight in the evening the ship went down.

This poem has a terse stoic clarity and a beautifully managed cadence (there is a perfectly controlled anapaestic lilt which sweetens the abrupt iambics), and it is somehow both placed and displaced. This is also true of 'The Strand', an elegy for Bishop MacNeice, his enlightened and liberal father. Here the Irish strand is a 'mirror of wet sand' which once caught 'his shape' as it now catches that of his son. 'But then as now,' MacNeice says, the foam blotted 'the bright reflections – and no sign / Remains of face or feet when visitors have gone home.' A strand is never quite a place, a really rooted locus, and that word 'visitors' is filled with a sense of dispossession – it is the word used in the West of Ireland to describe tourists.

On the page opposite 'Death of an Old Lady' in the *Collected Poems* there is a short and little-known poem called 'House on a Cliff' which is one of MacNeice's finest achievements:

Indoors the tang of a tiny oil lamp. Outdoors
The winking signal on the waste of sea.
Indoors the sound of the wind. Outdoors the wind.
Indoors the locked heart and the lost key.

Outdoors the chill, the void, the siren. Indoors
The strong man pained to find his red blood cools,
While the blind clock grows louder, faster. Outdoors
The silent moon, the garrulous tides she rules.

Indoors ancestral curse-cum-blessing. Outdoors
The empty bowl of heaven, the empty deep.
Indoors a purposeful man who talks at cross
Purposes, to himself, in a broken sleep.

The hard boxed circling rhythms build a terrible stoic isolation. The voice is variously and tautly cadenced in a cross between stress and quantitative metre – that word 'cross' stretches bitterly in so many directions – and there is a mysterious openness within or beyond the poem's mirror-like reflections of a dead closed universe. If this is one man facing his lonely mortality on the far extremity of an unnamed place, the 'ancestral curse-cum-blessing', the cross purposes and the broken sleep, suggest that the house is Ireland. Again, the silent moon and the garrulous tides obliquely suggest a Yeatsian reference to cold fanatic ideals and mob action. As in 'Death of an Old Lady', MacNeice recapitulates some of his favourite symbols – sirens, sea, wind, clock – in a manner that is almost playful. Although the demand for 'meaning' will discover and insist that 'the blind clock' is the pulse of an indifferent and mechanical universe – the earth's compulsion – the poem is best appreciated in terms of voice, atmosphere and a pure symbolism. It is a bitter and tragic poem with a freedom in its intensity that transcends its unflinching sense of cosmic indifference, malignity or mischief – the 'winking signal' of the lighthouse and MacNeice's favouritely ambiguous 'the siren' simultaneously warn and lure. If this poem fits that baffled and contradictory term 'Irish', it also has an asocial, even a derelict, quality which makes it difficult to place. It subverts any comfortable notion of belonging, and this is true of all MacNeice's poetry. The anguished sense of displacement that is so fundamental to his imagination means that many readers glance at him and then hurry on. Instead he needs to be read and cherished. There are many places that should be proud to lay claim to him.

In the Salt Mines: Louis' Pick

In the early days of radio drama two of the most successful plays were Tyrone Guthrie's *The Flowers Are Not For You To Pick* and Richard Hughes's *Danger*. Guthrie's play employed the device of a drowning man's recall of his past life – voices from his past alternated with the sound of the waves – while Hughes wrote about three people trapped in a mine. Interestingly, Louis MacNeice's last radio play, *Persons from Porlock*, has several scenes set in 'Skrimshank's Cave', and its central character, an artist called Hank, is a keen potholer who suffers from claustrophobia. Before the play was recorded MacNeice went on an expedition to the Yorkshire Moors to record potholing effects for the production. It was there that he caught 'that cold' as Auden calls it in 'The Cave of Making', his wise and beautiful tribute to his dead friend. The play was broadcast as MacNeice lay ill in hospital, his sister listened with great foreboding, and four days later MacNeice died.

For anyone interested in the life of this remarkable poet, these facts must combine in a tantalizing and ultimately mythic manner. This is because radio drama and MacNeice's life have a common image – the cave. At its best, radio drama is essentially an intimate, even claustrophobic, form, and so it is no accident that two pioneering radio playwrights should have chosen the sensation of being trapped as their subject. They must have known intuitively that for the radio listener slow asphyxiation is more convincing than the din of sword blades or the gadzooks of trumpets. Although a radio play can be set anywhere in the great outdoors it always sounds bogus when it is – the ear suspects that the clatter of horse's hooves is only a couple of coconuts plocking together, and the inner eye is puzzled by this deception. And so radio drama works best

Review of Barbara Coulton, *Louis MacNeice in the BBC*.

when the voices of its characters are contained within an echoing hollow – a cave, a tunnel, a pothole, or a living-room.

In MacNeice's imaginative topography it was the cave which dominated: his childhood was spent in Carrickfergus, a small town on the coast of Co. Antrim, an area noted for its basalt formations and caves. In 'Carrickfergus' MacNeice describes the place like this:

I was born in Belfast between the mountain and the gantries
    To the hooting of lost sirens and the clang of trams:
Thence to Smoky Carrick in County Antrim
    Where the bottle-neck harbour collects the mud which jams

The little boats beneath the Norman castle,
    The pier shining with lumps of crystal salt;
The Scotch Quarter was a line of residential houses
    But the Irish Quarter was a slum for the blind and halt.

The salt on the pier came from the local salt mines, and the metaphoric significance of those mines begins to show in Barbara Coulton's introductory account of MacNeice's early years:

A dream that he recalled much later followed a holiday visit to a salt mine which was like a subterranean cathedral, the men 'like gnomes in the clerestories'. In the dream he was imprisoned by the gnomes, and could escape only by finding a certain jewel.

As in 'Carrickfergus' this is partly an image of Unionist Ulster (there is a beautiful variation on that particular provincial servitude in Seamus Heaney's 'The Singer's House'). The jewel is probably what is being referred to in one of the potholing sequences in *Persons from Porlock*: 'I noticed a funny bit of crystal in there in the wall of the tunnel – No, my God, it's submerged!' And the submergence of that crystal must denote Hank's inability to find the jewel and so break out of the cave-system (he loses his life-line, which is a version of Ariadne's thread). Trapped in this labyrinth, Hank tries to swim against the underground stream – MacNeice is clearly reworking the 'caves of ice' and 'sacred river' in 'Kubla Khan'. In a sense, therefore, his 'persons from Porlock' are whatever private hobbies or distractions prevent the artist's exercise of the imagination, his disco-very of the jewel.

MacNeice treats this subject in 'Hidden Ice', where routine existence is overrun by the private hobby which should be free and separate from it:

> One was found like Judas kissing flowers
> And one who sat between the clock and the sun
> Lies like a Saint Sebastian full of arrows
> Fathered from his own hobby, his pet hours.

This fascination with the absorbing madness of the unchecked private hobby is an important theme in MacNeice's work, and *Persons from Porlock* his final oblique version of it. In the play, MacNeice refers to his dream of the salt cathedral, and he means that the mine of busy gnomes is really the institution in which he'd spent more than twenty years of his life – the BBC. Barbara Coulton astutely links the play with another of MacNeice's radio dramas, *Prisoner's Progress*, which involves a 'tunnelling to freedom, through a neolithic passage grave'. And this subject becomes dramatically clear once we place it in relation to *Rasselas* – MacNeice is exploring the dilemma of someone who knows he is trapped in the Happy Valley and wants to break out of it.

From this it should be apparent that I am by no means convinced that MacNeice's long and distinguished career in the BBC necessar-ily benefited his poetry. Certainly he made an immense and brilliant contribution to radio. Under Laurence Gilliam, the Features Depart-ment was a remarkable gathering of talent, and during the first six years of the Italia Prize, 'of fifteen entries chosen as the outstanding works of those years, fourteen came from the Features Department'. The programmes MacNeice scripted and produced were of the highest quality, and the position he occupied in relation to society was the egalitarian equivalent of a court poet. His plays and features are like masques created for a mass democracy, and his commitment to radio issued from his belief that the poet 'is only the extension of the common man'. In his working life he was applying the socialist and documentary aesthetic of the 1930s.

However, we must realize that all masques are designed simply to glitter in the moment. Like a piece of journalism, they are created for a particular occasion, and though they may be repeated their original freshness will always be missing. They are part of what MacNeice termed 'the yeast of culture', but they are ephemeral. If MacNeice was applying many of the ideals of the 1930s – commitment to a group, closing the gap between art and journalism – we still have to choose between his two identities of poet and distinguished servant of the BBC. And the problem is that those identities first overlapped and then fed off each other during his middle-age: his radio features sound like poems, while many of his poems sound like features.

Take his introduction to a programme called 'Portrait of Athens' which begins with the tinny note of a bell and the Visitor's comment:

So this is Athens. A nagging bell and a glaring sky. A box on the ear. A smack in the eye. Crude as a poster. Hard as nails. Yes, this is Athens – not what I expected.

There is a rich personal accent in these beautifully managed, knockabout speech cadences. And the ear gladly recognizes a punchy couplet in:

> A nágging béll and a gláring ský.
> A bóx on the éar. A smáck in the éye.

That pyrrhic foot – 'and a' – introduces the ghost of quantitative metre into the play of iambs and anapaests, and this mixed metre is characteristic of MacNeice's best poetry ('House on a Cliff', for example). Again, that last phrase, 'not what I expected', is both a dying fall and a superb moment of arresting colloquial thoughtfulness. It is magnificent radio journalism precisely because it comes so close to MacNeice's poetry.

However, if we transpose the relationship between journalism and art and examine these lines from the sequence of poems, 'Our Sister Water', we can see that their ersatz quality is the result of the application of documentary techniques to a subject that, at this point in the poem, should have passed beyond the journalistic:

Best in the West
Squelching round ankles, dousing the nape of the neck,
Ringing the jackpot of colour out of the mountains;
Best in the large or best when a girl in a shawl.
Barefoot and windblown staggers her way through the bog
With a bucket of windblown gold.

The image of the shawled girl is a piece of kitsch Irishness, while the 'jackpot of colour' is passable as a throwaway metaphor in a broadcast commentary – in cold print a sunset of fruit machines looks queasy and banal. When MacNeice admitted 'This middle stretch / Of life is bad for poets', he also meant that it was quite fun for boozy journalists – those tempting figures who wait beyond that famous line about the drunkenness of things being various. Journalism aims to live and die with the moment, but an art which addresses itself to the quotidian has to be intensely detached, intensely sure of itself – as MacNeice's vision usually was until broadcasting work began to invade his imagination.

He was a gregariously lonely man, and he appears to have needed team work and its inevitable concomitant, pub life, with increasing desperation. Two years before he joined the BBC he described his dream of community in the last canto of *Autumn Journal*:

Where the individual, no longer squandered
  In self-assertion, works with the rest, endowed
With the split vision of a juggler and the quick lock of a taxi,
  Where the people are more than a crowd.

And he came close to realizing that dream in his work for Features, which he described like this:

In this age of irreconcilable idioms I have often heard writers hankering for some sort of group life . . . we cannot but envy playwrights, actors or musical executants. And here again I for one have found this missing group experience, in a valid form, in radio. Radio writers and producers *can* talk shop together because their shop is not, as with poets, a complex of spiritual intimacies but a matter of craftsmanship . . . we are fully entitled to discuss whether the dialogue rings true, whether the dramatic climax is dramatic, how well the whole thing works. This is refreshing for a writer.

MacNeice's need to belong must in part have been due to his sense of deracination – he had left the salt mines and this meant that there was no existing community with which he could identify (it's crucial to recognize that he was born before partition and never came to terms with a divided Ireland). He dramatized his 'hankering' for group life in the figure of Hank in *Persons from Porlock*, and that life became a warm burrow which was also the great cathedral of the BBC.

Barbara Coulton's study is a valuable account of MacNeice's life as a creative member of an institution, and although her appreciation of his poetry is limited by that unhelpful term 'moving', she offers a diligent and comprehensive survey of his broadcasting career. Her chapter on MacNeice's Indian journey is excellent, and throughout she shows a warm and cherishing regard for her subject. There is in MacNeice's creative personality something that calls forth a strong and tender admiration, and the man himself was deeply loved by his many friends. This study should do much to rekindle interest in his life and work.

A Terminal Ironist: Derek Mahon

In 'Entropy' Derek Mahon included these images of the abject, almost snug moment before the final instant of cultural collapse:

> We have tried
> To worship the sun,
> To make gods of clay,
>
> Gods of stone
> But gave up in derision.
> We have pared life to the bone
>
> And squat now
> In the firelight reading
> Gibbon and old comics.

These stanzas have been cut from the version of 'Entropy' which appears in *Poems 1962–1978* and so Mahon has 'pared . . . to the bone' a poem already dedicated to the terminal and minimal. This ruthless refinement is one of the essential qualities of all Mahon's verse, and almost invariably he combines an exquisite absolutism with an arrogant nonchalance:

> I have been working for years
>   on a four line poem
>   about the life of a leaf.
> I think it may come out right this winter!*

Mahon aims at what Eliot terms 'A condition of complete simplicity / (Costing not less than everything)', and his poems are remarkable for their purity of style, the subtle lucid singing intelligence they display.

* 'The Mayo Tao' – a revised version of the prose poem 'A Hermit'.

Review of Derek Mahon, *Poems 1962–1978*

At some point in his brilliant youth Mahon must have faced the choice between perfection of the life or of the work – he chose the latter and made a religion of art. Thus he is an intransigent aesthete who rejects life almost completely and considers only the flotsam and jetsam along its fringes. In his magnificent reworking of 'April on Toronto Island' he sees a 'litter of tin cans / And oily fish-skeletons', and as groups of people stand on the wintry shore:

> Their faces dream of other islands,
> Clear cliffs and salt water,
> Fields brighter than paradise
> In the first week of creation –
> Redemption in a wind or a tide,
> Our lives in infinite preparation.

These figures cannot conceive of any compromise with this life, because like Mahon they must dream always of a perfect elsewhere.

In all Mahon's work there is only one poem which might, for what the terms are worth, be called warm and tender. Rather like one of Yeats's early poems, 'Glengormley'* sets the virtues of quotidian ordinariness – 'The terrier-taming, garden-watering days' – against the ideal reality of aesthetic heroism:

> The unreconciled, in their metaphysical pain,
> Dangle from lamp-posts in the dawn rain.

Mahon identifies with the unreconciled and the damned, and often there is a quality of still anguish in the bitter clarity and detachment of his work. Again and again he returns to motifs of silence, exile, utter clear-eyed despair, and versions of the artistic life. What he celebrates – and it's a celebration conducted in a temperature of absolute zero – is the perfection of art, an intense *quidditas* which exists outside history:

---

*In *Night-Crossing* this is dedicated to Padraic Fiacc. Whatever the reasons for it, the dropping of the dedication consorts oddly with the merely dandyish danglers from lamp-posts. The significant absence is a complex historical and personal bitterness – Fiacc's, not Mahon's.

> Perfecting my cold dream
> Of a place out of time,
> A palace of porcelain.

And he rejects any insistence that art should be socially relevant or politically committed:

> But the fireloving
> People, rightly perhaps,
> Will not countenance this,
> Demanding that I inhabit,
> Like them, a world of
> Sirens, bin-lids
> And bricked-up windows.

However, the poet and rioter share an occult identity in 'Rage for Order', and this is a version of Yeats's sense that every culture originally springs from the actions of 'violent bitter men'. Art, Mahon implies, has nothing to do with liberal ideas of decency, and his work has a quality that Yeats discerned in Joyce: 'a cruel playful mind like a great soft tiger cat'.

In order to arrive at his vision of art – 'Our afterlives a coming true / Of perfect worlds we never knew' – Mahon takes the negative way, and his rejection of sense experience is glanced at in 'The Voice':

> Do you hear the voice increase in volume
> and, as a March wind quickens the creaking trees,
> sing mildly to us without fear,
> content in the fact of death? Do you hear?
> What does it sing in the grey dawn? Nobody knows;
> but the voice is audible only to those
> whose hearts are emptied of property and desire.

This visionary voice is audible only to those who in Eliot's terms reject 'the practical desire' and follow this advice:

> To arrive where you are, to get from where you are not,
>   You must go by a way wherein there is no ecstasy.

> In order to arrive at what you do not know
>> You must go by a way which is the way of ignorance.
> In order to possess what you do not possess
>> You must go by the way of dispossession.

And in some ways Mahon resembles George Herbert, who characteristically creates a perfect poem which also abolishes itself in the last line ('Prayer' is the most obvious example of this self-annihilating technique). Herbert's poems set themselves aside in order to merge with the absolute reality of God, while Mahon's slip into the utter perfection of Art. Paradoxically, therefore, Mahon's work possesses an extraordinary humility – at the last moment his *non serviam* modulates into the finest idea of service. And perhaps his aestheticism has parallels with the dedicated fanaticism of a hunger-striker whose absolute personal pride must also involve a complete rejection of personal identity.

From his early poem 'Unborn Child' to the great masterpiece 'A Disused Shed in Co. Wexford', Mahon is fascinated by a place of pure being which exists outside history. It's a Jamesian subject and is treated in a sophisticated and paradoxical manner – the unborn child wants 'to live' and yet knows its days are numbered, the mushrooms are woken by a 'flash-bulb firing squad' and still beg us 'To do something, to speak on their behalf'. In 'An Image from Beckett' history and the still split second are identical:

> They will have buried
> My great-grandchildren, and theirs,
> Beside me by now

> With a subliminal batsqueak
> Of reflex lamentation.
> Our hair and excrement

> Litter the rich earth,
> Changing, second by second,
> To civilisations.

This is one of Mahon's finest achievements and an example of his uniquely terminal imagination: death and art are virtually identical in his work, and his mockery in 'Poets of the Nineties'* stems not from any moral criticism, but from an aesthetic position even more extreme than Dowson's and Lionel Johnson's. Mahon makes them seem like cosy rustic liberals, bland and incapable of a complete commitment to art.

Mahon's commitment is naturally evidenced in the type of book this is – somehow it feels like a selected and a collected edition, *and* a new volume. There is something terrifying about its wholeness. And yet if certain poems – 'My Wicked Uncle', 'April on Toronto Island', 'Rage for Order', 'Entropy' – have been brought to perfection, others have been nagged and tinkered into something less than their original spirit. For example, in 'In Belfast'† the line 'The spurious mystery in the knowing nod' becomes the too-obvious 'The hidden menace in the knowing nod'. And in 'Bruce Ismay's Soliloquy'‡ the cadence of the last line – 'Include me in your lamentations' – is flat and drab compared with, 'Include me / *Honoris causa* in your lamentations'.

With the exception of 'The Attic', 'The Return', and 'Three Poems after Jaccottet', Mahon's new poems are very disappointing – they tend to whine without much distinction. There is a very fine poem called 'Mythological Figure' which must have been dropped from *Night-Crossing* and which is included in this volume, and unfortunately Mahon's new poems don't match up to it. In it the mythological figure who 'ought' to have existed is condemned to sing whenever she opens her mouth. She begins to sing,

> and her gestures
> Flowed like a mountain stream;
> But her songs were without words,
> Or the words without meaning –
> Like the cries of love or the cries of mourning.

Only a rare and extraordinary imagination could invent such a figure.

*Originally titled 'Dowson and Company'.
†Now titled 'The Spring Vacation'.
‡Originally titled 'As God is my Judge'.

The Fuse and the Fire: Northern Protestant Oratory and Writing

In his maiden speech in the House of Lords, Edward Carson attacked the Anglo-Irish Treaty of 1921 and warned British politicians not to turn Ulster 'against the British connection'. With characteristic hyperbole, he urged them to remember that when 'through your laws, Ulstermen were driven out of Ireland and went to America, it was thirty-six Ulstermen, smarting under a grievance, who signed the Declaration of Independence'. More than fifty years later, in a short book entitled *America's Debt to Ulster*, the Rev. Ian Paisley described how 'Ulster men and men of Ulster stock' had a 'leading hand' in framing the Declaration of Independence. This pride in the Ulster Presbyterian contribution to the American Revolution was echoed during the 1980s in publications associated with the Ulster Defence Association, the chief loyalist paramilitary organization, and it issues from those contradictory emotions and beliefs that form the basis of 'loyalist' culture. Distrusting traditional definitions of Irish identity, that culture often aggressively presents itself as being simultaneously British and anti-British.

In order to establish the distinctive characteristics and values of Ulster loyalist or Protestant culture, it is necessary to abandon conventional ideas of the literary and the aesthetic and consider forms of writing that are often dismissed as ephemeral or non-canonical – familiar letters, political speeches, oaths and toasts, sermons, pieces of journalism, overtured addresses, the minutes of synodical and other meetings. All these texts are forms of cultural production which for a variety of reasons have remained unexamined for many generations. The consciously modulated and often passionate voices that speak out of these printed texts have not so far attracted that critical appraisal to which self-evidently literary texts are submitted, nor have they yet been gathered and reproduced by cultural historians; but they stand nevertheless as the distinctive achievements of a community.

From William Drennan's seminal letter of 21 May 1791, with its idea of a new republican society, to Carson's threatened Ulster independence, there is a curiously syncopated continuity of attitude, which cannot be subsumed under that overworked and misleading term 'tradition'. The eighteenth-century Belfast republican, Drennan, writes with a dissenting enthusiasm about the idea of independence, while the late-Victorian Dublin Unionist, Carson, speaks for his adopted province's grievances with a punitive earnestness. Separated by ideology and history, they share a passionate seriousness about politics and a self-justifying energy and sense of personal integrity that seem strangely innocent.

Drennan's symbol for an organized international republican movement – a 'caisson' – is ambiguous and revealing, and it may be read as articulating that type of Protestant imagination which he and Carson shared. A caisson is a large watertight chest used in laying the foundations of bridges in deep water, and for Drennan the term represents the idea of stability, secrecy, political and intellectual power, a new enlightened international order. However, the term also means an explosive device, a mine, and in that sense it is a highly unstable power, the embodiment of active revolutionary energy and enthusiasm. Drennan's imagination wants to destroy the old order and create a new society, an idea that derives ultimately from Pauline theology ('Therefore if any man be in Christ, he is a new creature: old things are passed away; behold, all things are become new', 2 Corinthians 5.17). At the root of Drennan's imagination is this idea of being born again, an idea that joins the personal life to the civic life; and, like St Paul, he sees epistolary communication as the essential medium for his ideas.

Commenting on Paul's statement in his Epistle to the Romans that the gospel of Christ 'is the power of God' (1.16), Ian Paisley states that gospel preaching 'is charged with the dynamic of heaven. Dynamite to be displayed in all its mighty potency must have the fuse and the fire.' He imagines the 'strongholds of Satan' toppling and the 'bulwarks of idolatry' collapsing. For Paisley, as for Drennan, ideas are a form of high explosive, and both writers share a detestation of 'torpid acquiescence', a fundamental hostility to Roman Catholicism, an intense commitment to the right of private judgement and a belief in a value they term 'energy' or 'the dynamic of heaven'. Like 'honest', 'independent' and 'pure', such terms represent key concepts in Protestant discourse and may be set against terms such as 'organic' or 'balanced', which feature so strongly in certain forms of British literary criticism and conservative argument. In essence, they express a constantly challenging or polemical mind-set and this is one result of a belief in the right of private judgement.

That belief also stimulates the frequent protestations of personal integrity that can disfigure Protestant discourse – in his 'Intended Defence', Drennan often insists on his 'pure intentions and honest principles', while Henry Montgomery speaks of himself as being 'an honourable and irreproachable man, who has raised himself to a station of honest independence by his *own exertions*'. Protestantism can protest its integrity too much and mask an argument with a series of self-images and personal testimonies. One result, though, of such self-addressed character references is to foreground consciousness as the subject of both writing and oratory and, by breaking down the barriers between printed text and speech act, impart a free-flowing, improvisatory texture to what is being said.

In 'The Intended Defence', Drennan speaks of 'that conscious mind, which is its own awful world', and although he is referring specifically to the burdens of the individual conscience – its solitary sense of guilt and damnation – there are moments in Protestant discourse when consciousness for its own sake, consciousness as subject, erupts and dominates. This sense of consciousness as process, as an end in itself, can be observed in much American writing, and it is rooted in puritan ideas of private judgement and personal testimony. Its effect is sometimes circular and narcissistic – Drennan, Montgomery and Henry Cooke can base arguments on their own affirmations of personal worth. This Presbyterian habit of insisting on one's integrity finds a philosophical justification in the work of Francis Hutcheson, but it can appear to be an over-personal and personalized method of argument. That enduring Presbyterian preference for the direct testimony of consciousness over formal argument creates a solipsistic universe gnawed at its edges by anger and incoherence. Such powerful frustrations can be observed in Paisley's discourse and in Harold McCusker's heartfelt manner of testifying against the 1985 Anglo-Irish Agreement.

This type of urgent, declamatory, polemical anger fuels the Rev. James Carlile's attack on 'an individual, styling himself Lord Castlereagh', an attack that is egalitarian in outlook and sometimes populist in expression ('Who or what was this Lord Castlereagh . . . ?'). Insisting on the right of private judgement and the principle of non-interference by the state, Carlile describes the manner in which the Synod of Ulster has reacted to Castlereagh's threat of withdrawing a grant called the *regium donum*, which the government made to the Presbyterian Church:

. . . here we are gravely deliberating whether we shall suffer the civil Government to interfere in our spiritual concerns – whether we shall barter what we believe, and what we have declared again and again to be, the spiritual interests of our people, for money – I say to barter them for money. O fatal day for the independence of the Synod of Ulster! O miserable degeneracy from the spirit of our forefathers! There was a time when, if the Sovereign himself, in all the pomp of royalty, attended by an armed force, had appeared within these walls, and held out such a threat, and had added to it the threat of fire and faggot, he would have met with a unanimous opposition to his interference, and not one of our number would have been found base enough to justify it, or to insinuate that we ought to yield to his requisition.

The appeal to 'the spirit of our forefathers' is one of the hallmarks of Presbyterian oratory (there is a similar reference in the Solemn League and Covenant of 1912), and the exclamatory, dramatic style of Carlile's speech has all the appearance of being sudden and extempore and therefore passionately sincere. This is an eruptive moment which begins with the recapitulatory emphasis *I say to barter them for money*. From this point, a volatile consciousness – that of the speaker fused with his audience – expands moment by moment and pushes far beyond conventional and restraining notions of decorum, propriety and 'gentlemanly civility'. Such an ethic is hostile to hierarchical codes of manners and expresses itself in a free unpolished vernacular. Its equivalent in the visual arts is action painting, and it is no accident that Jackson Pollock was of Scotch-Irish descent. (Elizabeth Frank notes in her study of the painter that the Scotch-Irish were 'historically dispossessed, rootless, and deeply Presbyterian'.) Pollock's father's credo – 'I think every person should think, act and believe according to the dictates of his own conscience without to [*sic*] much pressure from the outside' – is characteristically Presbyterian.

The puritan aesthetic that shapes vernacular discourse is founded on an anti-aesthetic of 'truth' or immediate divine inspiration. On the surface there is usually an appearance of directness and informality, but it is a carefully calculated illusion which can make the preacher resemble a method actor in his urgent authenticity and professions of personal sincerity. The church becomes a theatre where we witness an intense drama of consciousness and where a powerful sense of the absolute importance of the present moment – the urgent *now* of utterance – springs from the fusion of audience attention with the preacher's voice and gestures. The frequent dashes and exclamation marks that appear in printed texts signal an impatience with the fixity of print and a liberating ambition to make a primal reality of the spoken word. Like Emily Dickinson, the puritan writer wishes to substitute a series of exclamatory speech moments for the codified formality of print. This vocal aesthetic is a version of the argument in the third chapter of the Second Epistle to the Corinthians where Paul rejects actual inscribed letters through an imaginative assertion which abolishes the distinction between readers of written texts or 'epistles of commendation' and the writers of such texts. He asserts that 'ye' – the Corinthians he is addressing – are 'our epistle written in our hearts', and then draws a distinction between letters written with ink or 'in tables of stone' and those letters written 'with the Spirit of the living God . . . in fleshy tables of the heart'. This is an antinomian, born-again attitude which dedicates itself to 'the new testament; not of the letter, but of the spirit: for the letter killeth, but the spirit giveth life'. Paul contrasts this new spiritual text with the 'ministration of death, written and engraven in stones' (i.e. the Mosaic Law). This inscribed law is a veil that remains 'untaken away in the reading of the old testament'. Paul abolishes it and offers instead a new libertarian speech, 'great plainness of speech' as he terms it. Carlile's plea for 'very strong language' similarly insists on the necessity of a direct plain style, and he also follows Paul in his rejection of a formal, codified discourse. Like Drennan, Carlile is an enthusiast who wants to make everything new.

The published writings of the Rev. Henry Montgomery articulate a firm belief in civil and religious liberty and a liberal dislike of rigid official modes of faith. Montgomery delights in human diversity, loves natural scenery, respects other people's opinions and believes absolutely in the right of private judgement. He fears that Cooke and his supporters would create a 'dead sea' of Presbyterian conformity, and his legendary controversy with Cooke is a version of the battle fought in the 1790s between republicanism and loyalism. For all his professed belief in the British Empire and the Union with Britain, Montgomery's imagination appears to have a secret lien to the world of republican dissent that Drennan speaks for. He was Professor of English at the Belfast Academical Institution, which Drennan founded, and was closely linked to the liberal middle class of Belfast.

Contemporary witnesses noted that Montgomery's oratory was more polished than Cooke's, but that he lacked his opponent's ability to sway a large crowd. Persuasion rather than vivid rhetorical effect was a leading feature of his oratory and he left audiences feeling 'not so much delighted as improved'. Montgomery's biographer and son-in-law, J. A. Crozier, notes that Cooke spoke with a 'slow and rather provincial and drawling accent', and we may assume that Montgomery's speaking voice reflected his yeoman background and middle-class connections. It would not be stretching a point to see his quarrel with Cooke as anticipating Paisley's struggle with Captain Terence O'Neill, the Ulster Prime Minister (1963–9) whose 'nasal tones' the Antrim preacher-politician defied.

Montgomery's beliefs are defined by invoking what he terms the 'native purity and simplicity' of the early Christian church. For Montgomery, primitive Christianity knew 'no creed but that which came from on high', and his benign rejection of narrow systems of belief means that he places little emphasis on sin and damnation. Unlike Calvinist thinkers, he does not dismiss sense experience as irredeemably evil and is appreciative of natural beauty, preferring a fluid variousness to 'one unnatural and unwholesome calm'. This element of sensuous responsiveness in Montgomery's thinking is a significant feature of puritan libertarianism and finds its classic expression in Milton's evocation of Eden before the Fall. D. H. Lawrence's writings offer a romantic version of this type of primitivism, and the paintings of Edward Hicks and other early American artists also embody this puritan belief in a primally innocent world where human beings and animals live in harmony with nature and each other.

Like all Presbyterians, Montgomery repeatedly insists that he can never be a time-server and submit to human authority. It could be that Daniel O'Connell's attack on him as a 'fawning, cringing sycophant' touched this sensitive nerve and thus provoked the unusual vehemence of his reply to O'Connell. On the other hand, Montgomery's hostility to O'Connell can be seen as the frightened response of the liberal Protestant bourgeoisie to the threat posed to their property by O'Connell's mass political movement. As in his earlier 'Letter to Henry Cooke', where he identifies with Joseph Priestley against 'an infuriated multitude', Montgomery is affirming a liberal position midway between 'arbitrary power' and 'wild democratical theories'. If Montgomery's thinking is rooted in the Volunteer Movement and the United Irishmen, it also looks toward the liberal Unionist position now represented politically by the Alliance Party. In opposing Cooke's drive to consolidate and unify Protestant power in Ulster, and in opposing O'Connell's agitation for the repeal of the Union, Montgomery occupies a position that is exposed to attack by both romantic nationalism and populist unionism. In this changed political climate, the late eighteenth-century values articulated by both Drennan and Montgomery appear stranded and inert, accessible only to sentimental recuperation by literary antiquarians.

Where Montgomery's suasive style is scrupulous and decorous, Henry Cooke often resorts to hyperbole, brutal simplification and sensational imagery. Part stand-up comic, part atavistic Covenanter, part Wellington look-alike, he impressed contemporary observers with his visceral powers of argument and his ability to move huge popular audiences. Attacking O'Connell during the Liberator's famous visit to Belfast in 1841, Cooke used the date to invoke atavistic memories of 1641 and remind his audience of the massacres of Protestants that took place in that year. This type of headline-grabbing opportunism is also apparent in Cooke's attack on Arianism, where he seizes on the birthplace of Arius in order to dismiss his ascetic theology as a 'sickly exotic', bred like Cleopatra in the warm mud of the Nile. Here Cooke's thinking is based on a form of racial exclusivism that is as central to orthodox Ulster Protestant thinking as the idea of the pure Gael is to the ideology of Irish nationalism. (In 1985, for example, the leader of the Official Unionist Party, James Molyneaux, opposed Irish unity by arguing that Protestants and Catholics are racially different.)

Cooke followed traditional British Protestant thinking in viewing the Catholic Irish as barbarians and the Ulster Protestants as civilizers. In his private letters he refers to the 'great unwashed' who attended O'Connell's meeting in Belfast, exults at the eviction of 'savages' from their cabins on an improving landlord's estate, and distinguishes between the 'cool, logical' Northern Protestants and the 'excitable Celts' of the South. Developing the image of floodwaters as a metaphor for sin, Cooke exclaims:

It comes! – The flood! – dark, deep, and sudden. Merciful Heaven hath given it a voice: but the warning uttered, there remains not an instant for delay. He that flees may escape; but he that deliberates is lost.

Cooke's image is not simply religious in its application; it represents the gathering force of O'Connellite nationalism, and Cooke's hysterical, distinctly uncool development of the flood image articulates the most profound social fear in his audience, the fear of being forced off the land:

In lands exposed to frequent inundations, experience teaches to guard against their inroads. But, if the flood rise far above its ordinary level; or, if it descend with unusual violence, it overtops or bears away the mounds or barriers erected for its confinement: and, the destructive element once let loose, it sweeps away property and life . . .

Cooke then cites the twelfth chapter of Revelation, the New Testament book traditionally interpreted by Protestants as a prophecy of the rise of Roman Catholicism; this underlines the anti-catholic significance of the flood image.

For all his proud provincialism ('Look at the town of Belfast'), Cooke also aims to create an international Protestant identity in which Hus, Luther, Milton, Ridley, Latimer and the Scottish Covenanters are ranged against the power of Rome. The concept of heroic martyrdom is as deeply ingrained in Ulster loyalism as it is in the discourse of Irish nationalism. Ian Paisley has published a number of sermons on the Scottish Covenanters, who were, he states, 'bold, courageous, strong men . . . these were not the putty paper men of the twentieth century – these were the rugged men of the Reformation'.

If Cooke helped to lay the foundations for that failed polity, the State of Northern Ireland, it is not difficult to admire the gruelling and aggrieved search for identity that his long career embodies. He speaks for the moral north, and his attitudes and values are firmly rooted in Ulster. Craigavon's proud reference in his speech 'We Are King's Men' to 'our rockbound and turbulent coast' shows a similar form of regional nationalism, and both Cooke and James Craig (Viscount Craigavon) share a modernizing energy and belief in economic development. For them, Ulster is a paradisal garden occupied solely by hardworking Bible-reading Protestants. Craiga-von's remark, 'Britain's difficulty is Northern Ireland's oppor-tunity', inverts a standard nationalist shibboleth and implicitly links the Nazi threat with the bombing campaign that the IRA had recently mounted in Britain. It exemplifies the dialogical or polemi-cal nature of the Protestant imagination, an imagination that sees itself dramatically as pitched against certain powerful ideas that threaten its existence and values. Feisty, restless, argumentative, never quite at home in this world, that imagination has seldom shaped itself in traditionally aesthetic form in the North of Ireland. There, its characteristic forms of cultural production are the religious sermon, the pamphlet, the political speech; and it is because those forms have received such little attention that this selection of Protestant *écriture* is intended as an enabling initiative, rather than a canonical gathering of isolated texts.

The Crack

Anyone glancing at the sharp fissures between the street murals on the cover of Sally Belfrage's account of contemporary Belfast life – *The Crack: A Belfast Year* – might be forgiven for thinking that its title refers to that glum cliché 'the sectarian divide'. In fact 'crack' is a cohesive word widely used in Ireland to mean 'the talk, or the ambience, or what's going on'. For Sally Belfrage, Belfast speech is 'magical' and her tribute to the city's distinctive oral culture conjures up a world similar to the paradisal fantasy in Yeats's poem 'The Man Who Dreamed of Faeryland':

> There dwelt a gay, exulting, gentle race
> Under the golden or the silver skies;
> That if a dancer stayed his hungry foot
> It seemed the sun and moon were in the fruit.

As one exulting Belfast native exclaims: 'This is the *only* place to live. I tried Australia but I come back cause I missed the crack.' Belfast is 'magic' – local demotic for 'super' or 'marvellous' or whatever high superlative leaps instinctively off the tongue.

During her plunges into Belfast society Belfrage met terrorists, hoods, activists, paramilitaries, politicians and ordinary people. Many of them invited her in 'for a cup of tea and a wee yarn', and she was clearly bowled over by their voluble hospitality. She found Belfast people 'warm and involved and alive' and readily admits to loving them 'more than any group I had ever encountered'. Reading her transcripts of their talk and her sometimes starry-eyed descriptions of their looks, I became concerned that this might be another voyeuristic account of a society which has become highly visible during the last two decades. Belfast must be one of the most studied

Review of Sally Belfrage, *The Crack: A Belfast Year* (London: André Deutsch).

and self-conscious cities in the world – Belfrage found it packed with journalists, academics, social scientists, photographers, 'every kind of pundit'. Gallup pollsters have been busy, too, and in the mid-1980s they found that 39 per cent of Northern Irish people define themselves as 'very happy', as compared with 15 per cent of Italians and West Germans, and 10 per cent of Japanese.

Even when interviewing 'the most out-of-the-way people' Belfrage got used to the idea that she was the fourth interviewer they had had that week. In this city of life sculptures everyone is a speech artist swimming confidently in its waves of pure talk:

He hopped himself well up (dressed warmly) to go out for the messages (shopping). Then one thing led to another and this caper and carry-on and whenever he stopped at the pub, he hoovered up five pints and got poleaxed (jarred, puddled, punctured, paladic, plucked, blocked, blitzed, snattered, stocious, steamboats, elephantsed, arsified, blootered, lockjawed, or merely full). 'You know what yer mon's like, like.' – 'Och aye. Not a titter of wit.' 'Did you get the sausingers but?' – 'I'm only after goin' til the shop so.'

This speech collage captures the intense linguistic hedonism which many Belfast people share, and they emerge as lovers of junk food, children, white lemonade, lashings of tea, cigarettes, alcohol, history, song and an entity called 'people' – i.e. themselves.

This profound pride in being citizens of no mean city influences Belfrage's vision of the place as a kind of heavenly wreck:

In late spring in Belfast, the night comes so gently it hardly comes at all, and by midnight there is still a fringe of light along the mountains, with the rest of the sky a rich, clear indigo. It's the reward in the far north for the winters of the long night.

Knowing those mountains well and reading this romantic evocation of them shortly after visiting the city, I recognize that such perceptions depend on the mobile hell of double estrangement, flights back and forth over the Irish Sea, that starved feeling which English reserve and demoralization can occasion in migrant hearts. At such moments the expatriate and the tourist enter into a collusive pact and a shrewd new cultural commodity called *Ulster chic* is born. Where the Aran Islands used to be the focus of cultural authenticity, Belfast would now seem to be the deep navel of ethnic chutzpah. But to get from dulse and pampooties to the Ulster fry a lot of terrible events had to happen.

In the end, though, this is a fascinating and absorbing piece of reportage or rapportage which deftly allows as many voices as possible to jostle together. Belfrage is acutely sensitive to the rhythms of Belfast English, which she calls 'lilting and lyrical, inventive and funny – and optimistic, because of the upward inflexion, suggesting doubt or paradox, at the end of most sentences.' This sense of demotic energy and endlessly creative speech patterns makes me long to read an Ulster equivalent of the multitudinous voices in Norman Mailer's great oral epic *The Executioner's Song*. Belfrage may have helped prepare the ground for some future vernacular classic which will express the extraordinary experience which rips from out her writing. In the meantime *The Crack* is a spontaneously intelligent and loving tribute to a city which I continue to believe is the great good place, the *amor* that locks with *loci*.

Sublime and Ridiklus

> How beauteous mankind is!
> O brave new world
> That has such people in't!

Miranda's breathlessly innocent, admiring, Utopian address to various tainted politicians in *The Tempest* uses a word – 'brave' – which has dropped out of standard English. It's still current in Ulster English, one of many words which are a source of pride to citizens of the province. Here is C. I. Macafee's definition of *brave*:

1 said of anything fine or good of its kind; 2 specifically, of a person, bold, unconcerned, nonchalant eg *Afterwards, I meet my brave Andy walking down the street*; 3 in good health, improved in health; 4 before another adjective to intensify its sense: very

Ask someone how's their health and the response is 'Bravely.'

The editor goes on to list the phrases where the word signifies a great number: *a brave clatter*, *a brave drap*, *a brave few*, *a brave lock*, *a brave wheen*. Just running through those phrases makes me long for the crack and buzz of Ulster speech. And to read through this work – the first of its kind – is to think, Miranda-like, that a dictionary promises a new and better world.

There is something intensely irenic in this scholarly word-hoard, just as there is both mellowness and a sceptical irony in these stanzas from 'Traditions' in Seamus Heaney's *Wintering Out*, a volume which appeared in 1972, one of the very worst years of the Ulster troubles:

> We are to be proud
> of our Elizabethan English:

Review of *A Concise Ulster Dictionary*, ed. C. I. Macafee (Oxford University Press).

'varsity,' for example,
is grass-roots stuff with us;

we 'deem' or we 'allow'
when we suppose
and some cherished archaisms
are correct Shakespearian.

Not to speak of the furled
consonants of lowlanders
shuttling obstinately
between bawn and mossland.

Among the cherished archaisms is the world *miching* – standard English 'beaking', as in 'beaking off school'. It occurs in that famous phrase of Hamlet's, '*miching mallecho*', and is used commonly in Ulster speech. To notice this and other Elizabethan survivals is to recognize that the province's language has existed almost unknown to the wider world for several centuries. Only the recent, nearly three-decades-long troubles have hurt it into a dictionary, just as that violence has brought into being many poems, novels, short stories and plays, as well as news reports and television programmes. To read through this extensive compilation is to come across many words and phrases which embody an oral poetry – brief epiphanies snatched out of living, subtle speech.

From the classically simple *the night is set*, the fricative *the scrake of dawn*, the Shakespearean *a polished villain*, to the affectionate term for a tall, thin person – *skinnymalaink* – and the equally affectionate *scaldy* for an unfledged bird or someone with a short haircut, Ulster speech is packed with expressions that bond people in a language that's made up of English dialect, Scots and Irish words.

The verb *thole*, for example, which means 'to bear or endure patiently', comes out of Anglo-Saxon, and has a tough, physical, stoic texture missing from its standard English equivalents. *Skelf*, meaning a tiny wood splinter, especially in a finger, has a similar physicality. A young child upset by the sight of someone they don't know is said to be *making strange*, a phrase produced, I would guess, by the subtle and elaborate manners of country people. One of my favourite rural words is *lunk*, which is applied to close, sultry weather, and can also mean 'queasy'. I've never heard anyone use it, though I live in hopes that its very concrete and exact rendition of a certain climatic effect will catch on. Similarly, the word *boke* for 'puke' has a richness and a humour which is missing from estuary English (*dry boke* is the term for retching).

Finding the commonly used phrase *broth of a boy*, which is defined as 'the essence of manhood, a thoroughly good, capable fellow', I realize that Hopkins's homoerotic poem 'Harry Ploughman' draws on the term when he describes his 'Hard as hurdle arms, with a broth of goldish flue / Breathed round.' Hopkins wrote the poem in the North of Ireland, and though he appears to be designing a hunky English ploughman he's also celebrating the naked thew and sinew, as he termed it, of the language in its dialect or regional vernacular forms. The word *thoughother*, which is one of a whole series of Ulster words denoting untidiness, is used (in a different spelling) by Hopkins in the phrase 'all throughther, in throngs' from 'Spelt from Sibyl's Leaves'.

Dr Macafee's concise Ulster dictionary is a fine and substantial work, a monument to the sparky creativity of Ulster English, but it needs to be supplemented by James Fenton's excellent dictionary of Ulster Scots, *The Hamely Tongue*, which was published last year and has not attracted much attention. I also miss some of my favourite words in Macafee's text – *header* in the sense of someone who takes too many risks, *spacer* for someone who takes even more risks than a header, *raft* for 'a great deal', *spooly* for a harmless fool, and *dozer* for someone who is dull and stupid (this language is rich in terms of varieties of rain and fools). To say that someone is *no dozer* is to give praise in a characteristically Ulster fashion. I also missed *get langered* for 'get really drunk', and *half-cut* for 'fairly drunk'. It's a pity too that obscenities have been excluded. I also regret the absence of *ridiklus* which is used often with splenetic humour to deflate pomposity, as in 'I heard a speech Sir Patrick Mayhew give – it was absolutely ridiklus!'

Political Verse

We have been taught, many of us, to believe that art and politics are separated by the thickest and most enduring of partitions. Art is a garden of pure perfect forms which effortlessly 'transcends' that world of compromise, cruelty, dead language and junk cars which Manichaeans dismiss as mere politics. Art stands for freedom, while politics is a degrading bondage we must reject and escape from. Indeed, there is an influential school of literary criticism – appropriately, it dominates literary studies in the United States – which argues that the political and historical content of literature must be dismissed as 'extrinsic irrelevance'. The practitioner of close reading agrees with Henry Ford that history is bunk and enforces that belief with a series of fallacies – biographical, intentional, historical, 'personalist', ideological. Like intimidating heresies, these supposedly fallacious ways of reading literature are designed to hinder the reader who believes that there is often a relationship between art and politics, rather than a clear-cut opposition between formal garden and contingent scrapheap.

The poet who elects to write about political reality is no different from the poet who chooses love, landscape or a painting by Cézanne as the subject for a poem. The choice of a political subject entails no necessary or complete commitment to an ideology – Burns, for example, was a radical republican but he nevertheless based 'Charlie He's My Darling' on popular Jacobite songs about the Young Pretender. He could combine a dedicated egalitarianism with a pride in the House of Stuart that was both personal and national. And if Burns had been more extensively cavalier in his sympathies, Arnold might not have dismissed him as a 'Scotch' provincial who speaks in a bogus voice, lacks high seriousness and has mistakenly elected to write about 'a harsh, a sordid, a repulsive world'.

Burns is one of the most notable victims of the aristocratic, hierarchical, conservative tradition which Arnold and T. S. Eliot have floated as the major cultural hegemony in these islands. And although Eliot offered a strategic defence of Burns's verse, his subversion of Milton's reputation was a major act of cultural desecration (the subsequent modification in Eliot's attitude did not repair the damage). Both Arnold and Eliot adopt a romantic, curiously puritan and personal attitude to Milton – Arnold criticizes his 'asperity and acerbity, his want of sweetness of temper', while Eliot confesses 'an antipathy towards Milton the man'. Abetted by Leavis, the *Scrutiny* group, the New Critics and that reactionary theologian C. S. Lewis, Eliot was able to rewrite English literary history and almost obliterate the Protestant prophetic tradition. And as David Norbrook has pointed out in his brilliant, pioneering study *Poetry and Politics in the English Renaissance*, the Renaissance poetic tradition culminated in Milton, a figure whose

uncompromising republicanism places his views even today outside the conventional framework of political discussion in England. Eliot and Leavis did not flinch from a drastic solution: Milton must be declared to have been a bad poet, and 'dislodged' from the canon.

As Norbrook reminds those of us who still revere Milton as the greatest English poet and the most dedicated servant of English liberty, some of the major Renaissance poets were politicians. But this unsettling historical fact was pushed out of the cultural memory by a group of literary critics dedicated to a 'transcendental' vision which ostensibly depoliticized art.

This orthodoxy has meant that students of English literature have for several generations now been encouraged to believe that Milton's theology is entirely separate from whatever his political beliefs might have happened to be. And in any case, Milton had been smeared by T. S. Eliot as a master of 'a dead language' and was therefore a writer who might be respectably avoided. The ghost of an earlier *entryiste*, Edmund Burke, must have smiled at Eliot's enterprise, and Arnold's eccentric praise of that Irish counter-revolutionary as 'our greatest English prose-writer' is one of his more 'interested' or committed critical judgements, even though Arnold astutely balances it with a criticism of Burke's stylistic extravagance and 'Asiatic' provinciality.

Together, Arnold and Eliot ensured that the magic of monarchy and superstition permeated English literary criticism and education like a syrupy drug. Fortunately, the work of Christopher Hill challenges the bland, unhistorical, insidiously tendentious readings of Milton which have been dominant until recently, and in time it may be generally acknowledged that Milton is no more a non-political writer than Joyce was – or Dante, or Virgil.

One of the dogmas of the ahistorical school of literary criticism is the belief that political commitment necessarily damages a poem. Thus poets tend to be praised for their liberal openmindedness, their freedom from the constricting dictates of ideology. As Douglas Bush has shown, Cleanth Brooks transforms Marvell's 'Horatian Ode' into an expression of modern 'uncommitted' liberalism. Yet the two greatest political poems in English – *Paradise Lost* and *Absalom and Achitophel* – are works of the committed imagination. Milton was a republican, a regicide, the official propagandist of the English parliament, Dryden became a monarchist and a Tory after the Restoration. Their political beliefs are fundamental to their poems, and our reading is enriched by a knowledge of those beliefs and an understanding of the social experience which helped to form them (I say 'helped' because in the end we accede to a political position by an act of faith – Milton's essential faith was love of liberty, Dryden's love of order).

In the Western democracies it is still possible for many readers, students and teachers of literature to share the view that poems exist in a timeless vacuum or a soundproof museum, and that poets are gifted with an ability to hold themselves above history, rather like skylarks or weather satellites. However, in some societies – particularly totalitarian ones – history is a more or less inescapable condition. In those cold, closed societies a liberal belief in the separation of the public from the private life is not possible. Nor is it possible to believe that a poet may take only an occasional interest in politics, or adopt a position which in the West would be termed 'purely aesthetic and non-political'. The ironic gravity and absence of hope in poets such as Zbigniew Herbert, Różewicz, Holub, remind us that in Eastern Europe the poet has a responsibility both to art and to society, and that this responsibility is single and indivisible. The poet, in Joyce's special use of the term, is the 'conscience' of his or her society. Pasternak on Hamlet, Herbert on Fortinbras, Holub on the illusion that 'Hamlet will be saved and that an extra act will be added', all remind us that in certain societies to write poetry is to act socially, not to turn one's back on contingency. Here, symbols are deployed like ciphers in a secret code – the dissident Hamlet becomes an honorary citizen of the Eastern Bloc. He is the intellectual and poet-figure whose presence in a poem always implies the existence of the usurping tyrant, Claudius, who smuggled poison into the garden and caused the Fall. To initiate the analogy is almost to ghost the rumour that Stalin had Lenin poisoned.

The actor-Hamlet's nervousness is Pasternak's fear that by speaking out directly like Mandelstam he will join him in the Gulag. But in this exposed, public confrontation with the tyrant it is Hamlet alone who will die. And it was partly by adopting an 'antic' disposition that Pasternak survived the great purges and lived to translate *Hamlet*. Like Shakespeare, Pasternak saw 'art tongue-tied by authority', and by pretending to be merely voluble, eccentric, a harmless cloud-treader, he earned Stalin's protection. No one would blame him – Nadezdha Mandelstam never did – for in a sense he made a reality of the illusion 'that Hamlet will be saved'.

To consider Pasternak's career is to understand how completely the personal life can be saturated by political reality, for politics is like a rainstorm that catches us all in its wet noise. Only in a liberal democracy can we hope to dodge it and even there we may be misleading ourselves, or being misled by others – ageing New Critics, or those neo-Christians William Empson so despised.

Although the imagination can be strengthened rather than distorted by ideology, my definition of a political poem does not assume that such poems necessarily make an ideological statement.

defining a political poem

Instead they can embody a general historical awareness – an observation of the rain – rather than offering a specific attitude to state affairs.

And sometimes a political poem does not make an obviously ideological statement – 'To Penshurst', for example, conceals its politics behind a series of apparently innocent and 'natural' images.

Almost invariably, though, a political poem is a public poem, and it often begins in a direct response to a current event, just as a pamphlet or a piece of journalism springs from and addresses a particular historical moment. For example, in March 1681, the Whigs introduced the Third Exclusion Bill, which was designed to safeguard liberty by preventing James Stuart, the Duke of York, succeeding Charles II. Charles dissolved parliament (he had already removed it to royalist Oxford), and in July he imprisoned the Whig leader, Shaftesbury, in the Tower on a charge of high treason. Dryden was both Historiographer Royal and Poet Laureate, and he supported Charles in a prose-pamphlet, *His Majesties Declaration Defended*, and then in *Absalom and Achitophel*, which was published in mid-November and is said to have been undertaken at the King's request. The poem was published as a pamphlet and it aimed to prejudice Shaftesbury's trial at the end of the month. Like Auden's 'Spain' – also first published as a pamphlet – Dryden's poem was generated by the hurry of contemporary political events. It is in no sense disinterested or transcendental of society – quite the reverse, in fact, for it aimed to bring Shaftesbury to the scaffold. Politically, it is a brilliant dirty trick, an inspired piece of propaganda; aesthetically, it is a great masterpiece. But no one should call it 'pure'. The writer who prompts a judge, a jury and an executioner is necessarily guilty, and although Shaftesbury managed to escape to Holland, that distinguished libertarian is now only a faint presence in the historical memory. He has melted into Dryden's fiction, a fiction that invests him with something of the engaging *élan* of Shakespeare's Richard III – a dramatic character whose historical accuracy Josephine Tey and others have challenged.

Yeats's couplet on the poet's impurity, his responsibility for political violence, is a well-rubbed quotation, though few critics have tried to follow up the question, 'And did that play of mine send out / Certain men the English shot?' by placing the writings in their immediate social context. This is partly because literary history is almost a lost art and partly because many literary critics have no interest in biography or in history proper (for example, it seems likely that Yeats's insistence on art's superiority to politics was partly a ruse designed to mislead Annie Horniman, who funded the Abbey Theatre and was a British patriot). 'Easter 1916' is dated '25 September 1916' and Yeats began writing the poem after the executions of the fifteen rebel leaders which took place between 3 and 12 May 1916. Curiously, the most famous modern political poem was originally published as a sort of underground pamphlet – it was privately printed in a limited edition of twenty-five copies by Clement Shorter for distribution among Yeats's friends. Yeats waited another four years before publishing the poem, and in his seminal essay 'Passion and Cunning', Conor Cruise O'Brien argues that:

By the time when 'Easter 1916' and 'The Rose Tree' were published, in the autumn of 1920, the pot had boiled over. The Black and Tan terror was now at its height throughout Ireland. To publish these poems in this context was a political act, and a bold one: probably the boldest of Yeats's career.

It could be argued that Yeats displayed his characteristic cunning in waiting four years before releasing 'Easter 1916'. He had told Lady Gregory in a letter of 11 May 1916 that 'I had no idea that any public event could so deeply move me', but he did not hasten to express that emotion in public. However, in the autumn of 1920 an influential British Labour Party commission was inquiring into the conduct of the war, and by publishing his poem in the *New Statesman* Yeats aligned it with Labour's condemnation of British reprisals (it appeared two days before Terence MacSwiney, the mayor of Cork, died on hunger strike). In 1916, he would have had no definite idea what a future Ireland might look like – the Union may well have appeared rock-solid at that time – but the poem's publication on 23 October 1920 coincided with Lloyd George's first tentative moves towards a truce and a settlement. And, appropriately, that issue of the *New Statesman* was dominated by Irish politics (it contained several articles criticizing the British government's campaign of 'official terrorism' – i.e. the Black and Tan campaign). Yeats's poem is therefore part of a new political climate, and like *Absalom and Achitophel* it must also have helped to mould opinion. A statement which might have isolated and exposed Yeats in the autumn of 1916, now helped to consolidate links between British socialists and Irish nationalists.

Yeats was an intensely political writer and his frequent sneers at politicians, journalists and other 'groundlings' are part of his consistent deviousness, his influential habit of first affirming that art and politics are hostile opposites and then managing to slip through the barrier, a naked politician disguised as an aesthete. It is a self-confessed circus-act which appears to have fooled many spectators into believing that the poet was somehow above the vulgarities of politics. This element of populism, cruelty and calculated circus-like improvisation is an important characteristic of Yeats's work, and I would guess that Samuel Beckett had the great ringmaster in mind when he created Pozzo in *Waiting for Godot*. Yeats belongs, though, to a separate Irish tradition of political verse, and in order to consider the concept of the political poem it is necessary to define the various traditions which inform such poetry.

THE POPULAR TRADITION

In England, this type of political verse began long ago in the complaints and rebellions of the common people against those in authority. It shapes itself in anonymous ballads, popular songs, broadsheets, nursery rhymes like 'Gunpowder Plot Day', and its visceral energies can be felt in both Kipling and Yeats. It is the ground bass, the deep tidal pull, which underlies much political verse written in 'higher' or more 'official' modes. Often it can be witty, tough, idealistic, and resolute with a sense of egalitarian integrity:

> I mean the ploughman,
> I mean the plain true man,
> I mean the handcraftman.

This rich proletarian tradition looks to the prelapsarian Adam and Eve as ideal images of a just society, and these primal figures were invoked by John Ball in the text of the revolutionary sermon he preached at Blackheath in 1381. Adam delving, Eve spinning – the image became a radical, republican commonplace, and it was invoked frequently during the 1640s. In *Vox Plebis*, a work ascribed to the Leveller, John Lilburne, we read: 'For as God created every man free in Adam: so by nature are all alike freemen born'. The image of free Adam – an image often used pejoratively by episcopalians – passes from Milton and Marvell in the seventeenth century to Clough in the nineteenth, and Clough's ironic, half-admiring reference to 'Democracy upon New Zealand' in *The Bothie of Tober-na-Vuolich* is a late version of the ideal puritan commonwealth whose failure Milton probes in *Paradise Lost*.

One of the masterpieces in this tradition is John Clare's 'The Fallen Elm', a bitter and tender elegy which speaks for a dying social class – the agricultural labourers who were displaced by the enclosure acts. Like Jonson's 'To Penshurst', Clare's poem is conservative in its sacral sense of the value of tradition, and it gains enormously from Ann Tibble's restoration of Clare's original orthography:

> The common heath became the spoilers prey
> The rabbit had not where to make his den
> & labours only cow was drove away
> No matter – wrong was right & right was wrong
> & freedoms bawl was sanction to the song
> – Such was thy ruin music making elm
> The rights of freedom was to injure thine

Like a Luddite pamphlet, Clare's poem seems to rise up from a vast, anonymous historical experience, and we can see that experience expressing itself actively in this United English oath which E. P. Thompson cites in *The Making of the English Working Class*:

In a ful Presence of God. I a.b. doo swear not to abey the Cornall but the . . . Peapell. Not the officers but the Committey of United Inglashmen . . . and to assist with arms as fare as lise in my power to astablish a Republican

Government in this Country and others and to assist the french on ther Landing to free this Contray.

The Irish accent of the oath is a reminder of the close links between radical movements in these islands, and it is significant that the English Chartist poet Ebenezer Elliott should echo Burns in 'Drone v. Worker'.

It seems likely that Browning's 'The Lost Leader' is spoken by a Chartist, and the poem's lithe dactyllic rhythms are shared by many Irish rebel songs. Again, this poem was inspired by a particular occasion – Wordsworth's acceptance of the laureateship on 4 April 1843. The speaker of the poem voices the feeling that Wordsworth has betrayed 'us' – i.e. the working class. Browning had a non-conformist background and was a convinced Liberal (see, for example, the uncollected sonnet 'Why I am a Liberal'). He was briefly a student at University College and his poems show traces of Bentham's philosophy; they also manifest a distinctively Protestant fascination with the workings of the individual conscience. It is possible to discern in Browning's numerous portraits of Renaissance egotists both a traditional Protestant and libertarian obsession with the power of Italian Catholicism and a topical criticism of the individualistic ethos of Victorian England. Like Arnold in *Culture and Anarchy*, Browning is voicing – though less directly – an unease with the *laissez-faire* philosophy of 'doing as one likes'. In this he resembles Clough, who was deeply interested in political economy and hostile to an unbridled capitalist ethic.

Tragically, the popular verse tradition appears to be almost extinct in England now, though the work of the 'pop' poet John Cooper Clarke, and that of a number of poets who write in West Indian and reject standard British English, may be aligned with this type of political verse. Linton Kwesi Johnson on the Brixton riots of 'April nineteen eighty-wan' is like an echo of these lines from the early fifteenth-century 'A Song of Freedom':

> þin ffadere was a bond man,
> þin moder curtesye non can.

Euery beste þat leuyth now
Is of more fredam þan þow!

To read these poems with their deep libertarian instincts and demand for social justice is like discovering a hidden, living tap-root which permanently feeds a vigorous eloquence. Clare's lament for his 'music making elm' becomes symbolic of the uprooting of his class and of the loss of certain traditional English liberties. Anyone who has seen the Stars and Stripes flying over a piece of English common land will understand something of Clare's answer to the 'cant of tyranny'. The student of Ted Hughes's poetry will notice that it draws strongly on a popular vernacular, but his recent acceptance of the Laureateship suggests that he has been co-opted by the rival monarchist tradition.

THE MONARCHIST TRADITION

Despite T. S. Eliot's influence on the shape of English literary history, this is not the major tradition of political verse in England. It is important, but not as omnipotent as its supporters would have us believe. Although Spenser is a Protestant prophet, his poetry has been commonly aligned with that mystic patriotism, belief in social hierarchy and reverence for institutions 'sprong out from English race' which characterize monarchism. Spenser served the Earl of Leicester and he shared his patron's extreme Protestantism. Thus when Spenser looks forward to the 'new Hierusalem' and identifies the English as God's 'chosen people', he is expressing radical Protestant beliefs which were later held by Milton and the English republicans. Spenser's historical placing long before the Civil War enables him apparently to span both the Protestant and the monarchist traditions. But for Milton there was no doubt that 'our sage and serious poet Spenser' was fully committed to the puritan cause.

Shakespeare's conservative pessimism belongs to the opposing tradition, though there is a populist anger in Sonnet 66 which is radically disgusted and anarchistic, like much of Swift's writing.

This rejection of a corrupt public world is also offered in Ralegh's 'The Lie', and his anti-Spanish stance made him both a popular hero and, like Spenser, an influence on Milton. It would require a large and separate anthology to give a comprehensive account of Shakespeare's political vision and I have therefore included only two excerpts from *Coriolanus*, a play which has had a far-reaching influence on subsequent political verse. Its anti-populism is present in Hopkins's use of the verb 'mammocks'* in 'Tom's Garland', and although Eliot's 'Coriolan' is not one of his better poems, it must be noted that his designation of *Coriolanus* as Shakespeare's 'most assured artistic success' represents more than a disinterested aesthetic judgement. The hostility towards popular education which Eliot expresses in *Notes Towards the Definition of Culture* issues from his deep conservative loathing for democracy and his fear that education – which indeed comes under the influence of politics – will take upon itself the reformation and direction of culture, instead of keeping to its place as one of the activities through which a culture realizes itself.

Hopkins, though he called himself a 'communist' in the early 1870s, is essentially a right-wing patriot who is fascinated, like Kipling, by a vernacular energy and a primitivist vision of life. In a letter to Robert Bridges, he explicated 'Tom's Garland' and spoke of his indignation with 'the fools of Radical Levellers'. He also denounced 'Loafers, Tramps, Cornerboys, Roughs, Socialists and other pests of society', and informed Bridges that the model for his sonnet was Milton's 'caudated' sonnet 'On the New Forcers of Conscience'. Thus 'Tom's Garland' is a reply-poem which opposes that libertarian tradition of which Milton is the supreme exemplar in England. The working-class speaker in 'The Lost Leader' says 'Milton was for us', and though Milton's writings are often aligned with radical causes he was personally opposed to the Levellers and the Diggers. Hopkins, however, is in no sense a libertarian and he sees the working class as occupying a fixed position in the divine

---

*When Coriolanus's son tears a butterfly to pieces, Valeria says 'Oh, I warrant how he mammock'd it' (I.3.71).

social design – it is a lowly member of the body politic and leads a bestial, mindless existence, careless of the 'lacklevel' or inegalitarian nature of society.

The major figure in this hierarchical tradition is Dryden, and like 'Tom's Garland' *Absalom and Achitophel* answers Milton's radical vision, his belief in the free individual conscience. Following Milton, Dryden employs Mosaic imagery drawn from the Book of Exodus, and his comparison of David (Charles II) to 'the prince of angels' follows the Miltonic parallel with Satan. The political or topical use of imagery drawn from Exodus and other biblical books was commonplace in the seventeenth century, and Oliver Cromwell employed it in 1654 when he accused the English clergy of 'a design . . . to bring us again into Egyptian bondage'. Dryden was a civil servant under Cromwell and in the 1680s he inverted traditional puritan readings of the biblical account of the Garden of Eden by transforming Achitophel into Satan tempting the blushing Eve (i.e. Absalom who is the Duke of Monmouth). Dryden aims to bury English republicanism and Whiggery, and he compares the post-Restoration adherents of 'the good old cause' to fallen angels, fiends 'harden'd in impenitence'. Shakespearian drama is a major influence on the poem (it helps shape the subtle, often sympathetic portrait of Achitophel), and Dryden's account of Absalom's temptation is similar to Queen Isabel's defence of royal hierarchy in *Richard II* – a defence which Shakespeare is less than wholly committed to in the play.

Rebuking the gardener for his radical criticism of a corrupt aristocracy, the Queen cries:

> Thou, old Adam's likeness, set to dress this garden,
> How dares thy harsh rude tongue sound this unpleasing news?
> What Eve, what serpent, hath suggested thee
> To make a second fall of cursed man?
> Why dost thou say King Richard is deposed?

(III. 4.73–7)

For the monarchist, the deposition or execution of the lawful anointed king represents a split in society akin to a breach in nature.

Ben Jonson, writing from within the social tensions that were ultimately to lead to the Civil War, designs a utopian image of a feudal garden in 'To Penshurst', and like Shakespeare he is hostile to that new type of economic man which Edmund speaks for in *King Lear*. However, in *Richard II* Shakespeare's hostility is muted and offset by his sympathetic portrayal of Bolingbroke, and it is possible to detect a closet republicanism in *Julius Caesar*, a play that cannot be unconnected with fears for the post-Elizabethan future.

Jonson was hostile to republican ideas, acted as a government spy, and was in Frank Kermode's phrase a 'collaborator with Stuart absolutism', though his modern affinities are with the socially cohesive, paternalist strain within English conservatism. This paternalist idea informs 'To Penshurst', which is a classic one-nation poem, hostile to mercantile capitalism and recent money. Such hostility forms part of traditional or 'wet' conservatism, and it is also present in Swift's work. This anarchistic disdain for the cash-nexus also forms the opening section of *Maud* and it is an influential strand in Yeats's social thought. Like Jonson, Dryden and Pope, Yeats has a horror of the destruction of culture by the rough beasts of egalitarianism. Echoing Hobbes, Dryden imagines kings and governments falling to 'nature's state, where all have right to all'. It is no accident that Yeats should echo *Richard II*, as Hopkins does in the 'terrible sonnets', for he is reacting against that aggressive challenge to numinous hierarchy which Bolingbroke symbolizes. Bolingbroke/Cromwell/Robespierre/Lenin would be the paternalist conservative's thumbnail sketch of the continuity of tyranny, and we can sense in Dryden and Pope a cosmic terror at a levelling mediocrity bent on destroying culture, that 'ceremony of innocence' which Yeats celebrates in 'A Prayer for My Daughter'.

The conservative poet is naturally a pessimist and I would guess that the academic who rendered Ecclesiastes into English was not a member of the reforming puritan party within the Church of England. It is common for conservative historians, and particularly those who write about Irish history, to echo the preacher's statement, 'The thing that hath been, it is that which shall be; and that which is done is that which shall be done: and there is no new thing under the sun' (Ecclesiastes 1.9). For the conservative pessimist, intellectuals disturb the peace: 'he that increaseth knowledge increaseth sorrow.' This is a hard-line conservative position and it is weary with a quietist distaste for the topical and the new. Like many writers of pastoral, the conservative obscures political realities by professing an envy of the ignorant and by shuffling responsibility for historical suffering onto those who aim to increase knowledge by challenging received ideas. At times, the conservative pessimist echoes Eliot in *After Strange Gods* ('What is still more important is unity of religious background; and reasons of race and religion combine to make any large number of free-thinking Jews undesirable'), and we must note that Yeats, like Eliot and Jung, also believed in a concept of racial memory.

It was Eliot's influential ambition to express a unifying conservative vision in his religious verse and in his social and literary criticism. In 'Little Gidding' he imagines a cultural consensus where the English people are at last united 'in the strife which divided them'. Charles I – the beaten, broken 'king at nightfall' – combines in Eliot's historical memory with 'one who died blind and quiet', and that unnamed figure is the poet whose reputation Eliot did so much to maim. The regicide Milton is here allowed a ghostly presence in the canon as the ancient wounds are healed by Eliot's sacramental vision.*

In these salving lines Eliot appears to echo a consensual, Spenserian combination of the monarchist and puritan traditions, for now that the king and the blind epic poet have become part of the national memory, the opposing sides of an old argument can be seen 'folded in a single party'. It is a most poignant vision, and we must

---

*Cp. 'The anniversary of the execution of King Charles I was celebrated as normal on 30 January by the Society of King Charles the Martyr, an esoteric group on the rainbow fringes of high church/right-wing/monarchist/anglo-catholic frontiers who hope and pray for the late King's canonization. An altar was set up in Banqueting House in Whitehall – the scene of his execution supposedly consecrated by his spilled blood. Much gin was drunk. All in all, a funny sort of gathering for Mr John (Selwyn) Gummer to be found addressing, expressing his hope that the spirit of King Charles would enter the heart of the Bishop of Durham.' (Report in the *Guardian*, 2 February 1985.)

remember that it is an experience grounded in the British people's profound sense of national solidarity during the Second World War. Eliot aims to heal or 'associate' a split cultural sensibility, and whatever reservations we may have about his politics it is impossible not to admire his achievement in writing this type of religious and patriotic verse. However, that admiration ought not to make us collude with Eliot's displacement of the major tradition of English political verse, and we must be alert to the Burkean or High Anglican conspiracy which has so distorted literary history.

THE PURITAN—REPUBLICAN TRADITION

The puritan imagination is altogether more complex than its opponents suppose – its essential libertarianism can be ironic, playful, dedicated to the primal lushness of a new beginning, as well as paranoid, self-righteous, aggressive and intransigently committed. The puritan reads the Bible in a directly personal manner, and to such an eager imagination this psalm in the Authorized Version is a song of freedom that exults in the litheness of a released vernacular:

When Israel went out of Egypt, the house of Jacob from a people of
    strange language;
Judah was his sanctuary, and Israel his dominion.
The sea saw it, and fled: Jordan was driven back.
The mountains skipped like rams, and the little hills like lambs.
What ailed thee, O thou sea, that thou fleddest? thou Jordan, that
    thou wast driven back?
Ye mountains, that ye skipped like rams; and ye little hills, like
    lambs?
Tremble, thou earth, at the presence of the Lord, at the presence of
    the God of Jacob;
Which turned the rock into a standing water, the flint into a fountain
    of waters.

(Psalm 114)

Milton made a beautiful metrical version of this psalm when he was fifteen years old, and ten years later he adapted it into Greek heroic verse. That Stuart absolutism which Jonson helped to beautify, was for Milton a sojourn in Egypt where a 'people of strange language' oppressed God's chosen people, the English. And the parallel is made explicit in *Eikonoklastes*, where Milton compares Pharaoh's blindness to that of King Charles.

The true puritan rejects traditional monarchy and the authority of the Church, and looks instead to the Bible for sanction and inspiration. Puritan ideology draws often on these verses from St John:

And ye shall know the truth, and the truth shall make you free. They answered him, We be Abraham's seed, and were never in bondage to any man: how sayest thou, Ye shall be made free?

(8.32–3)

Milton echoes John in his sonnet defending his divorce treatises, and he does so in order to express his commitment to the free individual conscience. Like Cromwell, he believed in 'the free way', not 'the formal'. He is therefore opposed to 'a classic hierarchy' (the phrase refers in the first instance to the Presbyterian Church), and this is an influential libertarian idea. Yeats drew strongly on this tradition at certain moments in his career, and it informs his famous senate speech on divorce, where he invoked Irish Protestant rights 'won by the labours of John Milton and other great men'. Bernard Shaw also belongs to this resolute Anglo-Irish tradition, a tradition which paradoxically finds its most complete aesthetic summation in Joyce's superbly 'catholic' imagination.

In the closing years of the twentieth century we have the histories of many revolutions to remind us of the crimes committed in the name of liberty, and there are moments when Milton expresses that type of radical – not conservative – pessimism which can take a full look at those crimes. In *Paradise Lost* the forces of darkness occasionally voice their love of freedom with an affecting, but troubling sincerity. Thus when Mammon speaks of preferring 'Hard liberty before the easy yoke / Of servile pomp' (II.256–7), it is impossible not to feel that he is expressing a Miltonic credo. But as Christopher Hill argues, the fallen angels combine features drawn from both the royalists and those revolutionaries whom Milton believed had betrayed the republic, and here it is necessary to note that some Leveller leaders plotted with the royalists. Theology and politics fuse completely in the Protestant imagination, and it is essential that we read Milton in that knowledge, hard as Protestant hermeneutics are to convey in an England which appears to have forgotten its remarkable history. As Norbrook rightly insists, 'In abstract theological terms the debate between Calvinists and Arminians was abstruse and raised enormously complex philosophical issues. But it aroused deep passions amongst the laity because it had direct political connotations.' We wrong Milton's epic genius if we split *Paradise Lost* into different 'levels' or 'layers' of meaning and by doing so suggest that the poem's politics are separate from its theological vision. One of the things Milton learnt from Spenser's work was the *ennui* of allegory and we must not insidiously allegorize the greatest poem in the English language.

Adam and Eve in the garden is myth as history or history as myth – the ideal puritan republic is innocent of superstition and monarchy. When Satan enters the garden and sits 'like a cormorant' on the tree of life (IV.196), Milton is employing an image of greed which had traditional associations with 'hireling' clergy and which also possessed oppressive royalist associations for the poet. As Alastair Fowler notes, Milton must at least have heard the cormorant's cry, 'for just across the road from his house in Petty France the king's cormorants were kept in St James's Park'. And we may compare this composite image with the characteristic movement of Milton's mind at the close of *Areopagitica*, where he remarks that the Star Chamber 'is now fallen from the stars with Lucifer'. He wrote *Paradise Lost* after the starry empire had struck back.

Following Spenser, Milton imagines the English people 'Growing into a nation' – a nation that believes in 'free reason'. This rational liberty rejects the fate of Noah's younger son, Canaan, who became a 'Server of servants', and this is echoed in *Ulysses* when Stephen Dedalus casts himself bitterly as a 'server of a servant'. Indeed, the Book of Exodus provides one of the major mythic frameworks for Joyce's epic, and we should note how the idea of full republican nationhood is fundamental to both *Paradise Lost* and *Ulysses*. The critic who refuses to face this truth frankly is in danger of adopting a monarchist ideology of hierarchy with its accompanying values of rigid order and deference:

> Wolves shall succeed for teachers, grievous wolves,
> Who all the sacred mysteries of heaven
> To their own vile advantages shall turn
> Of lucre and ambition, and the truth
> With superstitions and traditions taint,
> Left only in the written record pure,
> Though not but by the Spirit understood.

(XII.508—14)

The Archangel Michael speaks rather like a New Critic as he voices the embattled puritan sense of how the written record can be falsified by the forces of reaction, and he then imagines the New Jerusalem which will be established by the revolutionary consciousness, or free virtuous reason:

> New heavens, new earth, ages of endless date
> Founded in righteousness and peace and love
> To bring forth fruits joy and eternal bliss.

(449—51)

In these prophetic lines, Michael echoes the Second Epistle of Peter where earth and heaven melt away: 'Nevertheless we, according to his promise, look for new heavens and a new earth, wherein dwelleth righteousness' (3.13). This prophecy is echoed in Revelation: 'And I saw a new heaven and a new earth: for the first heaven and the first earth were passed away; and there was no more sea' (21.1). At the end of *The Rainbow*, Lawrence evokes this Protestant prophetic tradition when he rejects industrial society in its entirety and describes Ursula Brangwen seeing 'in the rainbow the earth's new architecture'. This manner of interpreting the Bible contains much that is coldly self-righteous, and it informs 'Hibiscus and Salvia Flowers', where Lawrence witnesses in a distinctively puritan manner to his own swaying, contradictory feeling about Italian socialism. The destructive wish to melt the old social traditions in a consuming fire is a common Protestant form of political frustration – it is expressed at the end of *Samson Agonistes* and at the conclusion of 'In Memory of Eva Gore-Booth and Con Markievicz' where Yeats commands, 'Bid me strike a match and blow'. Intransigence, then a complete purging destruction, are the last stages of the élitist libertarian consciousness trapped within an imposed orthodoxy. A subjective individualism ends by abolishing itself along with the entire social order. At this point the traditional wisdom of the *via media* reminds us of the dangers of breaking the mould and making it all new.

If Milton is an example of the committed imagination, Marvell possesses an eirenic vision which is fluid and only sceptically involved with historical change. In his youth, Marvell appears to have been briefly converted to Catholicism by the Jesuits, and although he was a dedicated member of the anti-court party in the House of Commons his earlier commitment may partly explain the double-minded texture of his verse. His sophisticated ironies and his warm, green, distinctly vegetarian disposition resemble that form of Hinduism which rejects the world of the meat-eaters who mix sex, politics, war. For this type of mystic it isn't possible to make love instead of war – the two activities are cruelly synonymous. Marvell may therefore be said to embody something of the pacifist strain in English radicalism, but this does not mean that he 'speaks more clearly and unequivocally with the voice of his literary age than does Milton'. Eliot's remark is again part of his effort to taint the 'written record pure' with superstitions and false traditions.

Marvell's Protestant vision of history is evident in his miniature epic 'Upon Appleton House', where he symbolizes the English Church as the virgin Thwaites trapped in a convent – 'The nun's smooth tongue had sucked her in'. This is an echo of Spenser's papal Archimago who lives in a 'little lowly Hermitage' where he files 'his tongue as smooth as glas' and succeeds in parting the Redcross Knight from Una who is Truth. Both poets offer symbols of the English Church before the Reformation and we may compare their evocations of sinister enclosing houses with Milton's famous puritan refusal in *Areopagitica*, 'I cannot praise a fugitive and cloistered virtue, unexercised and unbreathed'. The rescue of the virgin Thwaites in Marvell's poetic narrative is therefore symbolic of the English Reformation, and this is given a local foundation by the fact that the Yorkshire estate of Nun Appleton was originally a Cistercian Priory which the Fairfax family acquired at the dissolution of the monasteries.

There are many echoes of *Richard II* in Marvell's poem* and he fuses these reminiscences of the prelude to Shakespeare's civil-war cycle with the classical Horatian theme of retirement and political apathy. His central concern, though, is to analyse the manner in which the individual consciousness within a polarized society can never be pure, can never make the transcendental exit from history. This is evident in stanza 46 where he looks over at Cawood Castle, the nearby seat of the Archbishop of York, and compares the act of seeing or 'sighting' the castle to the action of a field-gun ('invisible artillery'). Even eyesight is not innocent in a conceit which suggests that Marvell is lobbing cannonballs at the 'ambition of its prelate great'. The prelate is the enemy ('the episcopal arts begin to bud again', Milton warns in *Areopagitica*), and in what is really a metaphor for the political consciousness during a time of revolution,

---

*In the play, Bushy, Bagot and their accomplices are called the 'caterpillars of the commonwealth' (II.3.165), and Marvell's garden imagery and reference to 'caterpillars' (stanza 74) echoes this. His comparison of the woodpecker or 'hewel' to an executioner and his image of the 'traitor-worm' pick up the gardener's comparison of one of his men to an executioner, and the man's answering seditious question:

> Why should we, in the compass of a pale,
> Keep law and form and due proportion,
> Showing, as in a model, our firm estate,
> When our sea-walled garden, the whole land,
> Is full of weeds, her fairest flowers choked up,
> Her fruit trees all unpruned, her hedges ruined,
> Her knots disordered, and her wholesome herbs
> Swarming with caterpillars?

(III.4.40–47)

John of Gaunt's 'This England' speech is also a pervasive influence on the poem.

Marvell shows how such a consciousness sees politics everywhere, rather like a sexually obsessive imagination.

Nature is not innocent, and even grasshoppers, in a probable echo of Marvell's royalist friend, Lovelace, become giant cavaliers perilously balanced on 'green spires' (these grasshoppers also echo Numbers 13 where the children of Israel search for Canaan and hear a report of a land of giants that eats up its inhabitants). This pastoral phantasmagoria is full of strange distortions, like *Alice in Wonderland*, and Marvell shares with Carroll an affection for prepubertal girls. Dreaming of innocence – a prelapsarian innocence before war, sex, history – he suggests a sinister sexuality in the nun's invitation to the virgin Thwaites:

> Each night among us to your side
> Appoint a fresh and virgin bride;
> Whom if Our Lord at midnight find,
> Yet neither should be left behind.
> Where you may lie as chaste in bed,
> As pearls together billeted,
> All night embracing arm in arm
> Like crystal pure with cotton warm.

The lovely sexual narcissism of Marvell's walk through the woods has something of the ironic self-consciousness of a Hockney painting, and I can never read that line 'like some great prelate of the grove' without hearing a rich camp accent – Kenneth Williams dressed as a bishop and exuberantly intoning Marvell's words.

In a witty condensation of the Exodus theme, Marvell compares the 'tawny mowers' to the Israelites. The grass which they 'massacre' becomes the Red Sea (or Sea of Reeds as it is more accurately named), and the mowers are then transformed into Levellers. After the Israelites had crossed the Red Sea, 'quails came up, and covered the camp: and in the morning the dew lay round about the host' (Exodus 16.13). Marvell refers to this and to the biblical idea of popular discontent in stanza 51, and by introducing a mower who accidentally 'carves the rail' he offers a seventeenth-century version of the glib revolutionary adage, 'you can't make an omelette without breaking eggs'. The prophetic symbol of the mower mown suggests that those who execute kings will themselves be executed, and it anticipates the fate of the regicides under the Restoration.

Marvell's 'tawny' mowers are versions of the 'yron man' Talus in *The Faerie Queene*:

> But when as overblowen was that brunt,
> Those knights began a fresh them to assayle,
> And all about the fields like Squirrels hunt;
> But chiefly *Talus* with his yron flayle,
> Gainst which no flight nor rescue mote auayle,
> Made cruell hauocke of the baser crew,
> And chaced them both ouer hill and dale:
> The raskall manie soone they ouerthrew,
> But the two knights themselues their captains did subdew.
>
> (V.XI.59)

Talus accompanies Artegall, Knight of Justice, and his job is to carry out executions. Spenser based Artegall on Lord Grey, whom he served as secretary while Grey was lord deputy of Ireland and whose violent measures he supported. It is interesting to note that Talus tends to run amok, rather like an early Black and Tan, and it seems likely that Marvell is drawing out of the Spenserian echo a subliminal image of Cromwell's Irish policy. Spenser based Talus on Talos, the Bronze Man who was guardian of Crete, and the bronzed, sun-tanned mowers in Marvell's poem associate with this metallic image.

The poem's closing vision of the salmon fishers 'like Antipodes in shoes' is a literal embodiment of a popular folk image which was known as 'the World Turned Upside Down'. This phrase, which derives ultimately from St Paul, was applied to an inn-sign illustrating an unnatural state of affairs and alluding to the Antipodes. It often took the form of a man walking at the South Pole. There was a broadside ballad of 1646 entitled 'The World is Turned Upside Down', and the tune is believed to have been played when Cornwallis surrendered at Yorktown in 1781. Although Hill mentions the tune in his fine study *The World Turned Upside Down*, he does not note the popular source of this idea as an antipodean image.

When Queen Isabel in *Richard II* rebukes the gardener for speaking in a 'harsh rude tongue', we note the obvious link between accent and social class. It is a sign of Marvell's playful double-mindedness that he should give his egalitarian mower a polished, aristocratic, classical style in 'The Mower against Gardens'. By couching the mower's criticism of upper-class luxury and art in a language free of all dialect words, Marvell sets up a subversive argument in which the mower is trapped by the highly formal, artificial nature of the poem. This amounts to a reversal of Cromwell's preference for the 'free way', and we may compare it with Walt Whitman's choice of free, vernacular verse to express a populist democratic ethos. Perhaps, though, the mower has appropriated an aristocratic style, prior to occupying both house and gardens?

The mower's reference to the 'gods themselves' who dwell with 'us' aligns the poem with an anti-establishment attitude, and the puritan tradition often crosses over into the popular tradition with its sense of social and economic disadvantage. Bunyan's Valiant-for-Truth straddles both traditions, and as E. P. Thompson has shown, *Pilgrim's Progress* is, with Paine's *Rights of Man*, one of the two 'foundation texts of the English working-class movement'. As a further example of the links between these traditions, it should be noted that Bunyan remains a powerful influence within Protestant populism in the North of Ireland. Though upper-class in style and manner, Gray's *Elegy* expresses a compassion for the rural poor which makes it a part of the popular tradition, like Blake's entire canon with its firm biblical foundations and Miltonic vision. The 'dark satanic mills' of 'Jerusalem' echo Samson at the mill with slaves, and although 'The Tiger' is not limited to the sphere of politics, any reading of it must draw on David Erdmann's compelling historical interpretation of the poem which argues that Blake was thinking of Yorktown and also of Valmy (where the French people halted a counter-revolutionary Prussian invasion). The comparison of an awakened revolutionary people to a tiger was commonplace, and Erdmann cites a report in *The Times* of 7 January 1792, which said that the French people were now 'loose from all restraints and . . . more ferocious than wolves and tigers'. Here, it may be remarked that when Eliot criticizes Blake for lacking 'a framework of accepted and traditional ideas which would have prevented him from indulging in a philosophy of his own', he is really saying something like 'What a pity Blake was a radical Protestant prophet.'

In both versions of *The Prelude*, Wordsworth employs the tiger image in an agonized consideration of the September massacres, and although the 1850 version represents a defection from the poet's youthful belief in 'mountain liberty' and 'equal ground', we must respect the honesty of his intentions as he rewrote his early masterpiece. For the most part he strove to be true to his younger self, though his putative admiration for Burke's counter-revolutionary eloquence is notably absent from the 1805 *Prelude*. Yet in the 1850 version he retains his admiration for the revolution, and a Miltonic echo of the fallen angels is apparent in his description of the royalist counter-revolutionary officers 'bent upon undoing what was done' (IX.133). This is a direct echo of Adam's cry after Eve has eaten the apple, 'But past who can recall, or done undo?' (IX.926). For Milton, the eating of the apple historically symbolizes a servile acceptance of conformity, tradition, superstition, but the postlapsarian reference in Wordsworth's memory suggests a subconscious belief that the overthrow of Louis XVI was the primal sin. This feeling pulls against the major statement that the officers were misguided in their attempts to undo the done, or put the historical clock back. That major statement relies for its force partly on the use of 'bent' with its suggestion of a distortion. Wordsworth's mixed feelings about revolution lack the trepid delicacy of Marvell's vision, partly because Wordsworth casts himself so consciously as the inheritor of Milton's republicanism. There is a proleptically Yeatsian and very protestant cadence in that heroic invocation to 'The later Sidney, Marvel, Harrington, / Young Vane, and others who called Milton friend', and Wordsworth presents himself sternly in the line of succession to these 'moralists'.

Time and again, political poets divide on the issue of whether primal nature is a prelapsarian garden republic or a beneficent monarchy, and Clough clearly belongs with those utopians who nourish a belief in the pure republic:

> So that the whole great wicked artificial civilised fabric –
> All its unfinished houses, lots for sale, and railway outworks –
> Seems reaccepted, resumed to Primal Nature and Beauty.
>
> (*The Bothie of Tober-na-Vuolich*, IX.105–7)

Clough is a shamefully neglected poet who was closely interested in British, Irish, European and American politics. He undertook a detailed study of economics, and his criticism of *laissez-faire* attitudes are pertinent to the monetarist issues which now exercise Western society. A self-styled republican, socialist and feminist, Clough's nimbly ironic classicism always avoids a disablingly tendentious mode, and his sophisticated integrity unsettled the more devious cultivation of his friend Matthew Arnold.

In two sonnets composed during that year of revolutions, 1848, Arnold addressed his 'republican friend', saying 'God knows it, I am with you', but concluded that the day of 'liberated man' will not dawn at a 'human nod'. Although both sonnets are flawed by Arnold's lack of a distinctive individual style, they reveal that influential strain of religious pessimism which links him to Burke and Eliot and the later Wordsworth. Arnold, finally, is anti-intellectual because he is against those who seek to increase knowledge,* and one notes with frustration how in his criticism he will often stop himself from following through the implications of the issues he raises.

The intellectual eagerness and freshness of Clough's verse belongs with the Milton who feared that 'this iron yoke of outward conformity hath left a slavish print upon our necks; the ghost of a linen decency yet haunts us'. And although Clough later became an embittered reactionary, his major works were written at the height of his radical commitment during 1848 and 1849. It is an ambition of this anthology to redeem Clough from the neglect which his work

---

*For example, in 1882 Arnold recommended this motto to the students of Liverpool: 'Don't think: try and be patient'. Quoted in Chris Baldick, *The Social Mission of English Criticism*.

has suffered and to suggest his links with Auden in a tradition of upper-middle-class radicalism and sympathy with 'the old democratic fervour'. The 'gaitered gamekeeper' in Auden's 'Who will endure' seems almost a direct echo of the grouse-moor conservatism which is evoked at the beginning of Clough's *Bothie*, while the figure of the thin man 'clad as the Saxon' makes a link between the Scottish radicalism of Burns and Carlyle and the Chartist movement Clough so admired. Lowland Scotland is one of the most influential centres of the British Labour movement, though for Orwell Scotland suggested simply grouse-moors and ghillies, which is why he rejected his surname 'Blair' for the very English name 'Orwell'.

Auden presents himself in 'Letter to Lord Byron' as the inheritor of the republican tradition when he describes the Hobbesian ogre of Security:

> Milton beheld him on the English throne,
> And Bunyan sitting in the Papal chair;
> The hermits fought him in their caves alone,
> At the first Empire he was also there,
> Dangling his Pax Romana in the air.

Auden later crossed over to the monarchist or Anglo-Catholic tradition, and in the Christian ritualism of his post-war verse he combines this essentially reactionary vision with a Horatian celebration of political apathy and domestic life. This is the theme of 'In Praise of Limestone', where the volcano symbolizes romantic politics (specifically the Byron whom Bertrand Russell regarded as an influence on European fascism). Alluding to Goebbels' threat, 'If we are defeated, we shall slam the doors of history behind us', Auden rejects the politics of heroism, and his civilized vision of man in society is beautifully present in the closing image of the early poem 'From scars where kestrels hover', which sends the 'leader' or *Führer* to Cape Wrath and shows the host passing 'Alive into the house'.

The puritan–republican tradition ends in England with the early Auden, though some critics would claim that its inheritor is Tony Harrison. The diminution of this tradition is a tragic impoverishment, and so too is the attenuation of the rival monarchist tradition. Geoffrey Hill plaintively exemplifies a conservative Christianity in his lament for the past's 'Weightless magnificence' ruined by the recent concrete of the welfare state, while Larkin's lament for lost imperial glory is a deliberately drab, formal gesture of futility and resignation. Sadly, it would seem that political verse is virtually a lost art in England now, and it is difficult to admire the conservative vision of Charles Tomlinson and Donald Davie, though Davie's 'Remembering the Thirties' is a terse reply-poem which confusingly identifies that Coriolanian virtue 'courage' with the presumably pacifist 'vegetable king'. It is a mystifying conclusion offered by a conservative literary puritan who was later to join the Church of England and support the reactionary Anglicanism of *Poetry Nation Review*.

THE IRISH TRADITION

Curiously, the monarchist tradition within English verse is echoed by seventeenth- and eighteenth-century Gaelic poetry in Ireland. Egan O'Rahilly's *aisling* or vision poem 'A Time of Change' is a lament for the downfall of the native Irish aristocracy which followed from the defeat of James II at the Battle of the Boyne. The king who will come over the water in 'Reverie at Dawn' is James's son, the Old Pretender, and the lighting of the three candles symbolizes the restoration of the three kingdoms of Ireland, Scotland and England. The vision is therefore backward-looking and aristocratic, and although this may appear to be nationalistic the poet is in fact an adherent of the Jacobite order and an exponent of a distinctive type of Irish snobbery which we can variously detect in Wilde, Synge and Yeats. As Seamus Deane has argued, the Irish Catholic self-image is often expressed in terms of 'the aristocrat forced into the slum', and this is echoed in the patrician attitudes of many Irish Protestant writers.

The historical memory from which this self-image derives may be seen in Fear Dorcha Ó Mealláin's 'Exodus to Connacht', which is a response to the events that followed from an Act of Parliament which was passed in 1652. The Act ordered that all Catholics and many Protestant royalists above the rank of tradesman and labourer were to remove themselves into Connacht and Clare, where they were given small allotments. Any of those found east of the Shannon after 1 May 1654 might be killed by whoever met them. The move was made mostly during a severe winter and many hundreds died on the way.

The Irish Jacobite and the Irish rebel traditions of political verse are opposed by a populist Orange tradition which believes in hierarchy and deference – a deference to the new Williamite order which can be combined with hostility to England. That hostility is present in the reference to Bond Street dandies in 'The Orange Lily' and it is an expression of that aggressive feeling of cultural inferiority which still afflicts the loyalist imagination. Yeats in his *Autobiographies* mentions that as a child he first discovered 'the pleasure of rhyme' by reading Orange songs in his grandfather's hayloft, and his mature verse combines muscle-flexing Protestant triumphalism with an élitist dedication. His magisterial aristocratic style delights in certain intent cadences drawn from the ballad traditions of both Protestant and Catholic culture. And the more brutal qualities of that stylistic merging of peasant and aristocrat owe as much to the dark side of the Protestant imagination as they do to Yeats's reading of Nietzsche.

Yeats's 'The Fisherman' is, as Blake Morrison shrewdly notes, echoed formally in Seamus Heaney's 'Casualty', and the cadence of these lines

> They move in equal pace
> With the habitual
> Slow consolation
> Of a dawdling engine,

echo the definite 'They' and use of an adjectival rhyme in 'The Wild Swans at Coole':

> Unwearied still, lover by lover,
> They paddle in the cold
> Companionable streams or climb the air.

Marvellously, Heaney appropriates Yeats's high ascendancy rhetoric – a rhetoric that employs the swan-image traditionally symbolic of royalty – and spiritually repossesses Yeats's concern in 'The Fisherman' to find an audience of 'my own race'. The context is changed from the Anglo-Irish country house, Coole Park, to an Ulster Catholic funeral. The low, constant, diesel sound of the hearse's 'dawdling engine' becomes the outboard motor of the fisherman's boat in the succeeding lines, and it is also reminiscent of the ominously 'ticking' bicycle in 'A Constable Calls'. Reading these poems, we catch the pulse of a deterministic sense of history.

An Ulster Protestant poet once told me that Heaney's later work, made him feel 'lonely', and for the Irish poet who does not espouse a Unionist politics the temptation is to indulge an exclusive rhetoric of complaint and to offer images drawn from the jaded repertoire of romantic Irish nationalism. The pressures of tribal loyalty and 'complicity' are a permanent theme in Heaney's work, and his warmly inclusive vision has always rejected those nets of class, religion and ethnicity which Stephen Dedalus describes in *A Portrait of the Artist*. As the ghost of Joyce informs the poet in *Station Island*, 'That subject people stuff is a cod's game'. Noting that, we must also recognize the manner in which Heaney's work rises out of the post-partition Ulster Catholic community, out of a rural society which has always felt itself trapped within the modern concrete of the State of Northern Ireland. To oppose the historic legitimacy of that state and at the same time refuse the simplicities of traditional nationalism is to initiate certain imaginative positives and offer a gracious and civil trust.

The revisionist school of Irish history – a school hostile to Irish nationalism – is an influence on Paul Muldoon's 'Anseo', which is a classic critique of the enduring dominance of the heroic idea of Irish history. 'Meeting the British', a later poem, is coded for a nationalist account of that history and throughout Muldoon's work there is a cutting awareness of the long tradition of agrarian violence in his native county, Armagh. Like Marvell, Muldoon ironizes the theme of love and war, sex and politics, and there is a fascination in his poems with the idea of no man's land, the waste ground between the tribal factions or between 'a hole in the hedge / And a room in the Latin Quarter'.

Neither Heaney nor Muldoon write in the direct manner of Swift's 'Ireland':

> While English sharpers take the pay,
> And then stand by to see fair play.

Swift's couplet is still relevant to the circumstances of Irish political life and we may compare his analysis with this sentence from a political thriller by a recent Secretary of State for Northern Ireland:

The Irish fever, the worst variety known to man. It destroys all gentleness, truth, sensible calculation. When Englishmen catch it they get it worst of all. And Englishwomen.

It must be possible to imagine that there is a vision which lies beyond a self-regarding emotional Irish nationalism and an equally self-regarding British complacency, and in their very different manners both Heaney and Muldoon give that possibility a strict and definite shape. The cadences of Anglican self-esteem – 'all gentleness, truth, sensible calculation' – are as remote for them as they are for any Irish writer, and the rhythms of Irish English have yet to echo Hurd's combination of plainsong and pragmatism. Only nationalists, whether British or Irish, claim a monopoly of 'truth'.

THE SCOTTISH TRADITION

In 1649, Milton rebuked the 'blockish' Presbyterians of Belfast for their support of King Charles and reminded them that John Knox 'taught professedly the doctrine of deposing, and of killing kings'. This Calvinist doctrine is a major intellectual influence on the Scottish tradition of radical verse, and it has obvious affinities with the English puritan tradition. There is also a Jacobite tradition in Scotland which is hostile to English Protestantism, and as I have noted Burns temporarily occupies that tradition in 'Charlie He's My Darling'*. Burns's statement that the Tree of Liberty

---

*It seems likely that Auden's 'The Quarry' draws on the Jacobite tradition, though the reference to a 'parson' must mean that these are English red-coats moving through an English village.

> stands where ance the Bastile stood,
> A prison built by kings, man,
> When Superstition's hellish brood
> Kept France in leading strings, man,

is echoed by his remark in a letter about the executions of Louis XVI and Marie Antoinette: 'What is there in the delivering over of a perjured Blockhead and an unprincipled Prostitute to the hands of the hangman, that it should arrest for a moment, attention, in an eventful hour?'

Burns believes in 'equal rights and equal laws' and in 'For A' That and A' That' he 'slegs' an aristocratic hierarchy:

> Ye see yon birkie ca'd, a lord,
> What struts, and stares, and a' that,
> Though hundreds worship at his word,
> He's but a coof for a' that.
> For a' that, and a' that,
> His ribband, star and a' that,
> The man of independant mind,
> He looks and laughs at a' that.

Here Burns is echoing a passage in *The Rights of Man* where Paine says:

Titles are but nicknames, and every nickname is a title. The thing is perfectly harmless in itself, but it marks a sort of foppery in the human character, which degrades it. It reduces man into the diminutive of man in things which are great, and the counterfeit of woman in things which are little. It talks about its fine blue *ribbon* like a girl, and shows its new *garter* like a child.

Although Paine's sexual stereotyping now seems dated, his internationalist sympathies are enlightened and forward-looking. And Burns, like Paine, imagines that man 'the world o'er / Shall brothers be for a' that'. Nowadays we may be much more sceptical about the realization of internationalist ideals, but that scepticism can too easily become a hardened pessimism which helps to promote an exclusive nationalism.

Hugh MacDiarmid's Marxist internationalism is counterbalanced by a strong anti-English attitude which is the result of his commitment to Scottish nationalism. His hostility to the English tradition of 'sensible calculation' produces the arresting invective of that passage from 'In Memoriam James Joyce' which attacks English amateurism and the Arnoldian doctrine of the balanced 'disinterested' imagination:

> English official criticism has erected
> A stone-heap, a dead load of moral qualities.
> A writer must have optimism, irony,
> A healthy outlook,
> A middle-class standard of morality,
> As much religion as, say, St Paul had,
> As much atheism as Shelley had . . .
> And, finally, on top of an immense load
> Of self-neutralizing moral and social qualities,
> Above all, Circumspection,
> So that, in the end, no English writer
> According to these standards,
> Can possess authenticity.

MacDiarmid brilliantly savages that strain of Anglican whimsy and antiquarian eccentricity in English culture, and his parody of Arnoldian judgement is especially pertinent now that certain schools of literary criticism are being attacked for their blandness and subjectivity. The idea of balanced judgement is a reflection of consensus politics, and in a polarized society with high unemployment such a concept is bound to appear comically irrelevant. MacDiarmid's polemical imagination instinctively polarizes reality, and in this he has more in common with a European critical imagination than with English literary practice. The figure of the 'bewildered foreigner' represents that common European exasperation with the very professional English cult of the amateur. Again, MacDiarmid points to that tedious moralism which is such a dominant force in English literary criticism and which is so careless of formal beauty.

Nationalist feelings often shape the political imagination, and

Douglas Dunn's 'Washing the Coins' also draws subtly on the Scottish socialist tradition:

> I filled the basin to its brim with cold;
> And when the water settled I could see
> Two English kings among their drowned Britannias.

As in MacDiarmid, there is a rigorously Calvinist tendency in Dunn's imagination which expresses itself in his angry, disciplined attack on Sir Walter Scott for turning 'our country round upon its name / And time'. Scott's chivalric, kitsch conservatism is rejected as snobbish, hierarchical and 'mendacious'. Like Christopher Hill, Dunn is concerned with that popular experience which lies beneath the surface of recorded history – what Hill vividly terms 'the vast mass of the population, surviving sometimes in records when they are born, married, accused of crime, or buried, but otherwise leaving no trace'.

This sense of anonymous history is strong in Carlyle's work and it would appear to be a much more powerful manner of thinking and feeling in disadvantaged societies like Scotland and Ireland. It is connected with those ideas of piety and reverence for the dead which form such a significant part of the imagination those cultures share. Piety, though, can easily shade into sentimentality – it is a conservative, communal habit of mind which can be resistant to social change.

THE AMERICAN TRADITION

There is, sadly, a rather meagre tradition of political verse in the United States. Philip Freneau, who was a close associate of Thomas Jefferson, is the first American political poet, and his 'George the Third's Soliloquy' is ironically echoed at the end of Robert Lowell's *Day By Day* where Richard Nixon is compared to that reactionary British King. Freneau's new world republicanism is unfortunately shackled by the old world couplets he employs:

> For late I find the nations are my foes,
> I must submit, and that with bloody nose,

> Or, like our James, fly basely from the state,
> Or share, what still is worse – old *Charles's* fate.

The stylistic failure here demonstrates the difficulties which attend an effort to create a new style in a separate Anglophone culture, and it wasn't until later in the nineteenth century that American poets were able to break decisively with this distractingly formal, aristocratic idiom.

Whitman's free verse is remarkable for its Jeffersonian, populist confidence in republican democracy:

> Of Life immense in passion, pulse, and power,
> Cheerful, for freest action form'd under the laws divine,
> The Modern Man I sing.

This is a declaration of poetic independence, a dedication to life, liberty and the pursuit of happiness, and it speaks for the pleasure-loving side of the puritan imagination. Whitman's loose-limbed modern vernacular draws strongly on the rhythms of the Authorized Version and on native speech rhythms (modern American speech retains many cadences reminiscent of the early seventeenth-century speech which shaped the translation of the Bible).

At times, Whitman resembles an aggressive type of customs-officer who is trying to stop the importation of European ideas and attitudes. His suspicious question, 'is the good old cause in it?' ('By Blue Ontario's Shore'), is ambiguously poised between an imperative rejection of an English republican ideology and an affectionate sympathy for that cause.

The United States contains untold millions of blockishly reactionary people, and at first sight Robert Frost's 'Mending Wall' appears to express an obdurately conservative vision. It is invisibly dedicated to the Roman god Terminus, the lord of boundaries and limitations. Thus the neighbour's traditional adage, 'Good fences make good neighbors', is pessimistic and Hobbesian in its definite wisdom. It expresses a belief in good manners, decorum, formality and personal privacy, and this is naturally opposed to the sprawling libertarianism of Whitman. Such a belief is based on that concept of original sin which, despite Milton's application of it to kingship, remains one of the most powerful conservative arguments. Socialists tend to believe in sin but they usually draw the line at the idea of inheriting it.

Frost's imagination is foxy, and he deploys that cunning by transforming the subversive 'something' which doesn't love a wall into his own mischievous wish to trick and subvert his neighbour's dogma. The subversive something can be the force which rules a Hobbesian state of nature, but Frost upsets that identification by associating his neighbour with darkness and the primeval past (he is like an 'old-stone savage armed'). Thus this figure becomes primitive, not civil, man, and in making that identification Frost aligns himself with Noah Webster and Whitman in their rejection of the past. The neighbour appears briefly as a bone-headed reactionary so that his repetition of his father's saying is rocked slightly by the reservations Frost has insinuated during our reading of this sly, vernal poem.

If Frost often appears to belong inside the Georgian tradition of English verse, Robinson Jeffers can be placed within a European tradition of élitist criticism of democracy. Like T. E. Hulme, he expresses that rigid conservative belief in man's limitations and this is combined with a certain Coriolanian contempt for mass consumer society. Though his verse line is paradoxically based on Whitman's, Jeffers reins in the democratic expansiveness of that style by introducing a consonantal terseness and spartan abruptness which discipline each line by splitting it into brief complete units:

The quality of these trees, green height; of the sky, shining, of water,
    a clear flow; of the rock, hardness.

It is a poetry in love with 'hardness and reticence', a vision which is instinct with a prophetic conservative pessimism about the nature of man and the future of the United States. The sober, tight *pietas* of the statement 'The love of freedom has been the quality of Western man' helps to make Jeffers's prophetic vision of American freedom hooded 'like a kept hawk . . . on the wrist of Caesar' sound with a descriptive urgency. And the spondees in 'Bé gréat, cárve déep your héel-márks' give the line a tense classical texture, rather like the sudden deep jab of a chariot's wheelmarks on a sandy battlefield.

Like Hopkins, Jeffers is a sophisticated primitivist and is clearly a major influence on the work of Ted Hughes. This type of spartan conservatism draws inspiration from Aufidius's image of Coriolanus:

> he'll be to Rome
> As is the osprey to the fish, who takes it
> By sovereignty of Nature.

> (IV.7.32–4)

Such a vision is fascinated by the lethal mysteries of power and knows that the misplaced idealism of Woodrow Wilson must fade beside a Leninist marriage of ideology and *realpolitik*.

Jeffers is a critical analyst of American freedom and there is a relatively oblique criticism of that idea in the witty, anecdotal formality of Elizabeth Bishop's evocation of Trollope's visit to Washington during the Civil War. Reading this poem, we shudder like Eugenia in *The Europeans* and understand e.e. cummings's anarchic criticism of American patriotism. Bishop's sophisticated quietism – or her radical distaste – challenges the democratic Yankee triumphalism of much American verse, and 'Trollope in Washington' is in a sense a reply-poem to Whitman's massive corpus. Like that other patrician, her friend Robert Lowell, Bishop is a social critic who believes in original sin, not primal innocence.

A patriotic critic would judge her verse to be 'un-American' and in a sense she is a silent political poet – by not choosing the puritan freeway her delicately formal verse expresses a high, cultured reaction against American optimism. That pessimism is present throughout Lowell's public verse, which indicts America's 'savage servility', commercial vulgarity and disposable view of the individual human life. But the injustice which so disfigures American society is most persuasively criticized by Blues singers – they are the most authentic American political poets and their work challenges the more comfortable written tradition.

THE ANTI-POLITICAL TRADITION

Elizabeth Bishop's vision of what Yeats terms a 'measured quietude' makes her also a member of this family of writers, and many reply-poems belong here. The Horatian poem of retirement adopts by its very nature an anti-political attitude, and although it can be argued that such poems are essentially conservative since their deliberate apathy must uphold the status quo, such an absolutist reading usually wrongs the sacral moments of being which this type of poetry can offer. Politics, after all, is often relentlessly second-rate in style, language and personality, and the imagination which can derive ideological significance from the fall of a leaf is too earnest to appreciate the mysterious fragrance or mushroom odour of this type of verse.

Derek Mahon's 'A Disused Shed in Co. Wexford' belongs to this tradition, and the formal intuitions of *Dasein* which his verse embodies owe much to Elizabeth Bishop's work. Marvell's verse with its voluptuously vegetarian warmth belongs here, as does Southey's 'The Battle of Blenheim', which is both an anti-war ballad and a humanist vision of historical suffering. This is Mahon's theme in 'A Disused Shed', where the reference to the Irish Civil War and to Treblinka implicitly connect the political fantasies of romantic nationalism with European fascism.

Such poems issue from that condition of supremely unillusioned quietism – the wisest of passivities – which is usually the product of bitter historical experience and which is temperamentally different from disillusion. To be politically disillusioned is often to be cynical; to be politically apathetic is usually to be ignorant, but to possess no illusions is to understand a spiritual reality which is religious in its negativity. Beckett's characters occupy that bare drained landscape, as do many Russian and East European poets. At times their work resembles a type of elegant, ironic, highly sophisticated skrimshan-dering – this is the art of a prison-camp society, verse produced in a closed world without hope but with an obstinate integrity which simultaneously negates as it creates. These poets acknowledge that what they are doing appears to be a pointless activity, but they go on writing, sometimes visiting the West, perhaps effecting the slightest, most minimal changes in the ruling consciousness of their societies. Like prisoners tapping out messages along the heating pipes in a cell block, they speak to us in cipher from an underground culture we in the West have difficulty in comprehending, or which we can too readily twist to our own smug purposes. As Różewicz says in 'Poem of Pathos',

> A poet buried alive
> is like a subterranean river
> he preserves within
> faces names
> hope
> and homeland
>
> (trans. Adam Czerniawski)

The poet is like Aeneas in the underworld. Invisibly, secretly, his epic imagination draws on a mnemonic compulsion to preserve the past and the dead, and this is contrasted with the 'deceived poet' who relies on external influences and an individual or a lyric credo. Such a poet is woken at dawn like a man being arrested or a prisoner about to be shot.

Finally, there is the lying poet, the laureate whose work is propagandist and ripe for transmission by the Ministry of Culture. The possible self-reference here is a severe irony, like the poem's dismissive title, and this ironic insight into the nature of the committed action is also shared by Różewicz's fellow Pole, Joseph Conrad. The end of the first section of *Under Western Eyes* resembles 'Poem of Pathos' in its tragic sense of complete closure:

> An unhurried voice said –
> 'Kirylo Sidorovitch.'
> Razumov at the door turned his head.
> 'To retire,' he repeated.
> 'Where to?' asked Councillor Mikulin softly.

In this autocratic or totalitarian reality there is no private life, no domestic sanctuary, to retire into. Here, any and every action has a political significance which cannot be evaded, and this means that East European poetry is not finally 'anti-political' – it is instead the most advanced type of political verse. In confronting a sealed, utterly fixed reality the East European imagination designs a form of anti-poetry or survivor's art. It proffers a basic ration of the Word, like a piece of bread and chocolate in wartime.

Shakespeare the Catholic

There is a particular type of literary criticism – these days very rare – that aims to exist intensely as bravura performance, dramatic spectacle. It would be pointless to object that the performing critic is merely a rhetorician engaged in digging and falling into a subjective pit of empty images, further descriptions, meaningless or questionable value judgements. If we admire the critic's imagination then we are bound to attend to the performance – a performance that lives only, or at least most intensely, in a first reading. Go back over the text and much of it seems to have melted into a series of repetitive rhetorical gestures that are all dead letter, not living spirit.

This is Hazlitt's point in a little-noticed passage in an essay called 'Whether Genius is Conscious of Its Powers' where he argues that 'the stimulus of writing is like the stimulus of intoxication':

While we are engaged in any work, we are thinking of the subject, and cannot stop to admire ourselves; and when it is done, we look at it with comparative indifference. I will venture to say, that no one but a pedant ever read his own works regularly through. They are not *his* – they are become mere words, waste-paper, and have none of the glow, the creative enthusiasm, the vehemence, and natural spirit with which he wrote them.

Though it lacks Hazlitt's perfectly judged momentum and flexibility, Hughes's prose has a similarly vehement enthusiasm, a pulsing directness that makes him testify to 'the simple immediacy and as it were natural inevitability' with which his idea of Shakespeare's Tragic Equation grew in his mind, 'and which is no small part of what I would like to communicate to my reader'. Rooted in Yorkshire nonconformism, Hughes's prose is every bit as urgent as his poetry: it crackles like his thistles under a frosty blue-black pressure.

Review of Ted Hughes, *Shakespeare and the Goddess of Complete Being* (London: Faber and Faber).

In this type of criticism, the reading process becomes more than analogous to the act of writing – reading fuses with writing because it empathizes in a dramatic manner with the critic's struggle to express ideas, a struggle that resembles an actor's total expressiveness in relation to an audience. Such writing is conspicuous for its puritan theatricality – the term is not self-contradictory – for it carries always the preacher's sense of speaking to and through a deeply attentive audience. Both critic and preacher demand complete attentive assent, an act of faith. Once that assent is given the performance can begin, but it can continue only if the audience's attention is held. Like Emily Dickinson, Hughes aims to push writing beyond writing, he wants to melt its signs into free expressive performance, but unlike Dickinson he doesn't – at least in this study – know how to employ formal brevity as the foundation of unconditioned Being. Like his admired Cromwell, he sees the formal and the free way as opposites, not synergies.

Yet despite the length of the performance, this is mythic criticism issuing from a marvellously intuitive historical sense, and no matter how fixed, reductive, tedious and obsessive the applied template of the myth eventually becomes, it is the relentless hurrying drive of its communication – its 'pure, naked expressiveness' – that counts above all. What matters is less the figure in the carpet than Hughes's figuring out a pattern he discerns in many but by no means all of the plays. It's therefore essential we attend a show which features the Poet Laureate on the National Bard, partly because Hughes has a sense of his country's history that goes much deeper than that of any other living English writer. His huge study of Shakespeare, more than ten years in the making, is an extraordinary and unprecedented act of critical witness that spills out of an energy – a tragic energy – which has all but disappeared from current professional critical practice.

This tragic witness springs from Hughes's way of shouldering England's history as a burden of desperate Protestant guilt. He is haunted by a sense that not so very long ago this was a Catholic country which 'hardened into Protestantism'. The phrase occurs in a review of Max Nicholson's *The Environmental Revolution* which

Hughes published more than twenty years ago, a brief essay that links the 'fanatic rejection of Nature' with the 'subtly apotheosized misogyny of Reformed Christianity'. In a characteristically extempore passage, Hughes describes the attraction of its 'underground heretical life', a life 'leagued with everything occult, spiritualistic, devilish, over-emotional, bestial, mysterious, feminine, crazy, revolutionary and poetic'. For Hughes, the Reformation is the Fall, a gut belief he articulates in the brief essay which concludes his selection of Shakespeare's verse, published in 1971, where he remarks on the 'flukish character' of the Restoration, which disastrously imposed the 'mid-century tastes of the French Court' on the literacy and manners of a nation 'whose radical Englishness it had every reason to fear'. The prose of Milton was replaced overnight by the prose of Addison, which in all essentials is 'still our cultivated norm'. The full-stretch, vehemently un-Addisonian muscularity of Hughes's prose is a protest against civility that announces its pedigree – Bunyan, Milton, Lawrence – in an impulsive vernacular. It lacks subtlety, but it always confronts us with a bloody and engaged directness.

The tragic ground of Hughes's vision is his honest, agonized perception that Protestant England has as its national poet and prime cultural icon a poet and dramatist whom he believes was a deep, secret, committed Catholic. Drawing on a study by a Jesuit academic which ought to be better known – *Shakespeare's Religious Background* by Peter Milward – Hughes probes Shakespeare's Catholicism. Following Milward, he notes that his mother's family, the Ardens, were strongly Catholic and that the head of the Warwickshire branch, Edward Arden, was first implicated in a plot to assassinate Elizabeth I, then tried and executed. As a result, official persecution of Catholics in the area was renewed. Hughes notes that Shakespeare's father, John, was a recusant, and he also accepts as genuine a Spiritual Testament, found in 1784 and signed by John Shakespeare, which was a declaration of loyalty to the Catholic faith (Milward makes a convincing case for the document's authenticity).

Hughes's very sensitive feeling for the Catholicism of Shakespeare's family is the mainspring of his interpretation of the plays. He identifies Shakespeare's Venus with 'the archaic Goddess of the Catholic world' and with Mary Arden, his mother, arguing that Shakespeare was a shaman who witnessed to the 'prolonged, savage persecution and threatened extermination of the old Catholic tribe'. This tier of his argument leads Hughes to suggest with uncharacteristic hesitation that 'in so far as he was a shaman of that type, for that tradition, he was indeed not merely crypto-Catholic but committed to Catholicism with an instinct that amounted to fanatic heroism'. Shakespeare the secret Catholic, the Stratford burgher who, according to a tradition Hughes doesn't mention, 'died a papist' – the insight may not be original but it needs restating forcibly in a culture where Shakespeare is so often treated as a piece of Anglican heritage or as a second-rate Tory dramatist. It's an applied insight which gains authority not just from the active excitement of Hughes's prose, but from the puritan cast of his temperament, its Faustian agony. That agony is his enactment of what is essentially a buried national neurosis, a hang-up, that is the result of the damage done to Catholic England by the Reformation.

It's here that Hughes has a problem with his subject. If Shakespeare was a committed Catholic, ever and always, then the modern history of Britain looks from that point of view like a terrible series of violent suppressions and official lies where the English Catholics, like the Palestinians today, are the victims of a punitive nationalism. Hughes the primitive visionary believes that in many respects it has been downhill all the way since the Reformation, but his admiration for Milton's prose binds him to 'radical Englishness' and to many of the values unleashed by the break with Catholicism. However, he also supports things as they are, and rather like Lord Denning on the need to accept the guilty verdict on the Birmingham Six, he can't face the 'appalling vista' of a whole system – the culture that made and empowered him – which is built, from a Catholic point of view, on systematic lies and injustice. Yet he believes, as he says in the essay accompanying his selection of Shakespeare's verse, that the 'Shakespearean fable' is really the account of how in the religious struggle that lasted from the middle of the sixteenth century, to the middle of the seventeenth, England lost her soul. To call that event a 'dissociation of sensibility' is an understatement. Our national poems are tragedies for a good reason.

But the difficulty is that Milton embodies radical English national-ism, while Catholicism is identified, Hughes notes, with treason. Contemplating this crucial historical period, he states:

The psychoanalyst of this prolonged trauma would want to see the dreams. England's permanent state of war, the unrelenting threat of the armies and armadas of the Papacy, had two effects in particular that had consequences for those dreams. It created, for the first time in England's quite young history as a single state, an heroic, exalted, defiant sense of national identity. But in doing so it pushed that national identity towards a fusion with the Puritan hardcore – whose religious loathing of the common enemy could be relied on. Inevitably, a Puritan inclination came to feel like patriotic fervour and a Catholic inclination like a proclivity for high treason.

The association of Catholicism with active disloyalty to the state haunts Hughes's powerfully atavistic imagination, for at some level he believes in gunpowder, treason and plot. But as he worships Shakespeare he must work hard to exonerate him of treachery.

Hughes therefore recreates Shakespeare as another shamanic type who rises not out of the defeat of 'some ancient, rooted culture, some humiliated nationalism', but out of what he terms 'a histori-cally new spirit'. This revolutionary spirit is incarnated, he states, in Milton, Blake and Wordsworth, and at this stage in the critical rite Shakespeare begins to materialize as a prophet of the 'ascendent, revolutionary, Puritan will'. At the very end of chapter one, Hughes announces:

As a prophetic shaman of the Puritan revolution, in opposition to his role as the shaman of Old Catholicism, he experienced a second initiation dream, opposite to the first, and enshrined in his second long narrative poem *Lucrece*. That is presumably how he came to possess the extraordinary faculty of dealing with the visionary revelation of each side of the conflict from the point of view of the other. He was on both sides, simultaneously a major shaman of both types.

This double shaman is not so very far from Shakespeare the balanced Anglican, the multivalent consensus liberal able to see all sides of any argument, but it has the merit of being intensely felt within the raging hell of Hughes's nonconformist conscience. Shakespeare's simultaneity allows Hughes to announce that the *Complete Works* are 'modern England's creation story, our sacred book, closer to us than the Bible'. This sounds positively Victorian in its ringing sense of manifest destiny, but in the context of Hughes's urgent prose-style it comes across as authentic, immediate, like a voice crying out in the wilder spaces of exaltation. A voice anxious for the reassurance of a sacred text and lacerated by its sense of complicity with state crimes.

Central to Hughes's reading of Shakespeare is his interpretation of *The Rape of Lucrece* and *Venus and Adonis*, and although the reading later degenerates into a locked mythic patterning of boar, goddess, flower, storm, it is compelling and ought to be treated seriously. Arguing that in so far as it is a theological work *Venus and Adonis* seems to favour 'a Protestant (actually a Puritan) idealism', Hughes asserts that when it is read in the light of the later tragedies, the poem becomes a judgement, not of Venus, but of Adonis. Adonis's rejection of 'the Great Goddess of Divine Love turns out to be an error, for which he pays. Eventually, say the tragedies, it turns out to be an error that brings down the kingdoms of both Heaven and Earth.' This sounds like Lawrence out of the Book of Revelation, and it must be seen as a late example of rhapsodic criticism, the critic as prophet witnessing in anguish to the ills of his society.

By contrast, *The Rape of Lucrece* is a deeply Catholic poem which exposes the violent and violating nature of Protestantism. Lucrece is a figure Shakespeare's Catholic contemporaries 'would recognize without difficulty', while Tarquin is the imagination which despoils traditional holy places.

If Lucrece is meant to be associated with the Virgin Mary and with church architecture, then we need to attend to the lines where the 'fair temple' of Tarquin's soul is 'defaced' by the rape he has carried out. Troops of cares 'muster' to the 'weak ruins' of his soul and ask 'the spotted princess' – i.e. the soul – how she fares:

She says her subjects with foul insurrection
Have battered down her consecrated wall
And by their mortal fault brought in subjection
Her immortality, and made her thrall
To living death and pain perpetual . . .

Hughes quotes from this passage, but he does not give it any detailed analysis. What he does instead is to offer a great enabling interpretation of Shakespeare which hopefully will inspire scholars to apply it.

If we consider that image of a battered 'consecrated wall' in the context of Shakespeare's Catholicism, it has to carry a historical memory of the dissolution of the monasteries and the judicial murder of monks and abbots during the reign of Henry VIII (after the rebellion known as the Pilgrimage of Grace, for example, Henry ordered that the chief monks of Sawley Abbey were to be hanged 'out of the steeple'). The consecrated wall is similar to the multitude of examples which Milward lists where Shakespeare applies the word 'holy' to material objects 'in the sacramental sense used by Catholics and often ridiculed by Protestants'. The battered wall is linked in the poem to the image of the dead Lucrece's blood-surrounded body which 'like a late-sacked island vastly stood / Bare and unpeopled in this fearful flood'. This is an image out of the Henrician reign of terror and it anticipates many images in *Macbeth* – for example, Duncan's 'gashed stabs' that look like a 'breach in nature'. As Milward suggests, this is a probable allusion to Thomas Cromwell's 'ruthless spoliation of the monasteries'. Again, I would suggest that when Shakespeare speaks of 'key-cold Lucrece' bleeding stream' he means to activate a papal reference within the proverbial application of the term 'key-cold'. And I would further suggest that by making Richard III habitually swear by St Paul, Shakespeare aims to identify him as a cruelly vindictive Puritan. Taken together, Hughes and Milward promise a welcome counter-reformation in Shakespeare studies.

Because Hughes feels English history intensely as myth, he is not much interested in detailing events, and this partly explains the narrow, tunnelled quality of his critical vision. He has a unique sense of this period of English history and of the theatre it inspired – a theatre that materialized from 'the sheer uncontainable excess of this national struggle with conscience, this internal Inquisition in perpetual session'. But he tends to begin the historical myth with Queen Mary and end with the execution of Charles I. Hughes shies away from Henry VIII, and only in an appendix that discusses Shakespeare's and Fletcher's *Henry VIII* does he consider the founding monster of the English state:

In so far as Henry's rejection of the Papal Authority introduced the Reformation to England, his 'divorce' from the Catholic Church was the act which begot the Tragic Equation within the English psyche. And as such it became the creation story – in its immediate, non-mythic, realistic terms – of Shakespeare's dramatic universe.

After five hundred pages we return to the myth's beginning in the 'realistic terms' of actual history, but by now it is too late. Hughes cannot bring himself to examine the historical record and contemplate a monarch whose Stalin-like actions Jasper Ridley and other present-day historians detail. Even so, what is remarkable about Hughes is that he lets his imagination rip along the interface of two opposed ideas about the Reformation. The first idea, as J. J. Scarisbrick expresses it in his biography of Henry VIII, is that during Henry's reign 'a people accomplished what was, by any standards, a radical breach with its past and a remarkable act of national amnesis'. Hughes is tormented by this great forgetting because he knows that enormous wrongs were committed and that the population was not a unified 'people' as Scarisbrick suggests. But Hughes also knows that Henry had led England back into European affairs and exposed the country to what Scarisbrick calls 'the immense creative energies of continental Protestantism'.

Hughes's entrepreneurial imagination responds eagerly to those energies – indeed they flex continually in his prose. Noting this, we can begin to see that early in Thatcher's administration Hughes was drawn to Shakespeare because he knew that the British people were going to be subjected to a rerun of the Reformation, and that even the Shakespeare whose 'flexible opportunism' was 'nimbly attuned to market forces' would have hated the angry deconsecrations that were going to take place. In a sense, this is an epic prose poem born out of the experience of Thatcherism. Its batty syncretism will be much mocked ('It is not impossible that Shakespeare knew, through the Occult Neoplatonist route, the legend of Buddha's enlightenment', Hughes opines in a typical footnote), but for all its shamanic obsessions *Shakespeare and the Goddess of Complete Being* testifies to a horrible decade. I admire the stink of its Protestant guilt.

T. S. Eliot and Anti-Semitism

Looking at the University of Oxford's *Informal Guide* to the English faculty's lecture list for Trinity term 1996, I find that the Professor of Poetry, James Fenton, will give a lecture on 9 May entitled 'Eliot *v*. Julius'. It would be improper of me to anticipate Fenton's approach to Anthony Julius's compelling study, but I would hope that he will not see fit to mount another repudiation of this brilliant, passionately concentrated 'adversarial reading' of Eliot's work. I say 'another repudiation' advisedly, because Julius's book was rejected by Oxford University Press on the grounds that it might prove 'too controversial'. So much for scholarship, so much for free speech.

Hamish Hamilton, Fourth Estate and Harvard also sent the author letters of rejection – rejections that now seem compounded by the lack of attention which literary editors have given the book. I've seen brief notices in the *Jewish Chronicle*, the *Hampstead and Highgate Express*, the *Evening Standard* and a publication called *New Moon*. Instead of large reviews close to the publication date, there has only been this desultory attention, which includes a notably foolish review by Gabriel Josipovici in which he states that he would happily trade 'the whole of that impeccable philo-semite, Joyce (the darling of the politically correct), for just that one Sweeney poem of Eliot's'.

This type of insidious put-down is hardly new, and in a sense it replicates the treatment Eliot accorded to a book published in 1936 by Victor Gollancz called *The Yellow Spot: the outlawing of half a million human beings*. The title-page reads:

a collection
of facts and documents relating to three
years' persecution of German Jews,

Review of Anthony Julius, *T. S. Eliot, Anti-Semitism and Literary Form*.

derived
chiefly from National Socialist sources,
very carefully assembled by a group of
investigators.

With an introduction by
THE BISHOP OF DURHAM

The book was briefly and anonymously noticed in the *Criterion*, which Eliot edited, like this:

The Yellow Spot: The Outlawing of Half a Million Human Beings: A Collection of Facts and Documents Relating to Three Years' Persecution of German Jews, Derived chiefly from Nationalist Socialist Sources, very carefully assembled by a Group of investigators. With an introduction by the Bishop of Durham. (Gollancz, 1936.) 8s 6d cloth; 5s paper.

There should be somebody to point out that this book, although enjoying a cathedratic blessing, is an attempt to rouse moral indignation by means of sensationalism. Needless to say, it does not touch on how we might alleviate the situation of those whose misfortunes it describes, still less on why they, among all the unfortunates of the world, have a first claim on our compassion and help. Certainly no English man or woman would wish to be a German Jew in Germany today; but not only is our title to the moral dictatorship of the world open to question, there is not the least prospect of our being able to exercise it. More particularly, it is noticeable that the jacket of the book speaks of the 'extermination' of the Jews in Germany, whereas the title-page refers only to their 'persecution'; and as the title-page is to the jacket, so are the contents of the title-page, especially in the chapter devoted to the ill-treatment of Jews in German concentration camps.

A number of Eliot scholars – C. K. Stead, Ronald Bush, Julius himself – believe that the review was by Eliot. Christopher Ricks doesn't disagree with this judgement – whether or not Eliot wrote the review, he observes in *T. S. Eliot and Prejudice*, it has 'the stamp of his approval and the stamp of his tone'. Calling the anonymous notice 'shameful', Ricks expresses the hope that 'such cruelly self-righteous impercipience' was later recognized by Eliot to be among 'the things ill done and done to others' harm which once he took for exercise of virtue'. Like Ricks, I had interpreted that admonitory statement about things done to others' harm in 'Little Gidding' as an act of contrition by a great, self-torturing poet. Now, reading Julius,

I feel a deep sense of shame at my interpretation of those lines which the compound familiar ghost speaks in the aftermath of an air-raid. Accurately calling T. S. *Eliot and Prejudice* an 'honourable attempt' to engage with Eliot's anti-semitism, Julius shows the ways in which Ricks's critically very intelligent and subtle work takes anti-semitism for granted, and by implication holds it to be an 'undifferentiated hostility to Jews without history or discursive complexity'. Ricks's study is honourable because it seeks to redress those critics like Denis Donoghue, whose indifference to Eliot's anti-semitism makes them complicit in it, and it also forcibly rebukes the poet for his prejudices at a number of points in the argument. It is no part of Julius's intention to dismiss *Eliot and Prejudice*, but he notes how Ricks's essentially New Critical methodology limits his ability to place Eliot's attitudes within their social and cultural context. In one of a number of forceful remarks about the practice of literary criticism, he argues that what still protects Eliot is the New Critical reluctance to engage with 'what poems actually assert' and the deconstructionist refusal to accept that poems, at least sometimes, 'mean what they say'. (This last stricture hardly applies to Ricks.)

Reading that anonymous review of *The Yellow Spot* – I believe it is by Eliot* – I was disturbed by its sinister dismissiveness. As Julius points out, the review 'crawls with impatient distaste' and wilfully refuses to do its subject justice. This indifference is compounded by the manner in which the book's title is reproduced at the head of the review, so that the emphatically capitalized words suggest 'the billboard announcement of a Victorian melodrama', or the urgent canvassing of a 'fairground barker'. As we can see by comparing the actual title-page with the review heading, the typography was a contribution by the *Criterion*. This is a striking and significant substitution: Eliot used the lower-case *j* to diminish Jews in 'Gerontion', but here employed upper-case to mock their suffering. Imagine the extra effort (the subtitle does not follow the dictates of house style) which went into typing those initial upper-case letters.

---

*Wrong. As a result of the attention which Julius's book belatedly received, the author of the review has been identified as Montgomery Belgion.

The reviewer is suggesting the book's contents do not justify the alarmism of its jacket or title-page. Yet in addition to the Nazi threats of genocide which it quotes, he would have read this:

After covering about 5 kms the car . . . stopped and we were told there was some engine trouble. We were ordered to leave the car and line up on the side of the road.

Suddenly we heard 4 shots in quick succession, and crying and moaning. Then we were again bundled into the car and brought back . . . the bodies of those 'shot while trying to escape' remained in the ditch until Monday afternoon, guarded by a few Storm Troopers. All four of them had been shot in exactly the same way: a revolver bullet through the jugular vein.

Untouched by this evidence of atrocity, the reviewer also suggests that the chapter on the treatment of Jews in concentration camps is exaggerated. It's shocking to think that Eliot might have read this book, which contains many photographs of Jews being humiliated, as well as reproductions of anti-Semitic posters, slogans and cartoons, and then contemptuously dismissed the suffering it details. As Julius comments, this is a person who 'does not know how to speak of the Jewish dead; he is without pity'. After such knowledge, can there be forgiveness?

And yet the knowledge which Julius has amassed is not new – Ricks and many other critics have noted and discussed Eliot's prejudices. The reference in *After Strange Gods* to reasons of 'race and religion' making any large numbers of free-thinking Jews 'undesirable' has often been quoted and censured, but the fact that Eliot never allowed it to be republished has been taken as a repudiation of his earlier views. So too has a scene in the 1934 pageant play, *The Rock*, which presents a group of Blackshirts critically. But as Julius shows, the rejection of the Blackshirts' prejudices is a rejection of anti-Christian paganism. The play is not a plea for modern Jewry – it is an endorsement of Christianity in 'both its historical and supernatural forms'. *The Rock* is not Eliot's *Our Mutual Friend*.

By detailing the scope of Eliot's anti-Semitic remarks and images, and by examining what several critical generations have made of them, Julius breaks down the protective barriers that have been erected around Eliot's work. His argument is that indifference to the offence given by certain of his poems is, among other things, a failure of interpretation, and as he demonstrates, critical interpretation has to carry with it a knowledge of previous and conflicting arguments about Eliot's work. The critic who gives Eliot credit for dropping anti-Semitic verses from *The Waste Land*, the critic who commends him for not having tried to edit out of his earlier poems views which he later regretted, is carrying the weight of those developing arguments. There are critics who have found anti-Semitism in the 'Burial of the Dead' section of *The Waste Land*, and in the phrase 'sapient sutlers' in 'Mr Eliot's Sunday Morning Service', but where a more polemical writer would have gleefully enlisted them, Julius does not. A combination of steely fairmindedness and evident admiration for Eliot's art makes his study read at times like a judge's summing-up in a long and difficult case (Julius is a practising lawyer and previously acted for Diana, Princess of Wales in her divorce).

One of the most damning pieces of evidence is 'Dirge', the two verses which Eliot is sometimes praised for excluding from *The Waste Land*:

> Full fathom five your Bleistein lies
> Under the flatfish and the squids.
> Graves' Disease in a dead jew's eyes!
>   When the crabs have eat the lids.
>   Lower than the wharf rats dive
>   Though he suffer a sea-change
>   Still expensive rich and strange.

> That is lace that was his nose
>   See upon his back he lies
> (Bones peep through the ragged toes)
>   With a stare of dull surprise
>   Flood tide and ebb tide
>   Roll him gently side to side
>   See the lips unfold unfold
>   From the teeth, gold in gold

> Lobsters hourly keep close watch
> Hark! now I hear them   scratch scratch scratch

Rereading these verses in the light of the insults detailed in *The Yellow Spot*, I realize that there is a subliminal or implicit anti-Semitic rhyme on 'squids' and 'lids' which is similar to Kipling's poem 'The Waster', where, as Julius points out, when 'Jew' is the expected word, Kipling substitutes 'etc'.

The insult Eliot offers is layered and complex, because by placing the Jew underwater in 'Dirge' and 'Burbank with a Baedeker: Bleistein with a Cigar', Eliot makes literal the commercial cliché of bankruptcy: Bleistein has in every sense 'gone under'. The very name 'represents a financial diminishing; "Bleistein" means "Leadstone", Eliot's substitute for the more expected "Goldstein". This name along with "Silverstein", "Loanstein", "Diamondstein" and "Sparklestein", routinely appeared in American business jokes of the period. Jews were meant to be at home in commerce; Eliot's "Bleistein" is not.' The image of Bleistein's gold teeth in 'Dirge' picks up the fondness Jews were supposed to have for that commodity. Bleistein is a commercial failure, however, who lacks even a pauper's grave – a departure from the more usual fantasies of Jewish commercial power.

The trope appears again in the notorious lines in 'Gerontion':

> And the jew squats in the window sill, the owner,
> Spawned in some estaminet of Antwerp,
> Blistered in Brussels, patched and peeled in London.

In the pre-1963 editions of the poem, the initial of 'jew' was printed in lower-case, part of Eliot's belittling intention. His aim is to insult and exclude Jewish readers. As Julius shows, 'Gerontion's Jewish landlord is 'misshapen and cowering', and therefore an object of contempt who is associated through the sibilants in the opening lines I've just quoted with Shylock: 'And spet upon my Jewish gaberdine'. If the rented house in the poem symbolizes postwar European culture, as I think it fairly clearly does, then the landlord represents economic power which is in fact powerlessness. Gerontion – the name means 'little old man' – is an embittered Struldbug meditating on the chaos of the postwar Continent. In an exemplary close reading of the poem, Julius shows how Eliot condenses a whole series of anti-Semitic associations with leprosy and faeces. He also argues that it is a response to Browning's 'Rabbi Ben Ezra', a poem which celebrates wisdom and welcomes old age. Indeed Browning emerges as one of the heroes of this study – along with the massive counter-example of Joyce; he exposed anti-Semitism in his poetry and gave Jews voices where Eliot silenced them. Relentlessly Julius dissects the tissue of interconnecting prejudices and clichés which Eliot draws on in his verse. Yet he counts Eliot's poems as one of anti-Semitism's 'few literary triumphs' – a wryly disinterested judgement which raises some profound questions about the nature of art and about the redemptive ethic which informs a great deal of literary criticism. By enlivening fatigued topoi, Eliot gives a new malevolent life to stale rhetorical figures and enlarges the anti-Semitism of the interwar period. Admitting that he cannot celebrate the poetry which issues from Eliot's attitude, Julius concedes that 'with great virtuosity' the poet turns a whole cluster of vile clichés into art.

It's here that we approach something intractable and frightening which lies at the diseased heart of European culture. George Steiner raised this matter some years ago when he observed in a letter to the *Listener* that the 'obstinate puzzle' is that Eliot's uglier touches tend to occur at the centre of very good poetry. As Julius shows, neither Ricks in his comments on Steiner's remark nor Steiner himself is able to resolve the problem because for them 'art redeems'. Both Symbolism and New Criticism hold that poetic discourse is 'non-propositional and benevolent'. Here, it's worth noting that the Unitarian culture in which Eliot was nourished placed a high value on the concept of 'benevolism', and his rejection of that ethic in his critical writing must be connected with his furious distaste for Unitarianism – which he linked with Judaism – and for liberalism. Yet there still remains the question of art's capacity to redeem. How does Eliot the conservative Anglican answer it? As Julius demonstrates, he denied the redemptive nature of art in his 1928 preface to

The Sacred Wood, where he asserts that poetry is a 'superior amusement'. Later in the same paragraph, he says: 'And certainly poetry is not the inculcation of morals, or the direction of politics; and no more is it religion or an equivalent of religion, except by some monstrous abuse of words.'

There is something, I would suggest, both casual and significant about that colloquial or slightly ungrammatical use of 'no more', because it is a phrase which strictly demands to be followed by a clause beginning 'than it is' – e.g., 'no more is it religion than it is secular music'. In Eliot's sentence it functions on one level as an intensifier – a weightier version of 'nor' – on another it means 'no longer'. There's just the faintest *ou-boum* sound to this, because Eliot is signalling almost invisibly that something is absolutely finished now. Poetry is not sacral or ethical or civic, it's just a higher form of limerick. We're close to Bentham's equation – quantity of pleasure being equal – of poetry to pushpin. But as well as demoting poetry, Eliot also insisted on its diversity, and this opened up the possibility of a poetry of 'scorn and deflation' which made room for his quatrains.

As Julius notes, objections to those anti-Semitic poems can stem from the rejected aesthetic of the constitutional benevolence of poetry, but they may equally derive from an objection to 'works of defamation'. Hate poems are offensive, and the offence which Eliot's give has been largely palliated or ignored for more than seventy years. I can think of no other modern writer whose prejudices have been treated with such tolerance. Those poems have been in practically continuous print since they were first published, yet there has been no protest at this, and little protest at the poems themselves. Julius's adversarial reading is therefore a long overdue act of critical justice. Because Eliot has so dominated this century's poetry, and because his writings have been so central to critical practice and to English literature as an academic discipline, to subject him to this kind of investigation is to call a large part of our culture – root, branch and flower – into question. Eliot studies will never be the same post-Julius. His account must be read both for its sustained critical intelligence and scholarship and as a means of extending one's unease about the moral basis – if there is one – of Eliot's work.

Discussing the ugliness of 'Dirge', Julius demonstrates how compounded the insult is:

Bleistein has become food for the sea creatures. This is horrible in itself. With the corpse's popping eyes, the principal symptom of Graves' Disease, we have already entered the realm of the gratuitous. Sufferers of the disease have a fearsome, startling appearance. They are wild-eyed and appear demented. The hideousness of their demeanour would be aggravated if their eyelids were torn away, for example by crabs. It is the peculiar horror of 'Dirge', that it celebrates the putrefying of Bleistein, achieved furthermore not by natural processes but by animal ravaging.

In refusing compassion or respect for the dead, Eliot is like Creon in *Antigone*. Bleistein has no terrestrial grave, because he has 'no country', and in gloating over the circumstances of his decomposition, Eliot also celebrates the condition of Jews as 'stateless transients' during extended periods of Europe's history. Here, as in the reviewer's dismissive comments on the murders described in *The Yellow Spot*, Eliot is indeed 'without pity' and demonstrates that he possesses the imagination of an anti-Semite 'in the highest degree'. Indifferent to the martyrdom of German Jewry, he allies himself both with anti-Semites and with those who denied the reality of the persecutions in Germany. Discussing a footnote on the 'illusion' that there can be culture without religion, which Eliot added to the 1948 edition of *Notes towards a Definition of Culture*, Julius shows that three years after the liberation of the death camps 'Eliot has learnt nothing. Too many free-thinking Jews are undesirable; contact between Jews and Christians is undesirable because it fosters a damaging illusion.'

With this denial of Jewish suffering goes the slashing of certain artistic sources which lie at the root of much of Eliot's poetry. Thus *The Waste Land*'s violation of passages from *Antigone*, *The Tempest* and *Ulysses*, which are among its sources of inspiration, enacts the violation of Bleistein's body. Eliot deforms those texts. As Maud Ellmann has noted, he 'desecrates tradition' at the opening of *The Waste Land* – twisting Chaucer on the sweetness of spring – and aims to steal and blasphemously deface the works he pilfers. Frank Kermode calls that seminal poem a work of 'decreation', and the figure that Eliot aspires to be is that of decreator. The poem is not now – is no more – godlike, but is instead a vandal, a criminal, an annihilator of all that's made to a murderous thought in a dirty shade.

In arguing that Eliot's choice of *The Sacred Wood* as the title for a selection of essays derived from Frazer, George Watson quotes the following passage:

In this sacred grove there grew a certain tree round which . . . a grim figure might be seen to prowl . . . He was a priest and a murderer: and the man for whom he was looking was sooner or later to murder him and hold the priesthood in his stead. Such was the rule of the sanctuary. A candidate for the priesthood could only succeed to office by slaying the priest, and having slain him, he retained office till he was himself slain.

As Julius tersely states, Eliot is 'the candidate, murderer and thief'.

To notice this is to begin to align the supposedly classical Eliot much more closely with the complex, late romanticism of Yeats. If, tediously, we have grown used to critical accounts of the 'blood sacrifice' that helped to found the Southern Irish statelet, it's time we began to notice Eliot's complicity in the prejudices and massacres which contributed to the founding of various national identities in Europe. As James Shapiro argues in a formidable recent study, *Shakespeare and the Jews*, anti-Semitism is closely linked to the formation of Englishness. Eliot reinvented himself as an Englishman, and as part of that studied act of identity he used to wear a white rose on the anniversary of the Battle of Bosworth, in memory of Richard III, whom he regarded as the last English – because Plantagenet – king. Coincidentally, Shapiro quotes from a popular postwar textbook, *The Plantagenets*, in which John Hooper Harvey states that the Jews engaged in a series of 'most sinister crimes committed against Christian children, including murder (allegedly ritual) and forcible circumcision'. Harvey's prejudices must have helped shape his interest in the Plantagenets, and so probably did Eliot's. The immigrant writer felt that Englishness and anti-Semitism were closely related, and he chose to echo sentiments which, it's often alleged, were common among all classes in the country then. As Sartre observes in a passage Julius quotes, 'a destroyer in function, a sadist with a pure heart, the anti-semite is, in the very depths of his heart, a criminal. What he wishes, what he prepares for, is the death of the Jew.' And as *T. S. Eliot, Anti-Semitism and Literary Form* shows, Eliot's poetry 'delightfully' conceives of Jews as dead and 'broods on the killing of women'. His misogyny is closely connected to his hatred of Jews: by making women Jewish – Rachel *née* Rabinovitch, Lady Kleinwurm and Lady Katzegg – he overcame them; 'by subordinating them to Jews, he diminished them'. Empson in an essay in *Using Biography* and Julius in a comment on it argue persuasively that Eliot's hostility to his father's Unitarianism is one of the psychological causes of his hostility to Jews, but I think there is a deeper cultural base for it, in that a certain strain of conservative discourse tends to identify Judaism with Unitarianism and with other forms of Puritanism. One source, here, is Burke. In *Reflections on the Revolution in France*, two leading Unitarians of that period – Richard Price and Joseph Priestley – are attacked and anti-Semitic prejudice is mobilized against their enlightened form of Christianity by ringing changes on the name of the meeting-house – the old Jewry – where Price delivered his famous discourse 'On the Love of our Country' which praised the Williamite, American and French Revolutions and provoked Burke's polemic. Burke attacks 'money-jobbers, usurers and Jews', and identified Price's writings on economics and statistics with Jewish business activities. He had a particular hatred of Lord George Gordon, who led the anti-Catholic Protestant Association and who converted to Judaism. In *Reflections*, he refers to Gordon, the instigator of the Gordon Riots, as 'our protestant Rabbin'. He wants his readers to see reform and revolution as part of a Jewish conspiracy to destroy an organic, hierarchical society. Unitarianism and Judaism deny the divinity of Christ, and it is this denial which, at this late point in his career, incenses Burke, who opposes business, science, economic theory and new ideas. Implicitly, he dismisses Joseph Priestley's theory of matter as a form of energy by praising a sluggish lack of ideas and a sluggish social structure in *Reflections*.

I think, however, that this type of argument goes much further back. I have a hunch that Shylock is meant to be a satiric version of a Puritan businessman, and would guess that the Catholic Shakespeare is drawing on a prejudiced identification which must have been common in Elizabethan England. Certainly, the link is made in Charles I's reign by a writer called Henry Blount, whom James Shapiro quotes in *Shakespeare and the Jews*. In *A Voyage into the Levant*, Blount likens Jews to radical English Puritans, saying that Jews have 'light, aerial and fanatical brains, spirited much like our hot apocalypse men'. Eliot's reading in the Elizabethan and Jacobean periods would have made him aware that conservative, as opposed to radical, Englishness partly depended on this double repudiation. Unlike Yeats, who was entirely without anti-Semitic feeling, and who asked not wholly to be absorbed by the breath of a different rose, the dark rose, Cathleen ni Houlihan, Eliot wanted to be completely drawn into the white rose of Plantagenet England. If Yeats, very properly, is criticized for his heady and emotional nationalism, it's surely time that Eliot's embracing of a destructive energy was given more critical attention. The question, Julius insists, is whether we accept that art is capable of 'Gerontion', 'Sweeney among the Nightingales', 'A Cooking Egg' and 'Dirge', or surrender our claims to understand art's 'protean varieties'. For all its impressive scholarly detail, Julius's study is only the beginning of a long process of revisionist criticism which should diminish the overwhelming, stifling cultural authority which Eliot's oeuvre has acquired. I have been reading him for more than thirty years, and teaching him for more than twenty – his work seems endlessly subtle and intelligent, many of his cadences are perfect, but there is a malignity in it which is terrifying. It's so firm and so quiet, because like a true politician Eliot never apologizes and he never explains.

Strinkling Dropples: John Clare

A week or so back, in the fortress that is Broadcasting House in the centre of Belfast, I watched an actor scribble a few last-minute changes to the script of a radio play, then screw his face up and remark that his handwriting was nearly as bad as John Clare's. He went on suddenly to talk about some manuscripts of Clare's he'd seen in the Peterborough Museum – what an enormous poetic gift, what a sad sad life. 'You know that poem of his, "I Am"?' he asked me, and quoted the opening lines:

> I am – yet what I am, none cares, or knows;
>   My friends forsake me like a memory lost:–
> I am the self-consumer of my woes;–

Immediately and spontaneously another actor added:

>   They rise and vanish in oblivion's host,
>   Like shadows in love's frenzied stifled throes:–

And then a third member of the cast took up the quotation:

>   And yet I am, and live – like vapours tost
>   Into the nothingness of scorn and noise,

Caught off guard, for until that moment the occasion had had nothing to do with Clare, I struggled to complete this unforeseen recital:

>   Into the living sea of waking dreams,
> Where there is neither sense of life or joys,
>   But the vast shipwreck of my lifes esteems;
> Even the dearest, that I love the best,
> Are strange – nay, rather stranger than the rest.

I long for scenes, where man hath never trod
   A place where woman never smiled or wept –
There to abide with my Creator, God;
And sleep as I in childhood, sweetly slept,
Untroubling, and untroubled where I lie,
The grass below – above the vaulted sky.

Perhaps this is the way poets should be celebrated – out of the blue, in a break from doing something else, by an *ad hoc* group that has come together like a tiny cloud formation and will never meet up again?

It was an intensely moving moment and all the more so because across the water the England of national heritage, warm beer and critical theory has contrived to leave Clare's bicentenary almost unnoticed. A few events in his native Northamptonshire, an article in the *Guardian*, a short programme on the World Service, but otherwise hardly a whisper. No major biography or critical study, no important academic conference, no united voices singing in praise of England's greatest nature poet, a scandalously neglected figure who is one of the most important writers of the Romantic era. As Donald Davie has already pointed out, Jerome McGann's recent *Oxford Book of Romantic Period Verse* contains only one poem by Clare, a piece of jokey light verse entitled 'My Mary'. Cast out of the canon, lonely and unhoused, Clare has indeed been forsaken 'like a memory lost'.

How then do we celebrate this unique poet? Perhaps first by recognizing that Clare is not a poet with a complete, fully formed, canonical and settled reputation. Rather he is a writer whose achievement is still in a process of cultural formation – he is on a version of that legendary journey out of Essex, a journey out of obscurity towards posterity. In Yeats's phrase he has been 'sent out naked on the roads, and stricken / By the injustice of the skies for punishment'. The punishment is deeply unjust – it is a disturbing act of cultural amnesia and those who struggle to make reparation for the neglect of Clare's reputation have, I believe, as part of our experience of loving and cherishing and revering his work, a shared feeling of isolation. The dedication in the magnificent Oxford edition of Clare's early poems is 'To the John Clare Society and to all friends of John Clare'. It embraces a small scattered community that lives in the hope of seeing Clare one day as well-known, as quoted and visible, as his contemporaries Keats and Shelley. Meanwhile the experience of reading through the enormous Oxford edition of his poems – blessings on those devoted editors – is rather like entering scenes 'where man hath never trod'. So few critics have discussed these poems that we seem endlessly to approach them for the first time because, if an anthology piece is like an overcultivated flower, Clare's poems are like wild flowers or wild creatures on whom we have laid almost no percepts, no critical judgements. They do not shine through the patina of generation upon generation of readers and critics, but instead exist in unplaced, rather dislocated glimpses. Until perhaps we come upon this poem of loss and affirmation:

> I lost the love, of heaven above;
> I spurn'd the lust, of earth below;
> I felt the sweets of fancied love,–
> And hell itself my only foe.

> I lost earth's joys, but felt the glow,
> Of heaven's flame abound in me:
> 'Till loveliness, and I did grow
> The bard of immortality.

> I loved, but woman fell away;
> I hid me, from her faded fame:
> I snatch'd the sun's eternal ray,–
> And wrote 'till earth was but a name.

> In every language upon earth,
> On every shore, o'er every sea;
> I gave my name immortal birth,
> And kep't my spirit with the free.

'A Vision' tersely enacts what it felt like to be touched in both senses by poetry. In the act of writing, Clare becomes alone in the universe: 'I snatch'd the sun's eternal ray / And wrote till earth was but a name'. The vulnerable, uncertain, apologetic Clare – 'With ragged coat and downy chin, / A clownish, silent, aguish boy / Who even felt ashamed of joy, / So dirty, ragged, and so low,' – that exposed tramp-like figure is transformed into the giant Prometheus who seizes the fire and gives his name 'immortal birth'. This is a vision of true, not celebrity, fame – fame as Milton conceived of it – and in his poem Clare dedicates his gift to that heavenly applause. In his strict tetrameters there is something of an enormous Enlightenment ambition to recast history, the whole of human life and society, into a visionary but rational structure. His poem reads strangely like a cross between a lyric by William Blake and an architectural drawing by Thomas Jefferson.

Although Clare identifies with power here – the consuming power of poetry – it is much more usual for him to merge himself with the powerless and the weak. One of his finest poems, 'To the Snipe', expresses this sense of oneness in a subtly mystical manner:

> Lover of swamps
> The quagmire overgrown
> With hassock tufts of sedge – where fear encamps
> Around thy home alone
>
> The trembling grass
> Quakes from the human foot
> Nor hears the weight of man to let him pass
> Where he alone and mute
>
> Sitteth at rest
> In safety neath the clump
> Of hugh flag-forrest that thy haunts invest
> Or some old sallow stump
>
> Thriving on seams
> That tiney islands swell
> Just hilling from the mud and rancid streams
> Suiting they nature well
>
> For here thy bill
> Suited by wisdom good

Of rude unseemly length doth delve and drill
The gelid mass for food

And here may hap
When summer suns hath drest
The moores rude desolate and spungy lap
May hide they mystic nest

Mystic indeed
For isles that ocean make
Are scarcely more secure for birds to build
Than this flag-hidden lake . . .

Yet instinct knows
Not safetys bounds to shun
The firmer ground where skulking fowler goes
With searching dogs and gun

By tepid springs
Scarcely one stride across
Though brambles from its edge a shelter flings
Thy safety is at loss

And never chuse
The little sinky foss
Streaking the moores where spa-red water spews
From puddles fringed with moss

Free booters there
Intent to kill and slay
Startle with cracking guns the trepid air
And dogs thy haunts betray

From dangers reach
Here thou art safe to roam
Far as these washy flag-worn marshes stretch
A still and quiet home . . .

Here, Clare's animist vision tenderly sets out a marshy paradise
where in a beautifully unexpected verb 'tiney islands' are seen 'Just

hilling from the mud and rancid streams'. Into this paradisal place of 'little sinky' fosses come 'free booters' who are more than simply hunters, they are symbols of enclosure, plundering free-marketeers who have come to steal the common land and destroy the delicate ecological balance there. They have entered a marshy open-air church with its 'hassock tufts of sedge' in order to kill the spirit of place.

What is remarkable about this poem is that it uses an oxymoron dear to the hearts of all who love marshes and bogs – the paradoxical sense that such sacral places are both somehow heavenly and hellish. So Clare's marshes have 'trembling grass', an 'old sallow stump', 'rancid streams', a 'gelid mass'. This is a sulphurous terrain, a warm 'desolate and spungy lap', whose 'tepid springs' echo the line 'Startle with cracking guns the trepid air'. Within the forcefield of trepid/tepid, the marsh becomes warm like a fearful bird or animal: the delicate chiming of the two words fuses the land – birds/animals/wetness/body-heat – with that intensely sensitive spirit which Clare shares with the wild creatures. Out of this vulnerable ontological sense of utter remoteness issues the final bleak ironic passive vision.

> Thy solitudes
> The unbounded heaven esteems
> And here my heart warms into higher moods
> And dignifying dreams
>
> I see the sky
> Smile on the meanest spot
> Giving to all that creep or walk or flye
> A calm and cordial lot
>
> Thine teaches me
> Right feelings to employ
> That in the dreariest places peace will be
> A dweller and a joy

Clare is the poet of dwelling, of Being, of *Dasein*. He inhabits his native landscape with all the nervous intensity of someone who knows he's been evicted from where he belongs. He is therefore both the poet of place and displacement: 'Inclosure came and every path was stopt / Each tyrant fix'd his sign where paths were found.' Clare's oral writing – unpunctuated, shimmering with visionary dialect words like 'moozing', 'crumping', 'drippling', 'soshing', 'brustling' – this spoken poetry offers a sometimes angry, often anguished challenge to the rights of property and the bruising tread of the Lockean individualist. Like Emily Dickinson he is a poet of anxiety of consciousness.

The delicacy of Clare's imagination can be observed in a whole series of acoustic images – i.e. images of sound as process – which structure his poems. Take this marvellously clattery evocation of the sound of a carthorse's hooves – 'The toltering (hobbled/clumsy) bustle of a blundering trot' – or these lines describing a labourer's walk:

> While hard as iron the cemented ground
> & smooth as glass the glibbed pool is froze
> His nailed boots wi clenching tread rebound
> & dithering echo starts & mocks the clamping sound

This complete acoustic image from 'The Village Minstrel' catches the hammering sound of nailed boots in a particular cold atmosphere as they set up a quick shifting echo that builds back into the sharp heavy sounds. Sounds are changed by the dryness, warmth, dampness or coldness of certain atmospheres, as Clare wittily demonstrates in 'Haunted Pond', where 'poor amys dripping spirit' draggles:

> All wet & dripping from her watry bed
> Echo seems startd with the gushing tread
> As when our feet are wet squish squa[s]hing round

This is another of Clare's sound epiphanies which describes, I take it, the echo-less eerie intensity and yukkiness of the noise made by soaked wet shoes and clothes. Clare enjoys both pleasant 'suthering' sounds and those rebarbative 'grincing' scrapes made by the mower who leans over his shoulder and 'wetting jars wi' sharp & tinkling sound'. Here he describes someone walking along a plank over a wintry stream:

> as one steps its oaken plank
> The hollow frozen sounding noise
> From flags & sedge beside the bank
> The wild ducks brooding peace destroys

Again Clare is fascinated by the whapping intensity of sounds in cold air. His aural vision textures his poems, and this heightened sensitivity to sound patterns may be a gift that was at least partly the result of growing up in an oral culture. In his *Autobiography* he writes – but writes as if he is speaking to us directly here and now – that both 'my parents was illiterate to the last degree my mother knew not a single letter and superstition went so far with her that she beleved the higher parts of learning was the blackest arts of witchcraft'.

Within oral culture there is an instinctive suspicion of print culture because it expresses power and law. The classical scholar Eric Havelock has characterized the oral culture of Ancient Greece as a 'mnemonic world of imitation, aggregative, redundant, copious, warmly human, participatory'. Orality, Havelock shows, is one expression of those close kinship bonds which belong in the extended family that is a particular community. It speaks as a community, not simply an individual. The uniqueness of Clare's language – words like 'soodling', 'sloomy' or 'gulsh'd' say – expresses a communal vitality that is the living heart of a language. In his essay 'On the Origin of Languages' Rousseau argues that language becomes 'less passionate' as it becomes more regular, and he states that 'it is not possible for a language that is written, to retain its vitality as long as one that is spoken'. Dialects, Rousseau argues, tend to be distinguished by oral speech, while writing works to assimilate and merge them. In celebrating Clare's use of Northamptonshire vernacular, we celebrate the native genius of the English language – a language of dwelling or Being which we hear, to quote Yeats again, 'in the deep heart's core'.

Acoustic pattern, dialect, oral culture, the in-dwellingness of spoken language are all present in Clare's fascinated observation of birdsong – the cuckoo's 'pleasant russling noise', the heron 'cranking a jarring melancholy cry'. His work is packed with examples, even a twenty-two-line rather Joycean transcription of the nightingale's song. This elaborate sensitivity to sound is one expression of Clare's fundamental aesthetic because his poetics is essentially a poetics of process. What he delights in are not finished and complete patterns or shapes, but those patterns as they shape themselves, as they exist in process, in the music of their happening or becoming:

> . . . the gudgeons sturting by
> Cring'd 'neath water-grasses' shade
> Startling as each nimble eye
> Saw the rings the dropples made

Clare loves these slippery liquid happenings: '. . . where oaks dripping shade the lake, / Prints crimpling dimples on its breast'. He has a particular fondness for 'crimpling', 'crinkling', 'dimpling' surfaces and for 'fizzling', 'crizzling', 'crumping' sounds. Both sound and surface, both 'strinkling dropples' and 'chickering' sounds are related as percepts – as sense perceptions – and as processes. What we therefore get is a fusion of the processes of perception and the natural processes of sound forming and travelling, and of water, light or leaves moving. This may seem obvious, but it isn't. What these frequent images of process embody is a visionary, a mystical or religious attitude of mind and imagination. The best way I can think of describing it is by taking an example of the Hindu imagination – the technique employed by Satyajit Ray in films like *Pather Panchali* where the camera will dwell for a long time on, say, a water drop forming on a leaf, then the drop falling. In the *dwelling* on such a tiny event – something in process, in a state of becoming – we get this strangely perfect, intensely pleasurable fusion of Being and Becoming. We draw a sense of dwelling from within what looks and feels like changing cloud-shadow.

Clare is fascinated by this combination of movement and stillness:

Little trotty wagtail he went in the rain
And tittering tottering sideways he near got straight again
He stooped to get a worm and look'd up to catch a fly
And then he flew away e're his feathers they were dry

Little trotty wagtail he waddled in the mud
And left his little foot marks trample where he would
He waddled in the water pudge and waggle went his tail
And chirrupt up his wings to dry upon the garden rail

Little trotty wagtail you nimble all about
And in the dimpling water pudge you waddle in and out
Your home is nigh at hand and in the warm pigsty
So little Master Wagtail I'll bid you a 'Good bye'

The last stanza of 'Little Trotty Wagtail' contains a subtle internal rhyme which links the 'tittering tottering' nimble motion of the wagtail to the 'dimpling water pudge' – the little wind-stippled puddle. The two forms of movement are combined and identified, then focused on the word 'home'. This is therefore an emblematic poem of Being which is further rooted in the idea of dwelling by the phrase 'the warm pigsty'.

That favourite, haunted word 'home' appears twice in one of Clare's most beautiful lyrics, 'Clock A Clay'. As the ladybird sings of the buzzing fly, dew-pearled grass, quaking forests, sobbing winds and pattering rain, we come to recognize that these are familiar, loved symbols of process in the poems. Clare returns again and again as only geniuses can to the same subjects, themes, images. In 'Clock A Clay' we have a lyric of such tender, redemptive vision that to read it is like being gently initiated into one of the secrets of the universe:

> In the cowslip's peeps I lye
> Hidden from the buzzing fly
> While green grass beneath me lies
> Pearled wi' dew like fishes eyes
> Here I lie a Clock a clay
> Waiting for the time o' day

While grassy forests quake surprise
And the wild wind sobs and sighs
My gold home rocks as like to fall
On its pillars green and tall
When the pattering rain drives bye
Clock a Clay keeps warm and dry

Day by day and night by night
All the week I hide from sight
In the cowslips peeps I lie
In rain and dew still warm and dry
Day and night and night and day
Red black spotted clock a clay

My home it shakes in wind and showers
Pale green pillar topt wi' flowers
Bending at the wild winds breath
Till I touch the grass beneath
Here still I live lone clock a clay
Watching for the time of day

It is time we praised John Clare the Northamptonshire visionary to
the skies.

The Tender Voice: Thomas Hardy

In 1864, Gerard Manley Hopkins announced in a letter to a friend, 'a horrible thing has happened to me. I have begun to *doubt* Tennyson.' He then offered a scrupulous critique of *Enoch Arden*, one of the season's new books, and argued that it is an example of what he terms 'Parnassian'. This predictable style is 'spoken *on and from the level* of a poet's mind' and can never break into 'poetry proper, the language of inspiration'. For Hopkins, this inspired language is often abrupt, short-lived, intense, and when he argues that its beauties take the reader 'by surprise', he anticipates Hardy's poetic, his 'Gothic art-principle . . . of spontaneity'. Both poets hold to an aesthetic of 'cunning irregularity' and aim for a poetry of syncopated texture rather than melodious veneer. For them, the highest form of poetic language is rapid, extempore, jazz-like and 'funky'.

Although Hopkins initially intends the term 'Parnassian' to designate a plateau of self-parody, the reflex duplication of a settled and established poetic style – i.e. Tennyson being Tennysonian, Wordsworth being Wordsworthian – he is beginning, at the age of twenty, to define a poetic tradition which is anti-Tennyson and which one might term 'Gothic'. This involves arguing for a split vision of English poetry, so that we see on the one hand a high, melodic, vowel-based tradition which moves through Surrey, Spenser and early Shakespeare. It includes Milton, Pope, Wordsworth, Keats, Tennyson, Eliot, and it looks south to the Romance languages for its essential inspiration. By contrast, the Gothic tradition is northern and consonantal, and its roots are in the people rather than in the court. The Gothic poet writes poems that have a fricative, spiky, spoken texture, and this populist delight in rough,

Introduction to *Thomas Hardy: The Poetry of Perception*.

scratchy sounds is present in Brutus's description of Coriolanus's fame:

> All tongues speak of him, and the bleared sights
> Are spectacled to see him. Your prattling nurse
> Into a rapture lets her baby cry
> While she chats him. The kitchen malkin pins
> Her richest lockram 'bout her reechy neck,
> Clamb'ring the walls to eye him; stalls, bulks, windows,
> Are smother'd up, leads fill'd and ridges hors'd
> With variable complexions . . .

That collocation of 'kitchen', 'malkin', 'richest', 'lockram', 'reechy', and 'neck' has an erotic charge similar to Browning's 'the quick sharp scratch / And blue spurt of a lighted match'. Both poets bathe and luxuriate in certain squitchy sounds.

Sadly, this poetic tradition has not received much critical attention, and this is partly because one of its major figures is Anon, the ballad singer lost in the 'reechy' crowd. Students of literature tend to be familiar with Wordsworth's insipid literary ballads, but many critics and teachers ignore 'The Three Ravens', 'The Dilly Song', 'The Bitter Withy', 'A Farmer's Song So Sweet' and other anonymous masterpieces. As a result, many people have failed both to appreciate these wonderful aboriginal creations and to understand how literary English has been periodically refreshed by an Antaeus-like contact with the earth. This rich tradition has been pushed to one side or patronized as quaint and faintly comic.

If the Gothic is rooted in an oral culture, its early beginnings can also be discerned in two court poets – Skelton and Wyatt – who are remarkable for the thorny, thrawn texture of their verse. From Wyatt, the line passes to Donne, Jonson, Clare, Barnes, Browning, and then to Hardy, Frost, Edward Thomas and early Auden. Hopkins has a curious presence in the tradition because, though he was influenced by Barnes and Browning and admired Hardy's novels, his poems were published posthumously in 1918 and do not appear to have had any influence on Hardy's later work. The affinities between the two poets are family characteristics rather than direct exchanges between contemporaries.

It is essential, I believe, that we give more attention to the poetic tradition which Hardy and Hopkins belong to, partly because at present many literary critics appear to believe that literary tradition is the simple mountain range of 'great' authors and 'great' texts. The belief is that critics should overthrow what is sometimes termed 'the hegemony of canonical texts' or 'official written poetry, high cultural poetry'. These critics argue that the canon of English Literature is an oppressive instrument shaped by a literary establishment concerned to safeguard its class interests by promoting the bogus idea of a national culture. Although this argument is sometimes presented in terms which are aggressively simplistic and philistine, it can be argued that Tennyson's work ought to be severely reassessed from such a critical point of view. Imperialist, racist, reactionary, sexist (see that vicious poem 'Hail Briton!'), Tennyson is in brilliant command of a dead language. The words he marshals belong to a brigade of cheap, brittle alloys which lack any natural spring or give. With the exceptions of a few dialect poems and two Hopkins-like lines ('Break, break, break' and 'On the bald street breaks the blank day'), Tennyson's cadences are for the most part a species of Virgilian kitsch, all silvery angst and trim melody. And here it's worth applying Barthes' statement in *Writing Degree Zero* that however hard the writer tries to create a 'free language' it comes back to him

fabricated, for luxury is never innocent: and it is this stale language, closed by the immense pressure of all the men who do not speak it, which he must continue to use. Writing therefore is a blind alley. The writers of today feel this; for them, the search for a non-style or an oral style, for a zero level or a spoken level of writing is, all things considered, the anticipation of a homogeneous social state; most of them understand that there can be no universal language outside a concrete and no longer mystical or merely nominal, universality of society.

If the luxuriant and 'never innocent' author of *In Memoriam* is really a dubious cultural emanation – the Saxon gardener whom Joyce dubbed 'Alfred Lawn Tennyson' – we should realize that

Hardy belongs outside this institutional, official reality. He grew up in a rural society where most people spoke dialect and where illiteracy was normal. Nowadays we tend to regard illiteracy as abnormal and slightly shameful, but this is not the view held by most members of an oral culture. To them, writing is simply a special technical skill, like mending shoes, and you can always hire someone to do it for you. Thus when he was a boy Hardy used to act as a scribe for girls from his village who wanted to send letters to their lovers. Like many members of ethnic minorities in present-day Britain, he could move between two cultures – one illiterate, oral, traditional and knitted by communal and kinship bonds, the other progressive, educated, individualistic, private, and emotionally somewhat chill. Although some literary critics are at present busily sentimentalizing oral culture (Hugh Kenner's *A Colder Eye* is perhaps the first book of 'oral' literary criticism to appear in print), we ought to realize how difficult the tensions between the two cultures can be. If there are advantages to be gained, there are also strains to be taken and obscure hurts that can never quite heal. As a writer, Hardy was caught between a provincial oral culture of song, talk, legend, and a metropolitan culture of print, political power and what linguists used to term RP – i.e. Received Pronunciation or Standard English. And when Hardy asserted that a 'certain provincialism of feeling' was invaluable in a writer and set that quality against Arnold's idea of culture – an idea hostile to provincialism – he was referring to a mode of feeling that is bound in with song, dialect, physical touch, natural human kindness and what he terms 'crude enthusiasm'. He does not mean provincial in the Chekhovian sense of stifled ambition and anxious mediocrity. Nowadays, some literary theorists profess a belief in 'the interpretative community' and suggest that in such communities 'aberrant decodings' – i.e. mistaken aesthetic judgements – can be understood and corrected. Hardy would agree that community is essential to art, but would regard community as not residing in concepts of social success or personal achievement, perhaps not even in the printed word.

This fundamental suspicion of the educated and the metropolitan is present in 'Tess's Lament':

'Twas there within the chimney-seat
He watched me to the clock's slow beat —
Loved me, and learnt to call me Sweet,
  And whispered words to me.

How strange that last line sounds — as if Angel Clare could have whispered anything other than words, as if the words themselves were difficult, threatening, somehow wrong or bad or in a different language. And then we realize that Tess is speaking in a provincial accent, while Angel speaks in a standard educated language which lies outside her community. Angel's words are mere signs, flat counters that are not tied to anything that is communal or traditional. Indeed, they threaten that community as surely as the steam-thresher or the attitudes of Angel's *ficelle*, Alec D'Urberville. At some fundamental level, Hardy is exploring the conflict between language as Being and language as Instrument. Anyone caught in that conflict knows that while there are arguments for both views, it is wrong to break your ties with dialect, with the language of passion and kinship. The guilt which springs from that betrayal of Being can never be quite forgotten or forgiven.

This, it seems to me, is the subject of 'In the Servants' Quarters', which is a late-Victorian or Pre-Raphaelite version of Peter's denial of Christ:

'Man, you too, aren't you, one of those rough followers of the
  criminal?'

The opening line is keyed exactly to speech rhythms and to the grammar of speech which need not be logically sequential. Thus the girl speaks in a sudden, authentic, exclamatory manner which sounds highly volatile and which is true to the Gothic principle of surprise. This quick, fresh, original directness can be heard again after Peter denies all knowledge of the criminal:

'O, come, come!' laughed the constables. 'Why, man, you speak the
  dialect
He uses in his answers; you can hear him up the stairs.
So own it. We sh'n't hurt ye. There he's speaking now! His syllables

Are those you sound yourself when you are talking unawares,
   As this pretty girl declares.'

Peter lapses into dialect, into a Galilean accent, when he talks 'unawares'. This type of vocal surprise is one of the great beauties of daily speech and conversation and Hopkins catches it in 'The Handsome Heart', which is subtitled '*at a Gracious answer*':

> 'But tell me, child, your choice; what shall I buy
> You?' – 'Father, what you buy me I like best.'
> With the sweetest air that said, still plied and pressed,
> He swung to his first poised purport of reply.

In Hopkins's deft phrase the child's vocal grace is 'his first poised purport of reply', and there may be an echo here of Browning's 'first fine careless rapture' (the phrase would have been fresher when Hopkins wrote). Thus a child's quick speech, a thrush's song, possess a visionary spontaneity and perfection far beyond the marble levels of the Parnassian style.

This is what Robert Frost meant when he told a friend:

Both Swinburne and Tennyson arrived largely at effects in assonation. But they were on the wrong track or at any rate on a short track. They went the length of it. Anyone else who goes that way must go after them. And that's where most of them are going. I alone of English writers have consciously set myself to make music out of what I may call the sound of sense. . . . Those sounds are summoned by the audile [audial] imagination and they must be positive, strong, and definitely and unmistakably indicated by the context. The reader must be at no loss to give his voice the posture proper to the sentence. The simple declarative sentence used in making a plain statement is one sound. But Lord love ye it mustn't be worked to death. It is against the law of nature that whole poems should be written in it. If they are written they won't be read. The sound of sense, then. You get that. It is the abstract vitality of our speech. It is pure sound – pure form.

Frost is of course not the first 'English' writer to consciously listen for 'the sound of sense', though he is the writer who best and most intelligently articulates and explains the mystery. Like Hopkins, he believes in vocal epiphanies.*

---

*See also that slight poem 'In the British Museum' where a labourer looks at the Elgin Marbles and muses on how these inanimate objects once echoed the voice of St

It is significant that Peter's denial of Christ in Hardy's poem should also represent a denial of dialect:

– His face convulses as the morning cock that moment crows,
    And he droops, and turns, and goes.

Peter's droopy departure makes him resemble treacherous and deracinated figures like Angel Clare, Alec D'Urberville or Edred Fitzpiers. He has betrayed the Word, and my guess is that the socially mobile Hardy is exploring a personal guilt he felt at having denied something vocal and sacred. This is the meritocrat's guilt, the troubled conscience of the achiever.

In 'The Self-Unseeing' Hardy very tersely evokes the rural family culture – his mother smiles into the fire while his father plays a wild fiddler's reel that the child-poet dances ecstatically to. And although the opening stanza may appear to be flat descriptive statement, it is most beautifully and surprisingly cadenced:

> Hére is the áncient flóor,
> Fóotwórn and hóllowed and thín,
> Hére, was the fórmer dóor
> Whére the déad féet wálked ín.

The first line consists of a trochee and two iambs; the second line of a spondee, an iamb, and an anapaest; the third has the same pattern as the first line, a trochee followed by two iambs, but with an internal rhyme ('for' and 'door'); while the fourth line is a most marvellous and surprising line – a trochee followed by two spondees.

Hardy's lines draw profoundly on the folk imagination, and as in the ballad 'Finnegan's Wake' that imagination overrides the great division between life and death – it locates the resurrection in the self-delighting wildness of sheer rhythm. And this resembles Yeats's remark that passionate rhythm preserves and transforms personal emotion by lifting it out of history into the realm of 'impersonal meditation'.

—

Paul: 'Words . . . in all their intimate accents'. The line goes beyond its context to become a kind of symbolist, self-referring phrase. Hardy is describing his own poetry, his intimately vocal aesthetic.

According to Yeats, Robert Bridges was able to make common-place words magnificent by 'some trick of speeding and slowing' in these lines:

> A glítter of pléasure
> And a dárk tómb.

Hardy employs a similar effect in the lovely fourth line of 'The Youth Who Carried a Light':

> I sáw him páss as the néw dáy dáwned,
>   Múrmuring some músical phráse;
> Hórses were drínking and flóundering ín the pónd,
>   And the tíred stárs thínned their gáze.

The bunched stresses of that last line give it a gently magisterial permanence and meditative perfection.

Ultimately, Hardy is close to Yeats in the connection which he makes between vocal rhythm and mystery, and this can be discerned in a very fine, but little-known poem called 'On a Midsummer Eve':

> I idly cut a parsley stalk,
> And blew therein towards the moon;
> I had not thought what ghosts would walk
> With shivering footsteps to my tune.
>
> I went, and knelt, and scooped my hand
> As if to drink, into the brook,
> And a faint figure seemed to stand
> Above me, with the bygone look.
>
> I lipped rough rhymes of chance, not choice,
> I thought not what my words might be;
> There came into my ear a voice
> That turned a tenderer verse for me.

Although the last line is overloaded with a dragging 'ur' sound, it is that tender voice which we hear in all Hardy's greatest poems. And in order to be visited by that voice he had to rid his poetry of certain received idioms. It's as if the muse visits him only when he learns to reject the instrumental will (rhymes of 'choice') for a more intuitive, 'rougher' type of verse which is rooted in rural speech, the Dorset accent and the formally very sophisticated dialect verse of William Barnes. This can only be discovered through a surrender to natural magic and superstition, through a creative idleness rather than a forcing ambition. As in 'The Abbey Mason', chance forms an essential part of the creative process, a process which in this case has certain analogies with action painting. Hardy is saying that he had to allow words to choose him, rather than try to choose them by an act of the desk-bound will.

If I've stressed Hardy's passion for the human voice, his obsessive fascination with sight is no less remarkable. Somehow we must learn to marry these imaginative worlds of eye and ear so that we can both see and hear the lovely acoustic texture of Hardy's verse.

The Phallic Thumb of Love:
Whitman and Hopkins

Enormous, oceanic, seminal, benevolent, *spermatic* Whitman, so unapproachably approachable: how do we reach out to that imagination? Maybe by looking at what his work meant to that deeply undemocratic English poet Gerard Manley Hopkins.

On 18 October 1882, Hopkins wrote to Robert Bridges detailing what poems of Whitman's he had read:

I have read of Whitman's (1) 'Pete' in the library at Bedford Square (and perhaps something else; if so I forget), which you pointed out; (2) two pieces in the *Athenaeum* or *Academy*, one on the Man-of-War Bird, the other beginning 'Spirit that formed this scene'; (3) short extracts in a review by Saintsbury in the *Academy*: this is all I remember. I cannot have read more than half a dozen pieces at most.

This, though very little, is quite enough to give a strong impression of his marked and original manner and way of thought and in particular of his rhythm. It might be even enough, I shall not deny, to originate or, much more, influence another's style: they say the French trace their whole modern school of landscape to a single piece of Constable's exhibited at the Salon early this century.

The question then is only about the fact. But first I may as well say what I should not otherwise have said, that I always knew in my heart Walt Whitman's mind to be more like my own than any other man's living. As he is a very great scoundrel this is not a pleasant confession. And this also makes me the more desirous to read him and the more determined that I will not.

Admitting Whitman's influence in a strangely contradictory manner that both maximizes and minimizes it, Hopkins wants to persuade his friend that he is 'quite mistaken' about 'The Leaden and the Golden Echo', which he had recently sent him. Bridges will on second thought find the fancied resemblance to Whitman 'diminish and the imitation disappear'. Hopkins then distinguishes what he terms Whitman's 'irregular rhythmic prose' from his own use of sprung rhythm by offering a metrical analysis of Whitman's 'or a handkerchief designedly dropped'. This, he says, 'is in a dactylic rhythm – or let us say anapaestic':

for it is a great convenience in English to assume that the stress is always at the end of the foot; the consequence of which assumption is that in ordinary verse there are only two English feet possible, the iamb and the anapaest, and even in my regular sprung rhythm only one additional, the fourth paeon: for convenience' sake assuming this, then the above fragment is anapaestic – 'oȓ å hánd|kėrchîef . . .|.děsígn|ėdly̌ dró́pped' – and there is a break down, a designed break of rhythm, after 'handkerchief', done no doubt that the line may not become downright verse, as it would be if he had said 'or a handkerchief purposely dropped'.

Hopkins's point is acutely interesting, though it depends on a mnemonic compression of the fourth and fifth lines of this passage from the 1855 edition of *Leaves of Grass*:

A child said, *What is the grass?* fetching it to me with full hands;
How could I answer the child? . . . I do not know what it is any
   more than he.

I guess it must be the flag of my disposition, out of hopeful green
   stuff woven.

Or I guess it is the handkerchief of the Lord,
A scented gift and remembrancer designedly dropped,
Bearing the owner's name someway in the corners, that we may
   see and remark, and say *Whose?*

Hopkins was attracted to this idea because it expresses the idea of the world as a designed artifice, and it does so in a free-verse metre that is close to his concept of sprung rhythm. For Hopkins, the divine artifice and this rhythm that breaks with 'downright verse' – that is, traditional metrical verse – are identified. They are inscape and instress. But it irks him to discover this intense conjunction in an American homosexual Protestant democrat. Despite his own worship of the masculine (it's one of his most favoured terms of critical approval), he is uneasy about confessing his deep kinship with Whitman, whose 'lusty lurking masculine poems' must have burst on him with all the amazed force of self-recognition. His admiration for Whitman is laced with very complicated feelings which he briefly admits to in 'The Windhover', then represses.

Let's take that phrase in his letter to Bridges – 'there is a break down, a designed break of rhythm after "handkerchief"' – and consider its bearing on these lines from 'The Windhover':

Brute beauty and valour and act, oh, air, pride, plume, here
      Buckle! AND the fire that breaks from thee then, a billion
   Times told lovelier, more dangerous. O my chevalier!

By packing heavy stresses together – Brúte béauty, áir, príde, plúme – Hopkins breaks down, he demolishes, traditional rhythm. The 'fire' that is generated by this process of almost chemical decomposition is both the friction of divine inspiration and the instressing – the perception – of the type of sprung rhythm he perceives in Whitman. To employ that overused term, Hopkins is deconstructing the normative rhythm of 'in his ríding / Of the rólling lével únderneáth him stéady áir' (metrical marks added). Enacting the kestrel's plunge, this rhythm breaks into the 'savage' art and rhythm which Hopkins admired in Whitman (later, in the letter to Bridges, he mentions the poem 'Spirit that Form'd this Scene', where Whitman identifies his verse with the 'savage spirit' of Platte Canyon, Colorado).

The term *savage* is a central imaginative concept for Hopkins, as it is for Whitman, and he defines it more clearly as 'tykishness' in an 1888 letter to Coventry Patmore. Tykishness is 'an old Adam of barbarism, boyishness, wildness, rawness, rankness, the disreputable, the unrefined in the refined and educated. It is that that I meant by tykishness (a tyke is a stray sly unowned dog).' And later, in the Whitman letter, Hopkins applies this savage aesthetic to rhythm: 'Extremes meet, and (I must for truth's sake say what sounds pride) this savagery of his art, this rhythm in its last ruggedness and decomposition into common prose, comes near the last elaboration of mine. For that piece of mine is very highly wrought.' (Notice he introduces 'pride', as in 'The Windhover'.) Hopkins insists that the rhythm of 'The Leaden Echo and the Golden Echo', which he had sent to Bridges, resembles the rhythm of 'Greek tragic choruses or of Pindar: which is pure sprung rhythm'. The implication is that Whitman is a savage who lacks classical training, though my hunch is that, like Frost, he brought a classical imagination to his nativist subjects. Praising John Mulvany's portrait of General Custer, Whitman remarks that with all its 'colour and fierce action, a certain Greek continence pervades it'. And in 'A Memorandum at a Venture' and his brief note on 'The Perfect Human Voice' he again cites the Greeks. But Whitman coincidentally also shared Hopkins's admiration of a demotic rankness, remarking that slang is the 'lawless germinal element, below all words and sentences, and behind all poetry, and proves a certain perennial rankness and Protestantism in speech'. This, except for the Protestantism, is close to Hopkins's idea of the tykish and to his fascination with regional British and Irish vernaculars.

Hopkins cannot tell either Bridges or Patmore that Whitman's barbaric yawp represents for him danger – lovely danger – savagery, democracy, wildness, hugely attractive working men. The homoerotic in Whitman is both classical and modern: it promises a whole new liberated consciousness which both fascinates and terrifies Hopkins. Whitman's technique of breaking down or decomposition releases a 'brute beauty'. This is the 'barbarous . . . beauty' he almost howlingly desires in 'Hurrahing in Harvest', where, as William Darby Templeman has noted, his 'stallion stalwart' is a version of Whitman's 'gigantic beauty of a stallion, fresh and responsive to my caresses'.

There is a distinctive erotic image pattern in Hopkins which he expresses in 'Hurrahing in Harvest':

> what wind-walks! what lovely behaviour
> Of silk-sack clouds! has wilder, wilful-wavier
> Meal-drift moulded ever and melted across skies?

This may be a version of Whitman's winds with their 'soft-tickling genitals'. It's possible that Hopkins read some of the many passages in Whitman where he savours the sensuously healthy feel of his own body and delights in his physical selfhood:

The smoke of my own breath,
Echoes, ripples, buzzed whispers . . . loveroot, silkthread, crotch
    and vine,
My respiration and inspiration . . . the beating of my heart . . . the
    passing of blood and air through my lungs,
The sniff of green leaves and dry leaves, and of the shore and
    darkcolor'd sea-rocks, and of hay in the barn,
The sound of the belch'd words of my voice . . . words loosed to the
    eddies of the wind,
A few light kisses . . . a few embraces . . . a reaching around of
    arms. . . .

There is a similar crotchy, groiny, pubic exultation in Hopkins's 'Inversnaid', a poem that is cunningly keyed to Burns:

    Degged with dew, dappled with dew
    Are the groins of the braes that the brook treads through,
    Wiry heathpacks, flitches of fern,
    And the beadbonny ash that sits over the burn.

Hopkins also visualizes the male genitals in that curious half-line in 'The Handsome Heart' where the 'muse of mounting vein' – the boy's beauty – is carefully or strategically hallowed in order to make him appear more than a merely physical turn-on.

Both Whitman and Hopkins are strongly attracted to men in uniform. In 'I Sing the Body Electric' Whitman remarks on: 'The march of firemen in their own costumes – the play of the masculine muscle through cleansetting trowsers and waistbands.' Hopkins loves sailors, redcoat soldiers, 'hardy-handsome' labouring men in the informal uniform of their work clothes. He responds to these lines from 'I Sing the Body Electric' (1855) by adopting the words 'juice' and 'cleave':

Limitless limpid jets of love hot and enormous . . . quivering jelly of
    love . . . white-blow and delirious juice,

Bridegroom-night of love working surely and softly into the pros-
  trate dawn,
Undulating into the willing and yielding day,
Lost in the cleave of the clasping sweetfleshed day.

In Hopkins's 'Epithalamion', an unfinished poem with many long
Whitman-like lines, the unusual noun 'cleave' is more than simply
Devonian dialect:

We are leaf-whelmed somewhere with the hood
Of some branchy bunchy bushybowered wood,
Southern dean or Lancashire clough or Devon cleave,
That leans along the loins of hills, where a candycoloured, where a
  gluegold-brown
Marbled river, boisterously beautiful, between
Roots and rocks is danced and dandled, all in froth and waterblow-
  balls, down.

Both poems celebrate marriage and echo Genesis where Adam says,
'Therefore shall a man leave his father and his mother, and shall
cleave unto his wife: and they shall be one flesh. And they were both
naked, the man and his wife, and were not ashamed' (2. 24). There is
also an erotic charge in Hopkins's use of the dialectal noun 'cleave'
in the *Journals* where he mentions a 'cliff over a deep and beautiful
cleave'.

'Epithalamion' follows Whitman in its strategic blending of the
homoerotic and the heterosexual. As in 'Inversnaid' Hopkins
designs a sexualized riverscape – 'the loins of hills' – while the
'gluegold' river may be a version of Whitman's 'adhesiveness'.
Etymologically the verb 'cleave' derives from the Dutch 'beklijven',
which means 'to stick'. Whitman's celebration of semen – 'quivering
jelly of love . . . white-blow and delirious juice' – is caught up in
both 'gluegold' and 'waterblowballs'. Similarly, the Elizabethan use
of 'spend' in Hopkins's extraordinary image of the lark's song in
'The Sea and the Skylark' – 'till none's to spill nor spend' – must
have been in part prompted by Whitman's jismy celebrations. And
as Charles Madge has noted, the phrase 'all this juice and all this joy'

in Hopkins's 'Spring' derives from Whitman's 'Seas of bright juice'. Again Hopkins's 'roots' and the 'silk-beech' he mentions later in the poem resemble Whitman's 'loveroot, silkthread, crotch and vine'.

More than fifty years ago, Philip Henderson in *The Poet and Society* pointed to the 'often quite naked sexuality' of Hopkins's poetry. He stated that Hopkins found in Whitman 'that same overmastering virile energy and turbulence, that luxuriant sensuality, that devouring love of the physical beauty of men and the world which even the "particular examinen" of St Ignatius had failed to stifle'. Acutely, Henderson noticed that Hopkins's 'sensuality, consistently inhibited, gave rise in his poems to recurrent images of mutilation – "gash", in the sense of cut flesh, is one of his most-used words'. It could be argued that Hopkins also found an erotics of mutilation in Whitman's verse. And if we consider the extraordinary stream-of-consciousness poem which Whitman eventually entitled 'The Sleepers', we can perceive more clearly the profound imaginative affinity between the two poets. In 'The Sleepers' Whitman imagines the 'gashed bodies on battlefields' and, in this section of the 1855 version, he envisions a sailor trying to escape from a wrecked ship:

I see a beautiful gigantic swimmer swimming naked through the
    eddies of the sea,
His brown hair lies close and even to his head . . . he strikes out with
    courageous arms . . . he urges himself with his legs,
I see his white body . . . I see his undaunted eyes;
I hate the swift-running eddies that would dash him headforemost
    on the rocks.

What are you doing you ruffianly red-trickled waves?
Will you kill the courageous giant? Will you kill him in the prime of
    his middle age?

Steady and long he struggles;
He is baffled and banged and bruised . . . he holds out while his
    strength holds out,
The slapping eddies are spotted with his blood . . . they bear him
    away . . . they roll him and swing him and turn him:

His beautiful body is borne in the circling eddies . . . it is continually
   bruised on rocks,
Swiftly and out of sight is borne the brave corpse.

Whitman's beautiful swimmer is close to the drowned sailor who is
grotesquely dangled at a rope's end in 'The Wreck of the
Deutschland' (though his detail derives initially from an account of
the disaster in the London *Times*). The 'lovely manly mould' of the
drowned, 'brown-as-dawning-skinned' sailor in 'The Loss of the
Eurydice' is also close to Whitman's lines in 'The Sleepers', and,
though we have no direct evidence that Hopkins read this strange
and daring poem, there is a very curious phrasal coincidence which
suggests that he must have.

   Take the 'unrestrained phallic splendor', as Edwin Miller calls it,
of this passage from 'The Sleepers' (1855):

Well do they do their jobs, those journeymen divine,
Only from me can they hide nothing and would not if they could;
I reckon I am their boss and they make me a pet besides,
And surround me and lead me and run ahead when I walk,
And lift their cunning covers and signify me with stretched arms,
   and resume the way;
Onward we move, a gay gang of blackguards with mirthshouting
   music and wildflapping pennants of joy.

In 'That Nature is a Heraclitean Fire and of the Comfort of the
Resurrection' Hopkins begins with his Miltonic vision of a cloudy
war in heaven:

Cloud-puffball, torn tufts, tossed pillows flaunt forth, then chevy on
   an air-
built thoroughfare: heaven-roysterers, in gay-gangs they throng;
   they glitter in marches.

Hopkins is alluding here to Milton's sons of Belial 'flown with
insolence and wine' in order to relocate them as the, to him, unholy
alliance of Gladstonian democrats and Parnellite Irish nationalists
which existed during the 1880s. Considering Hopkins's lines in
relation to Whitman, it appears that his phrase 'gay-gangs' is

adapted from the great American democrat's 'gay gang' in order to give visionary expression to a new political and sexual consciousness that both terrified and attracted him.

Whitman's 'gay gang' is doubly spontaneous and unusual: 'gay' means 'exuberant and spontaneous' (the recent homosexual significance is obviously coincidental and inapplicable),while a 'gang' is a spontaneous social group. Even in the twentieth century the word has a colloquial flavour which must have appealed to Hopkins, who would have applied it to the gangs of workmen whose 'packs infest the age' in 'Tom's Garland'. It is hard not to link it with the 'tykish', with a demotic wildness, rawness, and rankness.

In the original version of 'The Sleepers', Whitman included a famous sexual passage after these lines:

Be careful, darkness . . . already, what was it touched me?
I thought my lover had gone . . . else darkness and he are one,
I hear the heart-beat . . . I follow . . . I fade away.

This is the culmination of the sweaty-lover passage which was retained, unlike this section:

O hotcheeked and blushing! O foolish hectic!
O for pity's sake, no one must see me now! . . . my clothes were
    stolen while I was abed,
Now I am thrust forth, where shall I run?

Pier that I saw dimly last night when I looked from the windows,
Pier out from the main, let me catch myself with you and stay . . . I
    will not chafe you;
I feel ashamed to go naked about the world.
And am curious to know where my feet stand . . . and what is this
    flooding me, childhood or manhood . . . and the hunger that
    crosses the bridge between.

The cloth laps a first sweet eating and drinking,
Laps life-swelling yolks . . . laps ear of rose-corn, milky and just
    ripened:
The white teeth stay, and the boss-toothed advances in darkness,

And liquor is spilled on lips and bosoms by touching glasses, and the
  best liquor afterward.

Hopkins's airy thoroughfare may be a version of the bridge which
Sin and Death construct in *Paradise Lost* (it is 'a broad highway or
bridge over chaos', which Satan says makes 'one continent / Of easy
thoroughfare'), and it may also draw on Whitman's phallic pier –
there is a sense of released, joyous, but distrusted sexuality in the
opening lines of 'That Nature is a Heraclitean Fire'. Beyond this
particular possible influence, I would argue that 'The Sleepers' was a
crucial poem for Hopkins. With its gashed bodies, its gay gang, its
beautiful naked, then beautiful bruised swimmers, its wrecked ship
and prophetic imagery of civil war, it contains several of Hopkins's
obsessive subjects.

Whitman describes the wreck like this:

The beach is cut by the razory ice-wind . . . the wreck-guns sound,
The tempest lulls and the moon comes floundering through the
  drifts.
I look where the ship helplessly heads end on . . . I hear the burst as
  she strikes . . . I hear the howls of dismay . . . they grow fainter
  and fainter.

Hopkins was also fascinated by shipwrecks, and in the closing lines
of 'That Nature is a Heraclitean Fire' he again imagines a wreck:

> Across my foundering deck shone
> A beacon, an eternal beam. Flesh fade, and mortal trash
> Fall to the residuary worm; world's wildfire, leave but ash;
>> In a flash, at a trumpet crash,
> I am all at once what Christ is, since he was what I am, and
> This Jack, joke, poor potsherd, patch, matchwood, immortal
>   diamond,
>> Is immortal diamond.

The penultimate line is an application of that principle of 'last
ruggedness and decomposition into common prose' which Hopkins
discerns in Whitman's verse. Hopkins is deliberately smashing the
rhythm, packing strongly stressed hard syllables together in order to

enact the break-up of body/ship/state so that the 'immortal diamond' of the soul can be made manifest.

Whitman similarly impacts syllables in the middle line of this maritime passage from 'Song of Myself', revised for the 1872 edition:

The hiss of the surgeon's knife, the gnawing teeth of his saw,
Wheeze, cluck, swash of falling blood . . . short wild scream, the
   long, dull, tapering groan,
These so – these irretrievable.

In a later version of 'The Sleepers', Whitman substituted the harsher rhythm of 'baffled, banged, bruised' for 'baffled and banged and bruised'. And in the last three lines of 'The Windhover' Hopkins further decomposes his rhythm into prose – into a prosaic alliterative rhythm which perhaps coincidentally releases a bleeding, cutting image:

   No wonder of it: sheer plod makes plough down sillion
 Shine, and blue-bleak embers, ah my dear,
   Fall, gall themselves, and gash gold-vermilion.

Ploughing represents the democracy of labour here, and its rugged rhythm is meant to contrast with the effortless aristocratic *virtù* of the kestrel's flight. Hopkins has transposed the sweep of the skate's heel into the blades of the ploughshare whose heavy movement is analogous to the scrape of his pen nib. In this final image we catch something of the sheer grind of Hopkins's life as a priest.

Hopkins's fascination with a 'wrecked' or decomposed rhythm must in part have sprung from his fascination with the democratic currents of the age. In 'Spain, 1873–74' Whitman characterizes Europe as a monarchical wreck:

Out of the murk of heaviest clouds,
Out of the feudal wrecks and heap'd-up skeletons of kings,
Out of that old entire European debris, the shatter'd mummeries,
Ruin'd cathedrals, crumble of palaces, tombs of priests,
Lo, Freedom's features fresh undimm'd look forth – the same
   immortal face looks forth.

Hopkins's contradictory political imagination viewed British civilization as a wrecking process – 'our civilization is founded on wrecking,' he told Bridges – but he also feared democratic energy. He saw that energy being celebrated in Whitman and knew that the American poet viewed the old European order as a wreck. Charles Madge remarked that in Hopkins, as in Whitman, 'locks blown in the wind have the significance of flames rising from the physical being and searching the air of nature with fingers and tongues'. This is an exact and just point, but we need to see that this obsessive image pattern in Hopkins is also a way of figuring the erotic – it is a kinetic imagery with a specifically homosexual basis.

Hopkins was consciously aware of this, but he could not admit it to Bridges. On 21 October 1882, three days after writing his Whitman letter, he wrote to Bridges again and referred, rather disingenuously, to his earlier letter as a 'de-Whitmaniser', saying, 'I believe it was stern and a bit of a mouther.' Six years later, he tells Bridges that he has finished 'Harry Ploughman', saying, 'let me know if there is anything like it in Walt Whitman, as perhaps there may be, and I should be sorry for that'. Hopkins is trying to hide his tracks and deny that he has written a deeply homoerotic poem.

'Harry Ploughman' strongly resembles Whitman in its admiration for brawny proletarian masculinity. It employs the rope and 'wind-laced' imagery which is pervasive in Hopkins's verse:

> Hard as hurdle arms, with a broth of goldish flue
> Breathed round; the rack of ribs; the scooped flank; lank
> Rope-over thigh; knee-knave; and barrelled shank –

In the fragment 'The furl of fresh-leaved dog-rose down', he writes:

> His locks like all a ravel-rope's-end,
>   With hempen strands in spray –
> Fallow, foam-fallow, hanks – fall'n off their ranks,
>   Swung down at a disarray.

This is a benign reworking of the relished images of the drowned sailors in 'The Loss of the Eurydice' and 'The Wreck of the Deutschland'. Whitman has a similar attraction to the weathered faces of working men, and in the preface to the first edition of *Leaves of Grass* he extends this to the body of the language itself. 'The English language befriends the grand American expression. . . . It is brawny enough, and limber and full enough.' He goes on to tell what the 'messages of great poems' are:

Come to us on equal terms, only then can you understand us. We are no better than you, what we inclose you inclose, what we enjoy you may enjoy. Did you suppose there could be only one Supreme? We affirm there can be unnumber'd Supremes, and that one does not countervail another any more than one eyesight countervails another – and that men can be good or grand only of the consciousness of their supremacy within them. What do you think is the grandeur of storms and dismemberments, and the deadliest battles and wrecks, and the wildest fury of the elements, and the power of the sea, and the motion of Nature, and the throes of human desires, and dignity and hate and love? It is that something in the soul which says, Rage on, whirl on, I tread master here and everywhere – Master of the spasms of the sky and of the shatter of the sea, Master of nature and passion and death, and of all terror and all pain.

It is difficult not to connect this passage, particularly its last sentence, with the opening of 'The Wreck of the Deutschland':

> Thou mastering me
>   God! giver of breath and bread;
> World's strand, sway of the sea;
>   Lord of living and dead;
> Thou hast bound bones and veins in me, fastened me flesh,
> And after it álmost únmade, what with dread,
>   Thy doing: and dost thou touch me afresh?
> Over again I feel thy finger and find theé.

Hopkins transposes the active 'I tread' into the passive 'the hurl of thee trod' in the second stanza, and in stanza thirty-two praises God in a voice that sounds like a deep clenched growl:

> I admire thee, master of the tides,
>   Of the Yore-flood, of the year's fall;
> The recurb and the recovery of the gulf's sides,
>   The girth of it and the wharf of it and the wall;
> Stanching, quenching ocean of a motionable mind;

Ground of being, and granite of it: pást áll
  Grásp Gód, thróned behind
Death with a sovereignty that heeds but hides, bodes but abides.

Both poets are celebrating a stormy greatness, and they do so by associating poetry with the 'grandeur of wrecks'. Their imaginative affinity is so deep that we need to recognize it as a conceptual relationship which is just as important as the simply one-way relationship of influence which Whitman had on Hopkins. There is a kind of whale song that flows between the two poets.

  Drawing on the account of the wreck which was published in the London *Times*, Hopkins narrates how

  One stirred from the rigging to save
  The wild woman-kind below,
With a rope's end round the man, handy and brave –
  He was pitched to his death at a blow.
  For all his dreadnought breast and braids of thew:
  They could tell him for hours, dandled the to and fro
    Through the cobbled foam-fleece. What could he do
With the burl of the fountains of air, buck and the flood of the
    wave?

The crucial, the odd, the deliberately unsettling, inappropriate, and bizarre word here is 'dandled', which, with baroque panache, Hopkins intends to signify the merciful creator acting behind the cruel, cold elements. He uses the verb again in the fragment 'The furl of fresh-leaved dog-rose', which concludes with this image of the desired man: 'And the sunlight sidled, like dewdrops, like dandled diamonds / Through the sieve of the straw of the plait.' In 'Binsey Poplars' not one poplar is spared

      That dandled a sandalled
    Shadow that swam or sank
On meadow and river and wind-wandering weed-winding bank.

Hopkins asked Bridges, 'Why did you not say that *Binsey Poplars* was like Whitman?' My hunch is that the 'sandalled shadow' is a beautiful male figure, maybe classical or biblical. He uses 'dandled' again in 'Epithalamion', shortly before the 'riot of a rout' of boys appears. The naked bathing boys are another 'gay gang', emanations of Whitman's beautiful naked swimmer.

It is my belief that Hopkins's style is one based on dialogue, and that he is in profound communication with Whitman, who is one of the most dialogic of poets. Hopkins would have written much more narrowly had he not read Whitman. The great poet of democracy enabled and inspired Hopkins, and he also prompted all of D. H. Lawrence's finest poems. We celebrate Whitman both as the founder of American poetry and as the heartener and helper of two major English poets.

Lawrence and Decency

During the First World War, Lawrence remarked, 'We are, have been for five centuries, the growing tip. Now we're going to fall. But you don't catch me going back on my whiteness and Englishness and myself. English in the teeth of the world, even in England.' Although he may well have changed his mind the next day and proclaimed that he was, and always had been, an Assyrian or a Pict, this assertion of Englishness must be taken at its face value and its distinctive oddity noted – Lawrence a distinctively *English* writer? English like Orwell, or Edward Thomas, or Jane Austen? The Lawrence who wrote 'England, My England' belongs to the England which begins at the river Trent, that great hyperborean tundra of mills, mines and factories which dreams itself as the territory of fierce, passionate, authentic feeling. For some reason, that northern part of England never seems quite English, and I don't think it did to Lawrence – he sought parallels for it in other countries, other cultures, different ways of feeling. In doing so, he obviously had to adapt a received concept of Englishness, and he did this by offending, deliberately and often, against one of the central tenets of Englishness – the idea that there is ultimately a law to which we are responsible, a law which is invoked in that mystic phrase 'you're going too far'. This admonition not to go too far is linked with the notion of decency and with the idea that there is a version of experience which is indecent and which lies 'beyond the pale'.

That phrase 'beyond the pale' is a metaphor which derives from the English settlement of Ireland, and it denotes 'that part of Ireland over which English jurisdiction was established'. And obviously the phrase has ancient colonial significances – to go beyond the pale is to stray beyond the bounds of Englishness and to join the ranks of what

Kipling, the Lawrence of imperial engineering, terms 'lesser breeds without the Law'.

How, then, did Lawrence go beyond the pale? One example – it's a famous one – is the letter he wrote to Katherine Mansfield when she lay dying: 'You revolt me, stewing in your consumption.' Another example is a letter of 1912 which he wrote to Edward Garnett from near Munich:

I had rather a nice letter from somebody – 'Hugh Walpole'. Is he anybody? Could I wring thee ha'porth of help out of his bloody neck? Curse the blasted, jelly-boned swines, the slimy, the belly-wriggling invertebrates, the miserable sodding rotters, the flaming sods, the snivelling, dribbling, dithering palsied pulse-less lot that make up England today. They've got white of egg in their veins, and their spunk is that watery it's a marvel they can breed. They *can* nothing but frog-spawn – the gibberers! God, how I hate them! God curse them, funkers. God blast them, wish-wash. Exterminate them, slime. . . . Why, why, why was I born an Englishman! – my cursed, rotten-boned, pappy hearted countrymen, *why* was I sent to *them*. Christ on the cross must have hated his countrymen. 'Crucify me, you swine,' he must have said through his teeth. It's not so hard to love thieves also on the cross. But the high priests down there – 'crucify me, you swine'. – 'Put in your nails and spear, you bloody nasal sour-blooded swine, I laugh last.' God, how I hate them – I nauseate – they stink in sourness.

They deserve it that every great man should drown himself. But not I (I am a bit great).

This Calvinistic curse is directed simultaneously against the English social and literary establishment and against Ernest Weekley; and the terrible phrase 'Exterminate them, slime' is so close to Kurtz's scrawl, 'Exterminate all the brutes', in Conrad's *Heart of Darkness*, that Lawrence appears to be consciously modelling himself on that demonic emanation. He appears to be living the disintegration of liberalism, and ironically we have to consider whether Lawrence's murderous directive is an essentially primitive attitude or whether it's not a naturally colonial attitude which happens to be turned against its own culture?

For Lawrence, such a curse was an invocation of the savage god, and we can see this in another letter which he wrote to Garnett five days later:

I don't want to come back to England. For the winter I shall get something to do in Germany, I think. F. [that is, Frieda] wants to clear out of Europe, and get to somewhere uncivilised. It is astonishing how barbaric one gets with love: one finds oneself in the Hinterland der Seele, and – it's a rum place. I never knew it was like this. What Blasted Fools the English are, fencing off the big wild scope of their natures. Since I am in Germany, all my little pathetic sadness and softness goes, and I am often frightened at the thing [originally 'savage'] I find myself.

Obviously this passage is a celebration of the delights of barbarism – of living beyond civility – though what's curious about it is the way Lawrence *socializes* love while at the same time denying social or civil values. It's as if the act of love becomes a revolutionary act against the English class system – indeed, against the whole of European civilization. And of course love across the barriers of class, culture, race, is often seen as a form of subversion.

What is fascinating about this letter is the way in which two voices play against each other in Lawrence's rapid sentences – the voice we hear in that phrase 'it's a rum place' is distinctively English in its attitude of decent, slightly ironic stoicism. The second voice is Frieda's – 'Since I am in Germany, all my little pathetic sadness and softness goes'. The syntax here isn't English ('*Seit Ich in Deutschland bin*', it would begin in German), and so this sentence, both in its grammatical structure and its content, expresses a very different attitude. It's almost as though the entire von Richthofen family is speaking in a bad translation here. The spirit of Nietzsche and of Prussian militarism has momentarily possessed Lawrence.

Another significant influence which modified Lawrence's Englishness was that of Synge, whose work he read during the Croydon years. *Riders to the Sea*, Lawrence said, 'is about the genuinest bit of dramatic tragedy, English, since Shakespeare, I should say'. And in a letter to Garnett he states:

I believe that, just as an audience was found in Russia for Tchekov, so an audience might be found in England for some of my stuff, if there were a man to whip 'em in. It's the producer that is lacking, not the audience. I'm sure we are sick of the rather bony, bloodless drama we get nowadays – it is time for a reaction against Shaw and Galsworthy and Barker and Irishy (except Synge) people – the rule and measure mathematical folk. But you are of them and your sympathies are with your own generation, not with mine. I think it is inevitable. You are about the only man who is willing to let a new generation come in. It will seem a bit rough to me, when I am 45, and must see myself and my tradition supplanted. I shall bear it very badly. Damn my impudence, but don't dislike me. But I don't want to write like Galsworthy nor Ibsen, nor Strindberg nor any of them, *not* even if I could. We have to hate our immediate predecessors, to get free from their authority.

That last recommendation – 'We have to hate our immediate predecessors, to get free from their authority' – is in several ways connected with the admiration of Synge which Lawrence expresses early in the letter. This is because Lawrence and Synge both deal with essentially Oedipal conflicts between a passionate instinct for freedom and a Law which they see as imposed, as not belonging to the essential conditions of life. Thus Synge praises the natural *sprezzatura* of the Aran islanders like this:

The absence of the heavy boot of Europe has preserved to these people the agile walk of the wild animal, while the general simplicity of their lives has given them many other points of physical perfection. Their way of life has never been acted on by anything much more artificial than the nests and burrows of the creatures that live round them, and they seem in a certain sense to approach more nearly to the finer types of our aristocracies – who are bred artificially to a natural ideal – than to the labourer or citizen, as the wild horse resembles the thoroughbred rather than the hack or cart-horse. Tribes of the same natural development are, perhaps, frequent in half-civilised countries, but here a touch of the refinement of old societies is blended, with singular effect, among the qualities of the wild animal.

This is Yeats's 'dream of the noble and the beggarman' and it is accompanied by a celebration of passionate rage, a rage which is nevertheless a communal activity: 'This grief of the keen is no personal complaint for the death of one woman over eighty years, but seems to contain the whole passionate rage that lurks some-where in every native of the island.' And describing an eviction Synge writes: 'these mechanical police, with the commonplace agents and sheriffs, and the rabble they had hired, represented aptly enough the civilisation for which the homes of the island were to be desecrated.' Were Synge not an influence upon Lawrence, we might describe this remark – especially the words 'mechanical', 'rabble', 'civilisation' – as clearly Lawrentian in tone. The quality both writers share is also apparent in the folk tale which Synge described and which provided the immediate inspiration for *The Playboy of the Western World*:

Another old man, the oldest on the island, is fond of telling me anecdotes – not folk-tales – of things that have happened here in his lifetime.

He often tells me about a Connaught man who killed his father with the blow of a spade when he was in passion, and then fled to the island and threw himself on the mercy of some of the natives with whom he was said to be related. They hid him in a hole – which the old man has shown me – and kept him safe for weeks, though the police came and searched for him, and he could hear their boots grinding on the stones over his head. In spite of a reward which was offered, the island was incorruptible, and after much trouble the man was safely shipped to America.

This impulse to protect the criminal is universal in the west. It seems partly due to the association between justice and the hated English jurisdiction, but more directly to the primitive feeling of these people, who are never criminals yet always capable of crime, that a man will not do wrong unless he is under the influence of a passion which is as irresponsible as a storm on the sea. If a man has killed his father, and is already sick and broken with remorse, they can see no reason why he should be dragged away and killed by the law.

Such a man, they say, will be quiet all the rest of his life, and if you suggest that punishment is needed as an example, they ask, 'Would any one kill his father if he was able to help it?'

Some time ago, before the introduction of police, all the people of the islands were as innocent as the people here remain to this day. I have heard that at that time the ruling proprietor and magistrate of the north island used to give any man who had done wrong a letter to a jailor in Galway, and send him off by himself to serve a term of imprisonment.

The conflict, clearly, is between artificial civil law and natural passion, between Pentheus and Dionysus, and Lawrence gives this an extreme expression in 'The Prussian Officer', where the young orderly's 'blind, instinctive sureness of movement' is contrasted with the officer's harsh rigidity. It is his celebration of this wild and lawless principle which makes Lawrence an essentially un-English writer, and some idea of this other identity can be perceived in a wry and gentle short story by V. S. Pritchett called 'The Fig Tree'.

The story is told by a nurseryman who remarks, 'It is well known, if you run a nursery, that very nice old ladies sometimes nip off a stem for a cutting or slip small plants in their bags. Stealing is a form of flirtation with them.' And then he reflects on this delicately erotic situation:

There was a myth at our Nursery that when a box of plants was missing or some rare expensive shrub had been dug up and was gone, this was the work of a not altogether imaginary person called Thompson who lived in a big house where the garden abutted on our wall. Three camellias went one day, and because of the price he was somehow promoted by the girls and became known as 'Colonel' Thompson. He had been seen standing on a stepladder and looking over our wall.

In mythic terms this thief, the not-altogether-imaginary person called Thompson, is Autolycus, and what's fascinating about this passage is the way it demonstrates how a naturally lawless principle can be easily accommodated within the English class system. When Thompson daringly steals something enormous – three camellias – he is immediately promoted to Colonel, and so Autolycus becomes an English gentleman who somehow exists both within and beyond the law. Lawrence's opposition between the officer and his Dionysian servant is wittily circumvented. It's a curiously Burkean perception.

As a nonconformist, Lawrence cannot rest content with this type of evasive Anglican compromise. He believes in a romantic puritan ethic of 'sincerity and a quickening spontaneous emotion' and rejects the idea of reserve. Partly this issues from that dissenting chapel-culture which Matthew Arnold so disdained, but it must also be an expression of that new climate of feeling and behaviour which George Dangerfield examines in *The Strange Death of Liberal England*. One of the starkest examples of this is the end of 'The Fox', where the young soldier allows a tree to fall on March's possessive companion, Banford. Human relationships, for Lawrence, are a form of bloodsport in which the weakest are destroyed, and his savage puritan romanticism might be summed up in the remark with which Heathcliff justifies his treatment of Isabella Linton: 'I have no pity! I have no pity! The more the worms writhe, the more I learn to crush out their entrails! It is a moral teething.'

Although Lawrence's enormous hatreds appear to belong to a Nuremberg rally, it might be more accurate to regard them as distinctively neo-colonial. Synge's Christy Mahon, for example, is a Parnell-figure who tries to strike the father dead and is then turned on and betrayed by his supporters, while Lawrence's Oedipal hatred of the establishment is that of someone who feels that he belongs to another country, or at least to a disadvantaged culture. It expresses something more than class antagonism and is perhaps an extreme form of puritan individualism. And in arguing that the 'big wild scope' of human nature is something which the English 'fence off', Lawrence has moved outside the pale into Synge's western world or into a German cult of the *völkisch*.

Lawrence embodies a Cromwellian opposition to formality, and this is one reason why his work appeals to Leavisite puritans rather than to Oxford scholar-critics. For example, Lawrence would reject vehemently this characteristically Oxford remark of Anthony Cockshut's: 'reticence is so undeniably necessary to civilised life, since without it the whole idea of what is fitting is lost'. Commenting on this statement, Russell Davies has remarked that it represents

the extremely English concept, widespread throughout our society, though most Europeans would call it aristocratically conservative, of appropriateness as an ideal in itself – the notion that situations impose their own moral order, and that to respect this, and to pattern one's behaviour accordingly, is to make one's optimum contribution to the health of civilisation. By this creed, there is a decorum beyond decorum, beyond convention; its demands are unspoken, and its essence is tact.

Lawrence is fundamentally opposed to decorum and convention – reticence is merely priggishness for him – and he everywhere insists on the untactful expression of personal emotion. Preaching out of an evangelical culture of moral fervour and plain speaking, he often resembles a demonic version of John Bunyan. In a sense he has succeeded in internationalizing that world of nonconformist provincialism which offended Arnold so deeply.

One of the most damaging results of Lawrence's insistence on intense experience is that his work is regarded as a body of doctrine which compels a moral assent. His writings are seldom discussed in a formal aesthetic manner, and Lawrence is seen throughout as a preacher who exhorts us to live. The work, therefore, can only be discussed by making 'life' into a critical term – which is what Leavis does – and this means that critical writing about Lawrence is often comically and stupendously naïve.

To take one example, in an essay on the short stories D. Kenneth M. Mackenzie points shrewdly to the parallels between Lawrence's 'You Touched Me' and *Washington Square*. However, he concludes by expressing a preference for Lawrence's story on the grounds that James's novel 'resigns itself to a spinsterish fortitude'. Once you accept the Lawrentian imperative of experience, then you have to believe that married people are somehow morally better than spinsters or bachelors (puritanism is traditionally hostile to the unmarried and the celibate). It also means that when you reach one of the decisive tests of literary sensibility – the end of *Washington Square* – you are bound to fail precisely because you judge Catherine Sloper to be a failure. That last sentence – 'Catherine, meanwhile, in the parlour, picking up her morsel of fancywork, had seated herself with it again – for life, as it were' – is a life sentence, but it is not what Lawrence or Leavis mean by life. It has nothing to do with some managerial notion of positive thinking or with the insistence that it is everyone's moral duty to have sexual experience, or any form of experience.

Looking through the shelf upon shelf of Lawrence criticism, I've begun to realize that his critics believe that he wasn't an artist at all – instead, he was an inspired natural genius whose experiences simply fell out onto the page. In his study of *The Prussian Officer*, for example, Keith Cushman draws these moral lessons from the stories. 'Odour of Chrysanthemums' is a 'moving statement about the human condition', and the two lovers in 'Daughters of the Vicar' embody 'the human salvation available through the dark mystery of the body'. In a rare aesthetic judgement, Cushman remarks that the 'highly visible symbolic framework' of the chrysanthemums is 'perhaps a little overdone'. However, he fails to notice that when the flowers make their last appearance – one of the men carrying the miner's body into the room knocks the vase over – Lawrence is deliberately killing off his leitmotif with a neat self-conscious flourish (that vase of chrysanthemums is resurrected in Virginia Woolf's 'The Shooting Party', which is obviously inspired by Lawrence and Synge).

Again, although Cushman makes the important point that *Riders to the Sea* helped Lawrence shape his story, he must retreat from the idea of tradition, culture and conscious craft which this implies by adding, 'nevertheless the main creative impulse came from Lawrence's own experience'. Here, Cushman is attempting to be true to what he believes is Lawrence's ethic and actual artistic practice, for to the romantic critic experience is all, and art is mere dishonest artifice. By identifying experience with the imagination, Cushman suggests that as an artist Lawrence was complete and entire unto himself – he didn't need to learn from anyone else. Yet, as Cushman has discovered, 'Odour of Chrysanthemums' went through *five* major revisions – Lawrence didn't rest content with the first published version but continued to alter, change and perfect it. And perhaps at last he felt able to pare his fingernails like Joyce's aesthetic god.

Lawrence's story is remarkable for its formal perfection, for the manner in which he develops the irony of Elizabeth Bates's remarks:

'But he needn't come rolling in here in his pit-dirt, for *I* won't wash him.'

'They'll bring him when he does come – like a log. And he may sleep on the floor till he wakes himself. I know he'll not go to work tomorrow after this.'

'No! – I expect he's stuck in there.'

These ironies are drawn together when the body is at last brought home and one of the children shouts down, 'Is he drunk?' With great sureness, Lawrence builds a sense both of narrative inevitability and ordinary event – a stagnant afternoon, routine actions, waiting and foreboding. And then, as Elizabeth goes to enquire of her neighbours, there is this tense and evasive narrative uncertainty – do the neighbours know or suspect that there's been an accident? Why are they so furtive, helpful, rather embarrassed? Are they really trying to avoid her? And the manager's remark when the body is brought home – 'He'd no business to ha' been left' – throws us back to Rigley's self-justifying speech:

'Ah left 'im finishin' a stint,' he began. 'Loose-all 'ad bin gone about ten minutes when we com'n away, an' I shouted "Are ter comin', Walt?" an' 'e said, "Go on, Ah shanna be but a'ef a minnit," se we com'n ter th' bottom, me an' Bowers, thinkin' as 'e wor just behint, an' 'ud come up i' th' next bantle—' He stood perplexed, as if answering a charge of deserting his mate. Elizabeth Bates, now again certain of disaster, hastened to reassure him.

Though they are in no way derivative, Lawrence's delight in Rigley's dialect and the fatalism that is felt here and throughout the story owe much to *Riders to the Sea*. What is unusual is the way in which Lawrence appears to have set his puritan belief in personal destiny and individual salvation aside and to be inspired by a pagan fatalism.

However, to talk of Lawrence's debt to other writers, to notice his irony and his delight in conscious art is — at least in the lost world of Lawrence studies — to entirely miss the point. For the Lawrentian critic all that matters is the 'doctrine', and this turns out to be merely a few catchphrases about the 'dark mystery of the body' and 'wonderful naked intimacy'. Lawrence the man is Lawrence the artist; his prose style is the biological energy of the life-force, the expression of pure, natural, original inspiration. Here, then, is one of the greatest English short story writers, and yet there is hardly a critical book on the stories (Lawrentian critics find the novels a much softer option, and this softness has spread far and wide over the academic study of literature with terrible destructive consequences).

In my view, one of Lawrence's most formally satisfying short stories is 'Samson and Delilah', a story that was surely inspired as much by *The Playboy of the Western World* as by the fluid gods of experience. Synge's play and the story share similar settings — a dark Celtic night, a man arriving at a lonely pub near the sea, the woman who keeps the bar, his relationship with her, her urging the men in the bar to tie him up. Lawrence uses the adjective 'celtic' several times in the story and he does so for reasons which any Cornish nationalist would approve. This imaginative territory is outside the pale, another country like Northtrentland. And its different ethic emerges when the sergeant reflects on Nankervis's return:

'A dirty action,' said the sergeant, his face flushing dark. 'A dirty action, to come after deserting a woman for that number of years, and want to force yourself on her! A dirty action – as isn't allowed by the law.'

This speech is made, significantly, at closing time, the time when the law tries to control Bacchus. Nankervis replies, 'Never you mind about law nor nothing,' and here he speaks like one of Synge's peasants. In *The Aran Islands* Synge describes the islanders' hostility to the law, and in *Playboy of the Western World* the widow Quin says to Christy's father, 'Let you give him a good vengeance when you come up with him, but don't put yourself in the power of the law, for it'd be a poor thing to see a judge in his black cap reading out his sentence on a civil warrior the like of you.' Like Nankervis, Synge's characters scorn or refuse to recognize the law.

Subtly, Lawrence shows Mrs Nankervis using legality as a weapon against her husband. Concealing her personal anger against him, she calls out in a bright businesslike voice, 'Time, please. Time, my dears. And good-night all!' He then sets this vocal tone against a more personal tone as Nankervis refuses to obey what he terms 'orders' and leave:

'I'm stopping here tonight,' he said, in his laconic Cornish-Yankee accent.
The landlady seemed to tower. Her eyes lifted strangely, frightening.
'Oh! indeed!' she cried. 'Oh, indeed! And whose orders are those, may I ask?'
He looked at her again.
'My orders,' he said.
Involuntarily she shut the door, and advanced like a great, dangerous bird. Her voice rose, there was a touch of hoarseness in it.
'And what might *your* orders be, if you please?' she cried. 'Who might *you* be, to give orders, in the house?'
He sat still, watching her.
'You know who I am,' he said. 'At least, I know who you are.'
'Oh, you do? Oh, do you? And who am *I* then, if you'll be so good as to tell me?'
He stared at her with his bright, dark eyes.
'You're my Missis, you are,' he said. 'And you know it, as well as I do.'
She started as if something had exploded in her.
Her eyes lifted and flared madly.
'*Do* I know it, indeed!' she cried. 'I know no such thing! I know no such

thing! Do you think a man's going to walk into this bar and tell me off-hand I'm his Missis, and I'm going to believe him?'

Really, this is an operatic passage – the anger on her part is furious and intense, and yet what is taking place between them is a form of courtship. Like lovers in an opera, they are conscious of their audience – ' "Yes," *sang* the landlady, slowly shaking her head in supreme sarcasm.' The young soldiers look on 'in delight', the sergeant smokes 'imperturbed'. When Nankervis is seized by his wife and she and the soldiers tie him up there is a curious description of the couple swaying together like a 'frightful Laocoon' (so the woman is a sea serpent, the man is Laocoon, who offended Apollo by marrying and having children). The rope is the Law, is Justice, because Nankervis is being punished – at least this symbolism holds true until he frees himself and we learn that the rope is made of 'a kind of plaited grass' which soon frays and breaks. It has associations with natural magic, with the plaits tied round corn stooks or haystacks (in Irish such a rope is a *sugan*). Until this point the rope is punitive, the instrument of Nankervis's humiliation and apparent rejection by his wife. Yet paradoxically she is also laying claim to him – the door which she shut 'involuntarily' earlier is surprisingly unbolted.

Also, if their first argument is a form of courtship, the tying-up is a form of marriage service with the sergeant deputizing for the priest. Afterwards, when they're reunited in the kitchen and Nankervis uses the variously ambiguous phrase 'I take you', we can almost hear the by now extremely ironic words 'as my lawful wedded wife'.

Thus we witness a ceremony, a form of decorum, and see that their experience has a natural pattern. In the end, it's a comic story with a wonderfully banal love-speech from Nankervis which insists on being read ironically – Nankervis's coarse cloying 'mindless' stupidity, his macho weakness and almost clucking admiration are beautifully created. However, at least one Lawrentian critic I've read sees Nankervis as the perfect epitome of natural aristocracy, a moral lesson to follow. For such critics – they are numerous and influential – Lawrence's work is remarkable for an inchoate intensity, and not for a formal beauty, a ceremonial irony. It's a rum do, Lawrence criticism.

Formal Pleasure: The Short Story

Although there are no great short stories which aspire to be novels, there are great novels which dream of becoming short stories. In the last paragraph of *Middlemarch*, for example, the epic narrative disappears into an invisible short story. Dorothea Brooke's

finely-touched spirit had still its fine issues, though they were not widely visible. Her full nature, like that river of which Cyrus broke the strength, spent itself in channels which had no great name on the earth. But the effect of her being on those around her was incalculably diffusive: for the growing good of the world is partly dependent on unhistoric acts; and that things are not so ill with you and me as they might have been, is half owing to the number who lived faithfully a hidden life, and rest in unvisited tombs.

Here, we have a fine and poignant definition of the different ambitions of the two forms. Where the short story, in Frank O'Connor's argument, deals with a 'submerged population group', has never had a hero, and often has an atmosphere of 'intense loneliness', the novel depends on figures like Dorothea who appear 'widely visible' both to the reader and to society. The novelist believes that there is a shaping, mutually sustaining relationship between the individual and history, while the short story writer is an unillusioned quietist who describes the hidden lives of powerless people. In his eyes, the novel is a trendy, optimistic, slapdash form held together by the affairs of history men and history women, while the short story, like the rest of us, is powerless before what happens to happen.

When Dorothea is presented as a failed public figure she quits the society of the novel and joins that submerged population from which the short story draws its characters. Yet George Eliot cannot quite let go of that Whig interpretation of history which sustains the

Review of Walter Allen, *The Short Story in English*.

nineteenth-century novel. Although Dorothea disappears into the private life, she has still somehow the power to influence history – her actions may be 'unhistoric' but they are nonetheless contributions to progress. In her ordinary social and domestic life she assists 'the growing good of the world'. It's as though we are asked to believe that the National Health Service was created not by political action but by small subscriptions of individual decency over a long period of time. On one level, the tantalizing ghostly conclusion of *Middlemarch* advances a nineteenth-century liberal argument for private philanthropy, and a 1980s version of the story would stress the monetarist case for the importance of the private sector. George Eliot clings to this argument because to relinquish it is to question the very existence of the novel form – a form which assumes that there is a hot-line connecting the individual to history. To doubt the novel is to doubt the optimistic assumptions of liberal humanism which, in George Eliot's intriguing formulation, traces historic influence back to certain overgrown and 'unvisited' graves in Highgate cemetery.

In a fascinating essay, 'The End of the Novel', Mandelstam sets the novel form against the Russian political experience of the first two decades of this century and argues that the novel is no longer viable. He suggests that the flourishing of the novel in the nineteenth century must be viewed as 'directly dependent on the Napoleonic epos' which caused 'the stock value of the individual in history to rise in an extraordinary manner'. Thus the 'typical biography of Bonaparte, the aggressive man of destiny', was scattered throughout Balzac's work in dozens of 'novels of success'. Writing in the mid-1920s, Mandelstam argues that this individualistic confidence is anachronistic:

It is clear that when we entered the epoch of powerful social movements and organised mass actions, both the stock value of the individual in history and the power and influence of the novel declined, for the generally accepted role of the individual in history serves as a kind of monometer indicating the pressure of the social atmosphere. The measure of the novel is human biography or a system of biographies. Very early on, the new novelist sensed that individual fate did not exist, and he attempted to uproot the social vegetation he needed, its entire root system, radicles and all. Thus the novel always suggests to us a system of phenomena controlled by a biographical connection and measured by a biographical measure.

Prophetically, Mandelstam announces that the future development of the novel will be 'no less than the history of the atomization of biography as a form of personal existence', and he adds that we shall also witness 'the catastrophe of biography'. He concludes:

Today Europeans are plucked out of their own biographies, like balls out of the pockets of billiard tables . . . A man devoid of biography cannot be the thematic pivot of the novel, while the novel is meaningless if it lacks interest in an individual, human fate, in a plot and all its auxiliary motifs. What is more, the interest in psychological motivation (by which the declining novel so skilfully sought to escape, already sensing its impending doom) is being radically undermined and discredited by the growing impotence of psychological motives in the confrontation with the forces of reality, forces whose reprisals against psychological motivation become more cruel by the hour.

Mandelstam's argument is that history has overwhelmed both the individual and the novel, and so we can no longer credit the novelist's assumption of a relation between the finely touched spirit and the growing good of the world. By implication, this is the case for documentary writing (Solzhenitsyn's *Gulag Archipelago*, for example), for superrealist fiction and for the short story. It also comprehends the last great novel in English, *Ulysses*, because that epic work is formally very close to the temporal restrictions of the short story – everything is concentrated into a single day. And, significantly, *Ulysses* began life as an idea for a short story about a Dubliner called Hunter.

The short story writer severs the connections between individual biography and history, and offers the fictional equivalent of those moments 'in and out of time' which break over the 'unmoving' lines of *Four Quartets*. Thus the short story is a static form which dips out of the historical process and presents epiphanies, specks of time, or brief complete actions. A disadvantage here is that a collection of short stories can offer a surfeit of chill privacies – rather like a gallery full of Hopper's paintings. Indeed, Bernard Bergonzi has argued in a discussion of the short story appended to *The Situation of the Novel* that the form tends to 'filter down experience to the prime elements of defeat and alienation'. This is an arresting generalization but it is based on that confusion of art and life which vitiates a great deal of literary criticism and which must bear some responsibility for the current state of literary studies. Bergonzi writes as a critic of novels when he first praises the adroit style of a collection of stories by Sally Bingham and then expresses doubt about how far it is based on 'direct observation' and how far it relies 'perhaps unconsciously, on established literary models'. 'Direct observation', like the term 'accurate rendering', presupposes that *within* a fiction there is a distinction between reality and the writer's vision of reality which is his style. Thus the novel is considered to be a deep form which is full of 'life', while the short story is a superficial form which is all mere 'style' and is therefore very limited in its capacity to 'deepen our understanding of the world, or of one another'. Here the critic of the novel speaks as a vitalistic moralist who is hostile to pure art: the results of this attitude can be seen in the tedious moral paraphrase which constitutes much literary criticism.

Stylistic self-consciousness and a playful awareness of 'established literary models' are essential to the short story, and many famous short stories declare or imply their relation to certain predecessors. Thus James's 'The Beast in the Jungle' and Joyce's 'A Painful Case' have a common root in Maupassant's 'Regret', which is a story of an old bachelor who has 'never been loved' and who at last sits down under some leafless trees and weeps. Both stories resemble reply-poems in that they alter Maupassant's terms (John Marcher and James Duffy reject the love they are offered). Similarly, Lawrence's 'Samson and Delilah' is in part a tribute to Synge's *The Playboy of the Western World*, and 'Odour of Chrysanthemums' is a version of *Riders to the Sea*. Katherine Mansfield's 'Marriage à la Mode' is a reworking of Chekhov's 'The Grasshopper', and Frank O'Connor has a story called 'A Story by Maupassant'.

Maupassant's short stories have what Sean O'Faolain calls a 'whip-crack ending' – they first mobilize and then satisfy an appetency and on re-reading give only a dead or feeble pleasure. Nevertheless, Maupassant is one of the great masters of the form, and in that ruthlessly brilliant story 'Two Gallants' Joyce set himself the demanding task of bettering Maupassant. In his opening paragraph – crowded streets on a grey warm Sunday evening, lamps like 'illumined pearls' – Joyce designs an impressionist image of Dublin as Paris, and this prepares us for a quasi-Parisian story out of Maupassant which involves two seedy *flâneurs* and a girl 'slavey'. Joyce appears not to be concerned to tell a story – the two men, Lenehan and Corley, talk hollowly, and Lenehan seems anxious that his companion should help him in some unspecified manner. Corley boasts of his friendship with a girl who gives him cigarettes and cigars, and pays their tram fares. Corley then meets the girl; Lenehan wanders about the streets and later meets up with his friend. So far the story exists simply as a sketch of fringe lives in Dublin, and it's only at the very last moment that it springs a completed plot on the reader. Anxiously, Lenehan asks, ' "Can't you tell us? . . . Did you try her?" ' And immediately we are reading the last paragraph:

Corley halted at the first lamp and stared grimly before him. Then with a grave gesture he extended a hand towards the light and, smiling, opened it slowly to the gaze of his disciple. A small gold coin shone in the palm.

As in a story by Maupassant, there is that snap of recognition – Corley has carried out his unspecified promise to Lenehan by scrounging the coin from the girl, and we can understand this only when we have read the last sentence. However, this ending goes far beyond the cut-and-dried surprise at the end of a story by Maupassant. It is an imagistic, epiphanic conclusion which also glows with a suggestive symbolism – Corley as policeman, Lenehan as paid informer or Judas, the girl as a tawdry emblem of Ireland betrayed. That small gold coin is the vanishing point into which every element in the story rushes, for what at first appeared to be a drifting formless sketch is at the last moment given tense and perfect form. This is what Sean O'Faolain calls 'the eloquence of form', and it is a recognition that is instinct with a sense of joy and aesthetic redemption. This formal pleasure has nothing to do with naïve realism or with the 'accurate rendering' of experience.

Poe describes this aesthetic experience best in his famous review of Hawthorne's *Twice-Told Tales*, where he argues that in the 'brief tale' an artist is able to carry out 'the fullness of his intention'. He aims at a 'certain unique or *single* effect' and ensures that every word tends to 'the one pre-established design':

And by such means, with such care and skill, a picture is at length painted which leaves in the mind of him who contemplates it with a kindred art, a sense of the fullest satisfaction. The idea of the tale has been presented unblemished, because undisturbed; and this is an end unattainable by the novel.

Poe's aesthetic argument is close to our experience of 'Two Gallants', and his analogy with painting is inspiring, for it suggests that the literary critic must follow the art critic in discussing style, technique, form and tradition, rather than content, the achievement of 'felt life' or imaginative sympathy. In a discussion of the origins of the modern short story with which he opens his study *The Short Story in English*, Walter Allen draws a helpful quotation from Poe's review of Hawthorne and he also remarks interestingly on Flaubert's influence. By his exemplary dedication to his art, Flaubert stressed that treatment is 'almost everything' while subject is 'relatively unimportant'. For him, the 'capital difficulty' was 'style, form, the indefinable beauty, which is the result of the conception itself, and which is the splendour of truth, as Plato used to say'.

Although the characters in many short stories lack the social status which characters in a novel almost invariably possess, those in Lawrence's stories are often redeemed from isolation by their commitment to a relationship. Instead of existing permanently on the fringes of society, they acquire through that commitment the living confidence we associate with characters in a novel. In such stories as 'The Horse Dealer's Daughter', 'Fanny and Annie' and 'You Touched Me', the characters begin to emerge from that condition of fugitive downtrodden privacy which is the underground world of the short story. And like George Eliot in *Middlemarch*, Lawrence gives to his provincial characters a momentousness of treatment which never admits to any sense of inferiority about their relation to the capital.

Lawrence's stories have received scant critical attention. This is because critics ignore formal questions and fatuously concentrate on intensity and flux and on that doctrine of the dark mysteries of experience which the novels preach. Unfortunately, Walter Allen subscribes to this novelistic view when he states that most of the stories in *The Prussian Officer* are 'products of Lawrence's day-to-day experience in the Nottinghamshire and Derbyshire coalfields'. And Allen's mistaken belief that short stories are paraphrases of experience is responsible for a critical method which does little more than glue moral comment to expansive summaries of numerous stories. However, he quotes aptly, communicates a ripe sense of enjoyment, and discusses a wide range of writers – he pays a deserved tribute to Henry Lawson, though his exclusion of John McGahern is mystifying. In first tracing the beginnings of the modern short story to Scott's 'The Two Drovers' and then arguing for its influence on Mérimée's 'Matteo Falcone' he valuably gives the form a solid historical foundation which future critics must attend to. For it is only by combining formalism with the historical sense that literary studies can survive the deep-seated crisis of confidence which in their different ways Allen's study and the split in the Cambridge English Faculty represent.

Writing to the Moment: Elizabeth Bishop

The publication of Elizabeth Bishop's *Selected Letters* is a historic event, a bit like discovering a new planet or watching a bustling continent emerge, glossy and triumphant, from the blank ocean. Here is an immense cultural treasure being suddenly unveiled – and this hefty selection is only the beginning. Before the millennium is out, Bishop will be seen as one of this century's epistolary geniuses, like that modernist Victorian, Hopkins, whom she lovingly admired and learnt from.

Bishop was a compulsive correspondent (in one day's record binge she fired off forty letters) and her partying dedication to this supremely social craft hasn't simply extended letter-writing as an art form, it has also added a shimmering series of poems in prose to the canon of her work. Yet even as admirers and reviewers rush to start the necessary process of praising single letters and excerpting their many startling, bravura passages, some critical attention needs to be given to the art of letter-writing as Bishop practised and taught it.

Discussing 'my new seminar, on "Letters"!' with Arthur Gold and Robert Fizdale, she said the course would consist of 'just *letters* – as an art form or something. I'm hoping to select a nicely incongruous assortment of people – Mrs Carlyle, Chekhov, my Aunt Grace, Keats, a letter found in the street, etc. etc. But I need some ideas from you both – just on the subject of letters, the "dying form of communication".' In the Harvard course catalogue for 1971–72, her seminar was listed as '*English 2902. Conference Group: Letters – Readings in Personal Correspondence. Famous and Infamous, from the 16th to 20th Centuries.*' As Robert Giroux points out in his introduction, Bishop collected books of letters by Hopkins, Wilde, Woolf and many others, but it would be interesting to learn what

Review of Elizabeth Bishop, *One Art: The Selected Letters*, edited and introduced by Robert Giroux; and Elizabeth Bishop, *Collected Prose*.

critical works she included on the course's reading-list. Are there any such critical works? And is there a poetics of the familiar letter? Or do we simply enjoy a writer's published letters and then treat them as sources for biography and critical discussions of their literary works? Do letters possess what has been disdainfully termed 'literarity'? Or do they, as I believe is true, construct themselves on an anti-aesthetic, a refusal of the literary? Is their rhetoric a rejection of rhetoric in the interests of brief, in-the-moment, authentic certainties? Are letters not written against posterity as throwaway, disposable, flimsy unique holographs which aim to flower once and once only in the recipient's reading and then disappear immediately? The merest suspicion that the writer is aiming beyond the addressee at posterity freezes a letter's immediacy and destroys its spirit. Posterity – the gathered jury of posthumous readers – feels cheated and refuses to be impressed. What the posthumous reader desires is a privileged entrance to each text's primal, absolutely best performance, a cross-wired connection which is yet somehow random – what Charles Lamb in his essay 'Distant Correspondents' calls 'this grand solecism of *two presents*' where '*my Now*' collides with '*your Now*'.

In her youth, as Brett Millier shows in her pioneering biography *Elizabeth Bishop: Life and the Memory of It*, she experienced that solecistic collision as tragic when she received a postcard from a rejected male lover a few days after his suicide. The card read simply 'Go to hell, Elizabeth.' And after Bishop's death a letter arrived from Mary McCarthy denying in unconvincing detail that she had based Lakey in *The Group* on Bishop. Less drastically, in responding to published letters we need to take into consideration the relationship between writing and reception, and the dynamics of the relationship which existed between the correspondents. The long, competitive love which existed between Bishop and Lowell, the parabola of her relationship with Marianne Moore, are the best examples in *One Art* of this dynamic textuality. Very many letters derive their fascination from this type of dialogic energy – a momentary, sometimes momentous communicativeness that stretches them like soap bubbles sent blobbing up into the sunlight of unique, unrepeat-able relationships where each letter occurs as a historic moment whose taut nowness can be immensely exciting.

Within the tidal pull of the reading process, we do address these questions, even if they're seldom consciously or critically formulated; but more often letters are regarded simply as source material for the writer's literary work. In them can be discerned the seeds of future lines, images, whole poems. Thus the source for the images of gassy marine blueness and stoved boats in that brilliantly laidback poem 'The Bight' can be found in a letter to Lowell.

In the letter (15/1/48), Bishop writes: 'The water looks like blue gas – the harbour is always a mess, here, junky little boats all piled up, some hung with sponges and always a few half sunk or splintered up from the most recent hurricane. It reminds me a little of my desk.' But to treat this consummate sentence as simply a gloss on the poem, a 'nugget of description' as David Kalstone terms it in *Becoming a Poet*, where he cites part of the letter, is to diminish Bishop's prose by making it anterior to, and therefore also lesser than these slightly uneasy lines. 'Some of the little white boats are still piled up / against each other, or lie on their sides, stove in, / and not yet salvaged, if they ever will be, from the last bad storm / like torn-open, unanswered letters.' Rather we might note how in her prose the half-rhyme gas/mess helps structure the sentence, while the nimble phrasal rapidity of 'junky little boats all piled up,' and the complex of chiming sounds – junky/hung/sponges/sunk – tense the prose into an exact expressive arc. And we can also notice how she moves from the hurricane wreckage – she was fascinated by hurricanes – to the laconic, cunningly self-reflexive glance at the, it's implied, letters, abandoned poems and torn-open envelopes on her desk. In 'The Bight' this becomes the wittily Baudelairean line: 'The bight is littered with old correspondences.' Nature is strewn with tired symbols just as her desk is scattered with manuscripts and the detritus of the personal life. Yet the prose sentence isn't a staging-post towards the poem: it exists in its own right as a type of Imagist poem every bit as perfect as Pound's 'In a Station of the Metro'. It should therefore be accorded aesthetic autonomy – complete autonomy I nearly said, except that the letter as art form is based on the concept of impossible completion, and in any case the idea of the totally self-sufficient work of art is an aspiration not a reality. A letter is very often a me saying to a you 'this is the next best thing to us talking together'.

How privileged – and no doubt envious too – Lowell must have felt in reading this sentence written for him and no one else in the whole world. For a letter is an often-unexpected gift, a gift not bought but made especially for the recipient and therefore unrepeat-able, however the writer may recycle phrases in other letters or in subsequent poems. The sentence is Bishop's and hers alone, but it leaps out as if she is an actor or a dancer, inspired by the intelligence and attention of her audience of one. For there is – it scarcely needs emphasizing – a keenly performative element in the epistolary art, a mutuality which ought never to degenerate into a self-conscious cosiness or a mutual preening.

It's the achieving, even competitive element of mutuality and sharing which shapes this passage from a letter to Marianne Moore which Bishop wrote from Key West:

The houses here, with all their scrollwork that looks as if it were cut from paper, are very pretty, and everyone has rows of magnificent plants all across the railings of the lower verandahs. The little cottages where the Negroes live have the most gorgeous plants of all. The plants appear to have 'sapped the strength' of everything else in town. Down the street is a very small cottage I can look right into, and the only furniture it contains beside a bed and chair is an enormous French horn, painted silver, leaning against the wall, and hanging over it a pith helmet, also painted silver. The Negroes have such soft voices and such beautifully tactful manners – I suppose it is farfetched, but their attitude keeps reminding me of the *tone* of George Herbert: 'Take the gentle path,' etc.

Paper – like its 'binary' opposite hurricane – is one of Bishop's favourite images. Here it symbolizes the dwellings' 'frail improvis-ation', as Kalstone perceptively terms it in his commentary on 'Jerónimo's House', the poem that links with this passage, as well as embodying the fragile flimsiness of the sociable art of letter-writing and the blacks' vulnerable gentleness which reminds her of the opening of Herbert's 'Discipline': 'Throw away thy rod, / Throw away Thy wrath: / O my God, / Take the gentle path.' In 'Jerónimo's

House' the dwelling – like a wasps' nest of 'chewed-up paper' – contains an old French horn repainted with 'aluminum paint', writing-paper, 'lines of light', radio voices, four pink 'tissue-paper roses', and it is characterized as a shelter from 'the hurricane' which is nature's 'wrath' – a noun voiced with an *ah*-sound in black American and non-standard speech. But the hurricane we can tell by relating the poem and the letter also symbolizes both white violence and the approaching war. And when she identifies the gentle manners of the Key West blacks with the quietly spoken texture and profound sanctity of Herbert's poetry, Bishop is drawing two of her most cherished values together. Rooted in the deft, the patient energies of the speaking voice, her unobtrusively baroque aesthetic is deeply humane.

In her very helpful study *Elizabeth Bishop: The Biography of a Poetry*, Lorrie Goldensohn quotes a letter (13/3/65) which Bishop wrote to Grace Bulmer Bowers, in which she rebukes her favourite aunt for following southern opinion about Martin Luther King. Writing from Brazil, she informs Aunt Grace that she has no idea how the rest of the world feels 'about how the US treats its colored people – and particularly here, where there is no problem at all'. Then she tells a story from her days in Key West:

Don't forget I did live in the south. – My dear old laundress's (black) son was murdered by the Key West police because one of them wanted his wife. – Everyone knew this and nothing was done about it. The laundress was given her son's body in a coffin, straight from jail – She said 'I looked at his arm – Miss Elizabeth, – it wasn't an *arm* any more . . .'

This very revealing letter is not included in *One Art*, though in the absence of a complete canon of Bishop's letters it is unfair to criticize Giroux unduly for his selection. Even so, this omission is hard to explain. We glimpse her radicalism – her attitude to the Spanish Civil War for example – only fitfully, though it's cheering to note Bishop's contemptuous hatred for Governor Reagan. Every time she sees him on TV she plans to leave California immediately.

Another locus of absolute value which emerges in the letters is vegetation (the letter to Moore and 'Jerónimo's House' both celebrate her vegetable love, a love that is sometimes expressed by the gift of seeds). Writing to Moore from Brazil, Bishop says: 'Here are some seeds I've been saving for you since the tree bloomed last month – an enormous tall thin tree with a bright green trunk (like some of Rousseau's trees that have green trunks as well as leaves) with feathery plumes at the top and bright yellow flowers.' The improvisatory vegetal texture of this passage makes the tree – 'a *Sabotiera* – supposedly because the French made sabots from the wood' – seem to shoot up as she writes, while the comparison to one of Douanier Rousseau's paintings introduces another of the most important values in her humane aesthetic – primitive painting which she collected, wrote about and revered (notice how precisely she points to Rousseau's green trunks). The ferny 'love-nest' that is Jerónimo's house is one of her most delicate and assured studies in the naïve. Yet the existence of that poem does not relegate the epistolary passage which so clearly precedes it to a class of minor or secondary writings that simply minister to the poems. To argue this is not to assert the once-current idea that all is 'text' without value judgements – it is to point to a cultural space that critical theory may in time occupy. We need a poetics of the familiar letter, as we need a wider poetics of prose style, and it is crucial to notice that Bishop began to reflect on prose style in the letters she wrote and the notebook entries she made while an undergraduate at Vassar.

At the age of twenty-two, she read Maurice Croll's classic essay 'The Baroque Style in Prose' – it was first published in 1929 – and quoted extensively from it in a letter (20/11/33) to the poet Donald Stanford where she begins to elaborate her theory of poetry (unfortunately Giroux doesn't print this letter in full). As Lorrie Goldensohn shows in *Elizabeth Bishop: The Biography of a Poetry*, she also transcribed passages from Croll's essay into her notebooks. She was drawn to Croll's discussion of the means by which baroque prose writers aim to portray 'not a thought, but a mind thinking', and she would have been attracted to the parallels he draws between this prose style and the visual arts, El Greco especially. Discussing the 'curt period', Croll says that it aims at an energetic, upward, spiralling movement of mind, because the baroque writers knew that an idea separated from the act of experiencing it 'is not the idea that was experienced'. This idea of expressive motion, a paradoxical form of always-unfinished processive completeness or constantly deferred closure, underlies Bishop's poems and the letter form as she practised it. The result is an ontological style where ideas are not fixed and complete – existing somewhere *out there* – but are instead experienced here and now as part of a process, part of the writer expressing her being-in-the-world, her sense of *Dasein*. In rejecting polished Ciceronian periods, the baroque writer aims to embody 'the nerves and muscles of speech alone'. Such writers deny that a sentence's only mode of progression is 'the logical one' and aim instead at a revolving, upward motion of the mind 'as it rises in energy' and views the same point 'from new levels'. This spiral movement, Croll argues, is a characteristic of baroque prose. Disdaining revision, these writers depend upon 'casual and emergent devices of construction', broken symmetry, a progression that adapts itself to the movement of a mind 'discovering truth as it goes'. As a description of the epistolary form this is accidentally quite just and accurate, and Croll's essay stayed with Bishop as a talismanic value all her life.

If we apply this concept to Bishop's letters, we can see that she aims always at an impromptu spoken texture so that she is imaginatively inside, enwrapped by, what she is saying, rather like an action painter working furiously within, not outwith a canvas. So writing to two of her dearest friends, Kit and Ilse Barker, she wishes she could sit down to some tea 'right this minute because as you see I have a sort of talking jag on'. This is the most succinct image for her letters, because rather like one of her drinking-bouts these talking jags express and enact her addictive communicativeness, her aim to achieve an illusion of complete immediacy. In this she follows Samuel Richardson, who famously defined his epistolary method through Lovelace's remark in a letter to his male confidant: 'I love to write to the moment.' In *Pamela* and *Clarissa*, Richardson develops a puritan anti-aesthetic of artless naturalness and authenticity. Like Defoe and Bunyan, he disguises his artfulness while expressing, as they do, the almost unbearable intensity of the moment, the now, of consciousness. He lets the free individual conscience loose in an intensely dramatic manner, and indeed his definition of the epistolary method derives from the experience of theatrical performance (as well as being an epic figure partly based on Milton's Satan, Lovelace also belongs in a dark Restoration comedy where he is both character and actor). In letters – and Richardson understood this with a guilty, fascinated anxiety – the self wears the mask of the performing self, making an artful naturalness seem artless, as though self and mask are the same.

Bishop's puritan temperament – what she called the 'New Englander herring-choker bluenoser' in her – seizes on the letter form because like the sermon and the journal it expresses that culture with its ethic of the true, the real, the directly representational. This ethic she both recognized and at times distanced herself from, as when she remarks in her memoir of Marianne Moore, 'Efforts of Affection', that at times Moore's 'scrupulous and strict honesty could be carried to extremes of Protestant, Presbyterian, Scotch-Irish literalness that amazed me'. In the poem 'Seascape' with its Calvinist lighthouse, Bishop also ironizes puritanism, whose work ethic she lightly alludes to in her description of letter-writing as 'kind of like working without really doing it'.

Scribbling on an airmail form is a self-subverting act, so when she remarks to Moore that the mail from Rio de Janeiro to Petropolis – a distance of less than forty miles – often takes two weeks, she then immediately adds that this isn't a complaint about the mails because they are part of 'the really lofty vagueness of Brazil . . . where a cloud is coming in my bedroom window right this minute'. The cloud entering the bedroom window right this minute – write to the moment – adds a perfectly calculated, Magritte-like fogginess to her remark (the three dots, we assume, are Bishop's and not the identical three dots of elision which Giroux annoyingly employs to signal that he has cut a passage). By introducing a cloud at this point, Bishop simultaneously gives aesthetic form to her perception and changes the framing effect into a self-consuming process that literally comes out of the frame to obliterate everything.

Writing again to Moore from Naples, Florida – lovely place-name

– Bishop marries topographical description with a similar idea of the pointlessness of the letter-form:

On the way down we took a very slow train from Jacksonville here. All day long it went through swamps and turpentine camps and palm forests and in a beautiful pink evening it began stopping at several little stations. The stations were all off at a tangent from the main track and it necessitated first going by, then stopping, backing up, stopping, starting again – with many puffs of white smoke, blowings of the whistle, advice from the loiterers around the station – all to throw off one limp bag of mail.

With its beautifully assonantal swamps/turpentine camps/palms, this may be the first faint glimmer of her poem 'Florida', yet it exists in its own right as a fable-like symbolic cameo which is more than topographical description, more than 'all this accumulation of exotic or picturesque or charming detail' whose presence in her writing Bishop later confided to Lowell might make her become a poet who 'can only write about South America'. She wants to 'use everything' and keep on living in Brazil while remaining a New Englander at the same time (the South American Church gives her 'deep Protestant shudders'), and she is anxious that Moore will think that she has once again 'presented myself as the grasshopper-type girl, but you know I have a *serious nature*, really, Marianne. I can't help letting these details, however inappropriate, distract and entertain me.' Note that verb 'presented' – this is the inky self performing on its paper stage, writing itself into existence with the help of a highly intelligent audience of one.

If the concept of performative self-presentation is part of the epistolary aesthetic, so too is the term 'detail' – *deTAIL* in emphatic American speech – because for the baroque imagination it is the manner of any detail's presentation which is as important as the thing itself, even supposing that it could ever be isolated as a discrete entity independent of the manner in which it is stylistically experienced. Here the closing lines of her favourite Herbert poem, 'Love Unknown', illustrate the effect she sought:

> Wherefore be cheered, and praise Him to the full
> Each day, each hour, each moment of the week,
> Who fain would have you be, new, tender, quick.

Introducing a wholly unexpected stress on 'new' in the last line, Herbert twists the routine iambics into a novel and surprising baroque rhythm which breaks the iambic mould in order to release the quickened Christian spirit.

It is this spirit of newness and nowness Bishop seeks always in her letters, and it has as much to do with the pulsing energy of her style as with the many 'true' and 'real' details she flourishes within that style. Trueness and realness are fundamentally important to her as a bluenoser (the blue snail shells in 'Crusoe in England' she emphatically and excitedly told an interviewer were 'true'), but they belong within the provisional architecture of her prose – a prose that grows energetically, stretching itself out like vines, creepers, lianas, or shooting up like the green sappy italicized – therefore new tender quick – tree called *Sabotiera*. So when she twice mentions 'paper' in constructing the perishable clapboard of Jerónimo's house, she is drawing attention to the random, fugitive, ephemeral nature of the epistolary form – like Jerónimo's tissue-paper roses – as well as to the fragile nature of the house itself – a flexible writerly dwelling (unlike Yeats's stiff tower) which is both an ontological symbol and an emblem of the improvisatory throwaway aesthetic of letter writing: 'END. I loathe these airmail-letter forms. Now to see if I can fold it.' Rather like Różewicz's 'The poem / is finished / now to break it', this enforced closure is part of the act, part of its theatrical presence, its bursting nowness, as well as being a sweeping external gesture that empowers itself by cancelling what has just been said.

On the other hand, this final paragraph in an early letter to Frani Blough is deliberately overdone and campy:

Methinks that Frani needs refreshing, so let us repair to the farewell or closure. Taps – after fleeting shades of purple, blue marigold, and burnt henna have given way to deep, deep night blue. The sunsets are glorious. Oh, and here is a sample of female correspondence from *Diana of the Crossways*. (Just as I went to get the book, Judy called up – we're going to be in the poorhouse with these long-distance calls. And it's Saturday, not Friday, and she was about to go to the movies with Peggy): 'I am shattered, and I wait panting for a reply. I have no more time (space), it is my life I cry for. This is your breast,' my Frani! Come!!

Though it's self-consciously theatrical, this is doubly and brilliantly spontaneous as she goes to get *Diana of the Crossways* and the phone rings making her prose spiral into the final exclamation. This is writing to the moment within the moment within the moment, because what Bishop aims always to represent is 'that intense consciousness' or 'momentary concentration of sensation' which she also seeks in her verse.

These two paragraphs from another letter to Frani Blough from New York are perfectly to the moment in their concentration and intensity:

I've been back since last Wednesday, camping out in an apartment devoid of furniture, gas, ice, and hooks to hang things on. Telephone and ice are supposed to arrive this afternoon, but I see no signs of them and losing one's temper to make people do things is too much to expect in this weather. Margaret and her mother feed me now and then, otherwise I'd dry up & starve. I saw Mary & John at Margaret's the night I came back, and then they went off for a most mysterious weekend in Yonkers. Margaret and I believe that they are visiting the shady Mr. Russek in his hideaway – he's wanted by the police just now on two or three different charges. Mary wouldn't say where she was going, just feebly excused herself with 'Oh, it's so *comic*.'

Ah, the telephone man just arrived and is now taking off his coat and rolling up his sleeves to get to work. The prospect of actually getting in touch with anyone by such a simple and civilized expedient will be a little too much for me, I'm afraid . . . I have to buy a piece of furniture a month and the problem is, which is more necessary to my hospitality, two chairs or a table? I hope you'll come to see me often. The telephone man is running up against all sorts of difficulties – he can't find the spot where the telephone is meant to come into the place. He's crawling in the closet with a flashlight just now. Now he's gone over to see the landlord, leaving me to guard his discarded clothing.

This is the young Bishop writing tersely decisive prose – those packed firm stresses in 'furniture, gas, ice, and hooks to hang things on' – while at the same time describing in a Richardsonian manner the arrival of the telephone engineer, that facilitator of yet more communication (some six years later she began the practice of making miserable drunken late-night phone calls to her friends). In these paragraphs the detail and the drama are perfect and complementary – what we see is Bishop constructing her living-space even as she writes. Her being-in-the-world must be affirmed through letter-writing, and although we can identify most of the characters ('Mary' is Mary McCarthy, 'John' her first husband Harold Johnsrud, 'Margaret' Bishop's friend Margaret Miller), the letter is more vivid – more 'found' or random – if they remain freefloating, unidentified characters like the shady and mysterious Mr Russek. It's a movie-like moment, maybe some comic or slightly bizarre black-and-white detective thriller where the gas, the ice, the phone, the closet hooks, are empirical details which aspire to be moments of ontic inscription even as they express the rawness of setting up on your own in an apartment in the big city. It's poised between comedy and a threatening newness and strangeness, as the aspirant writer sets out in life, riding the raft of what's happening right here, 'just now'.

This letter to Frani Blough has an exacting decision in its style and attitude, but what we very often prize in letters is a zany spontaneity, a randomness of being alongside a vulnerable, risky, disposable, chancy or chanced-upon quality – that 'letter found in the street' Bishop included in her Harvard course.

Unfortunately, Giroux's cropping of many of the letters in the selection works to prevent that impromptu quality which is also present in the boxes made by an artist Bishop greatly admired – Joseph Cornell – who practised what he termed a 'metaphysics of ephemera' and created what Bishop in her translation of Octavia Paz's poem to Cornell, 'Objects & Apparitions', calls 'Monuments to every moment, / refuse of every moment, used: / cages for infinity', lines that also recall Jerónimo's papery house. For some reason I can't fathom, this sentence from a letter she wrote from Spain in May 1936 takes on an epiphanic force and vividness, a type of 'found' or Cornellian quality that is still too deliberate to be purely random:

So we caught the bus back to Madrid, and after a very strange drive through miles of deep oily-blue-colored flowers, with a radio playing loudly in the ceiling of the bus, I arrived feeling very light-headed and went to the Poste Restante, where I found the *Pangolin*!

The *Pangolin* is Moore's new volume of poems, but for me those oily-blue flowers are the deep centre of this sentence's monument to a moment. Perhaps they stand out because blue is her favourite colour and because oil in her poems becomes the sacral chrism of dwelling and being, of *Dasein*? Or perhaps this is just one out of many painterly moments in *One Art*? Or the flowers may be simply but mysteriously one of those chance authentic details glimpsed on a journey – details which in the natural gesture of her style create that 'naked communication' she prized in Dylan Thomas's poetry? Or this could be a more successful version of a passage in another letter to Moore which Bishop wrote a few months later from Cape Cod:

A great many Portuguese Negroes live near me and come around in very high-set, polished old Fords selling blueberries and raspberries that go beautifully with their black faces and blue denim clothes.

This rather overdoes the blueness she prizes – to impress either Moore or posterity. Either way there is a too-glossy, heritage, self-conscious, rather patronizing quality to the image.

Again a much later letter to Moore from Brazil is too aesthetically self-conscious: 'But today the sea is so blue and the breakers so perfect, with pinkish rainbows showing over them diagonally here & there. Very few people on the beach, because it is "winter". – One man has a kite up, transparent bluish-gray with a white tail – it must be cellophane. It looks like something up out of the water itself. Here is Lota & I must fix us some lunch. She sends you her regards.' This is stilted – really because Bishop is postponing making comments on Moore's new book of poems, and this gives her style a slightly guilty evasiveness and an uneasy, marking-time effect. There is a listless, nervy, slightly forced atmosphere to the writing here, which in turn opens up almost limitless interpretative possibilities (no wonder the first and greatest psychological novelist in English chose the epistolary form for his infinitely subtle analyses of motive and feeling).

A rather different moment of self-consciousness occurs when she tells Moore that there have been

several more fringes of hurricanes for excitement. I was sure I had described waterspouts to you long ago – maybe I'll develop it a little, since I hadn't. They move across the surface of the water very rapidly and the water in the base of one looks white and foaming. (This is about one half a mile away, the closest to one I've been.) They are translucent and you can see the water or mist or whatever it is going up inside in puffs and clouds, very fast, just like smoke up a chimney – and the top of the chimney is lost in a storm cloud. They look particularly awesome on a calm bright day, of course.

Somehow this doesn't quite work, perhaps because it's too clinical, too undramatic and uninvolved. But the idea of the baroque spiral which she discovered in Croll's essay on prose style may be influencing her here, as well as this journal entry Hopkins made on 10 August 1872:

I was looking at high waves. The breakers always are parallel to the coast and shape themselves to it except where the curve is sharp however the wind blows. They are rolled out by the shallowing shore just as a piece of putty between the palms whatever its shape runs into a long roll. The slant ruck or crease one sees in them shows the way of the wind. The regularity of the barrels surprised and charmed the eye; the edge behind the comb or crest was as smooth and bright as glass. It may be noticed to be green behind and silver white in front: the silver marks where the air begins, the pure white is foam, the green/solid water. Then looked at to the right or left they are scrolled over like mouldboards or feathers or jibsails seen by the edge. It is pretty to see the hollow of the barrel disappearing as the white comb on each side runs along the wave gaining ground till the two meet at a pitch and crush and overlap each other.

Here Hopkins is searching for pattern in both nature and aesthetic perception – it is hard, he adds, for the eyes to 'unpack the huddling and gnarls of the water and law out the shapes and the sequence of the running'. Bishop, in less detail, is seeking to enact a baroque concept of spiralling motion which she prized in Hopkins's verse and prose, and she is also modelling her observation on Hopkins's highly stringent, almost cubist perceptiveness. She is not merely observing – she is searching out a natural figure for her style. It may be slightly picky to suggest that this passage is in a theatrical sense too 'cold' or prompted, but in registering an unease here I want to make the point that a poetics does operate when we read a letter and that we naturally feel a shade resentful towards a prose that seems studied. Like the method actor, the gifted correspondent has to appear negligent of effect, completely unstudied and unrehearsed.

No doubt Bishop addressed this matter in her seminars, perhaps under the topic of the 'found' or 'impromptu'.

What we demand in a letter is writing rather than the written, speaking not the spoken, the mind in action, not the mind at rest. To achieve this effect, Bishop sought what her beloved Hopkins terms the instress of speech – 'Father, what you buy me I like best' as he expresses it in 'The Handsome Heart' where that oral response or speech-bite has a perfect conversational pitch and spontaneity. Similar vernacular sentence-sounds can be felt throughout the volume: 'Well, I must make myself a dish of tea', 'the harbour a pale, pale milky blue', or the moment when she says to Moore, 'I should like to tell you where we ate':

on the porch of a little tumbled-down white-washed shanty, owned by Aunt Seline, who served chicken, rice, beautiful rose-red tomatoes, etc., salad bowls of raw oysters. She is 77 years old, a Cuban Negress; there are two rooms in her house, decorated in the Spanish way with nothing but palm-leaf fans and straight chairs set against the walls. She has one lantern to cook by, and one for people to eat by; sometimes she brings things out on the porch, sometimes she hands them through the window. 'Heah's your cream', she said, handing out a little tin of condensed milk. Green glowworms crawled all over the porch screens as we ate . . .

The green glow-worms are very attractive but they are not essential details, for it is the phrase 'Heah's your cream' which literally concentrates value for Bishop. Aunt Seline's black vernacular transforming the condensed milk into cream is a rich epiphany, because in Bishop's joyous, loving admiration the black cook embodies the milk of human kindness which inspires yet another marvellous poem in prose, complete with a decorative frame of glow-worms like a naïve painting. And in *Songs for a Colored Singer*, the cycle she wrote for Billie Holiday, Bishop shows that one of her muses is black and sings the Blues. When she taught students taking her poetry classes metrics, it was the opening line of a Billie Holiday song – 'I hate to see that evenin' sun go down' – that she chose as her example of the iambic pentameter. It was the homesick speech rhythms of the Blues that enraptured this orphaned poet who was always searching for a home.

One of the finest examples of Bishop's deployment of speech in her letters is this paragraph addressed to the painter Loren McIver:

Loren – here it comes – will you do something for me? I feel I simply cannot live much longer unless I have a wool jacket in *Black Watch* plaid. There was one at Abercrombie's I almost bought, then thought I was being extravagant, also I didn't think the plaid was authentic. But they're all over the place now, and since one of the first things I remember about you is that little book bound in plaid you had on the Cape, I feel you're the natural victim for this commission. Will you? I want just a regular sack coat, I guess you call it, or blazer – like a boy's, or a boy's would do if there aren't any girl's right. I like dark buttons better than brass but it doesn't matter – I can change them . . . I have charges at Best's, Saks, Bonwit, but since that's involved maybe they'd send it C.O.D. In fact I think the best place would be Brooks Brothers – you know me, nothing but the best . . .

Reading this is like listening to a breathlessly urgent message on an ansafone. It is so helterskelter authentic that we feel we're hearing Bishop's voice live – its pauses, stroking trills and sudden luxurious lunges. Again this is a poem in prose, a beautifully pitched speech aria, though that triplet of editorial dots again interferingly rounds it off with a trailing closure that introduces a kind of accidental tweeness like a *hi/bye* signature tune.

The sheer stamina and creative flow of Bishop's correspondence can be felt also in the various unrehearsed, spot-on critical remarks she will suddenly throw out. Disliking the way Wallace Stevens, for all his gifts, 'occasionally seems to make blank verse *moo*'; she loves Donne's manner of giving 'a weird clearness' to a thought, finds that Auden's *About the House* has 'a kind of determined coyness about the indignities and comforts of old age (a little early, I think)', and admires Lowell's 'weird gift – just when you think a poem is falling apart it suddenly saves itself and appears perfectly clear and dazzling'. Though she likes Robert Fitzgerald the scholar, his verse 'never seems to ignite' and mostly reads 'like very superior translations from the Latin', while Randall Jarrell whom she in many ways admired has unfortunately adopted

Corbière's system of hysterical punctuation. I'm afraid Corbière has been a bad influence on him, bringing out more & more of his rather maudlin, morbid streak. Maybe it's a combination of Corbière & trying to write

NOT like Cal [Lowell] . . . The originals – what a child – may have reminded him of Cal. If you haven't read Corbière, do, by all means. He is really a marvellous poet & these 'adaptations' only give the poorest idea of what he's like.

Such off-the-cuff remarks are essential imaginative glimpses of her deepest aesthetic intuitions, darts of intense life which remind us how fundamental the critical is to the creative act.

What also emerges is a series of talismanic topics that she returns to again and again. As well as George Herbert, Hopkins, wild vegetation, black Americans, Bishop locates her most profound values in friendship (so many loyal and devoted friends she had), primitive art, Paul Klee, hurricanes, thunderstorms, seeds, light, Great Village in Nova Scotia where her mother's family, the Bulmers, lived, and also cooking, at which she excelled. Her Aunt Grace, to whom she dedicated 'The Moose', that gentle reply-poem to Frost, is a talismanic figure too, as well as a dearly loved relative.

There is a concentration of some of her most cherished values in this account of Christmas in Brazil with the lover who gave her more than a decade of happiness there, Lota de Macedo Soares:

Christmas here was very nice – we had a couple of guests – I stuffed the turkey – I received the Phaidon *Vermeer*, among other nice things – It was a hot day with intermittent thunderstorms, and late at night we made a few calls on our elderly neighbors – much kissing and hugging, hand-kissing, and little glasses of *caocaça*, while the rain poured down and an enormous frog called the 'Blacksmith' lived up to his name just beyond the porch in the garden. There is also a bird that makes an even louder metallic noise – like Arthur Rank's gong, only right in your ear. People even keep them in their apartments in Rio. – Oh, I have seen one good movie, *Jeux Interdits*, did you see it? The last night we were in São Paulo, and too tired to think any more, Lota and I were lured into *Quo Vadis* because the sign said it was 'refrigerated,' as they call it here – and I had yet to see anything outsize. But don't – even as a joke – don't go. It is too disgusting.

She excels at this type of impromptu description, except description seems too formal and external a term for a prose that speaks itself actively all inside what's happening in the moment. The ironical, consumerist, ultimately campy movement from the gonging bird to the movies is brilliantly accomplished – we are in the roaming, associative, free-ranging play of conversation here, not riding the rails of consecutive logical development. This is the witty, unstable, shifting ground of being, a state of continuous perceptual process which seems always to possess a heightened alertness.

What Bishop craves is the local and permanently rooted, so in a letter to Lowell she bemoans the changes in Great Village and says that the 'dying out of local cultures' seems to her one of the most tragic things this century. In Brazil small towns 'far inland on the rivers were real centers; they had teachers of music and dancing and languages — they made beautiful furniture and built beautiful churches. And now they're all dead as doornails, and broken-down trucks arrive bringing powdered milk and Japanese jewelry and *Time* magazine.' This is a version of an earlier letter to Lowell where she describes a day's voyage through the doldrums:

The water absolutely slick and flat and the flying fish making sprays of long scratches across it, exactly like fingernail scratches. Aruba is a little hell-like island, very strange. It rarely if ever rains there and there's nothing but cactus hedges and prickly trees and goats and one broken-off miniature dead volcano. It's set in miles of oil slicks and oil rainbows and black gouts of oil suspended in the water, crude oil — and Onassis's tankers on all sides, flying the flags of Switzerland, Panama, and Liberia. Oh, our tug was named *La Créole Firme* and one young engineer had a nice tattoo, simply MY MOTHER. I guess that will be enough about our trip.

This is one of her ecological visions, where international finance overwhelms local culture. Yet she was fascinated by oil and in 'Filling Station' insists that the floor is 'oil-soaked, oil-permeated / to a disturbing, over-all / black translucency'. For her, oil is an oxymoronic symbol which concentrates both Being and the destructive exploitation of nature. It empowers her addictive travelling and yet creates guilt-feelings about her constant changing of places. But the smell of gasoline left behind in 'The Moose' is the vision's closure. Moose *and* the acrid smell of gasoline, she is saying, not moose versus gasoline — it's a version of her persistent theme of nature and art, nature and consumption. When she describes a day in the oily doldrums, she is creating another outstanding poem in prose for Lowell.

Right from her undergraduate days, this type of effortless prose design was one of her aesthetic ideals. It's there in this paragraph from an early letter to Donald Stanford:

It is a wonderful cold night here. I live up in a tower (that isn't a figure of speech) and so have a fine view of the stars and the smokestack of the power plant. A ladder goes up out of our living room or lobby onto the roof and once up among the elaborate Victorian iron railings, it's a very nice spot to smoke a dishonest cigarette. We are gradually filling the gutters with butts.

The lonely tower gives way to the laconically guttural last sentence which perfectly balances the denied rhetorical and symbolic figure that is simultaneously introduced and cancelled at the start of the paragraph. And with its complex assonance of gradually/gutters/butts, that last sentence has perfect sentence-sound.

Over forty years later, Bishop throws off one of her most magnificent epistolary arias:

Sat. afternoon I went to the first wedding of my life – in a church & *all like that*. I found it pretty depressing, I must say. Do you know that little J. who worked in Kirkland House? She was the bride – the one with bright red hair. Her sister, 16, who looks exactly like her only younger & bigger, has red hair, too – only a prettier shade (I adore red hair). Almost the best thing about the wedding was when they were all standing up in front of the church – and the afternoon sunlight came in and lit up the sister's hair – a wonderful, almost blinding glow of red hair, almost through the ceremony. But it all took about 15 minutes. Seems shocking to me. Then a country club. All salt-of-the-earth New Englanders, I'm sure. Slight differences in caste between the parents of the bride and those of the groom – from Texas & slightly 'poorer.' *That* mother-in-law looked stiff & papery, just like poor Mrs. Nixon . . . We hadn't cared for the Putney Inn the night before, so ate at a Howard Johnson's on the way back – dozens of skiing (I think) families and innumerable children, all guzzling french fried potatoes with ketchup and gigantic mounds of ice cream and whipped cream and so on – revolting but fascinating. But yesterday was really heavenly – deserted fields, huge rolling fields, soft snow, not too cold, and bright sunlight – everything dazzling. The snow sparkles like diamonds, with colored lights – but then when you ski into the shade of the woods the dazzle doesn't stop – just turns to fewer but more intense glints of bright blue and purple. It was lovely. I fell down only once and I must confess to feeling pleased when Alice – who was trying to 'show off,' I fear – also fell down once. I thought I'd be lame, but I'm not.

The prose is typically spontaneous and improvisatory, but at the same time her painterly eye organizes it like one of the superrealist paintings that were emerging in the early 1970s. The Howard Johnson's interior is like a typical superrealist diner crossed with the aesthetic lavishness of the Emperor of Ice Cream revisited – not the 'Baskin-Robbins banana-nut ice-cream' demanded at the end of Paul Muldoon's 'Immram', but a tackier, cheaper confection whose 'gigantic mounds' glisten ironically at the reader as she shares the reality imagined/reality recreated joke with her friend, the poet Frank Bidart. The stiff and papery mother-in-law – like the first lady, Pat Nixon, we assume – is overlaid on the composition like a cartoon or a cut-out reproduction which in the New England context allusively ghosts the dry sinister puritanism in some of Andrew Wyeth's paintings. The rapid dashes introduce a slightly jerky, almost home-movie quality, before the final skiing passage which is pure technicolour pleasure. The transitions from the mounds of ice-cream and whipped cream in the claustrophobic interior with its guzzling consumers is neatly managed, and in 'revolting but fascinating' Bishop is reworking one of her own favourite lines – 'awful but cheerful' in 'The Bight' – a line she wanted Alice Methfessel to have inscribed on her tombstone. And as in that poem and many others, her eye consumes detail in order to try to look beyond the act of consumption to somewhere impossibly innocent and beautiful. The light, that 'almost blinding glow of red hair', the snow-dazzle, Elizabeth and Alice each falling 'only once' as they ski away from a straight, salt-of-the-earth, New England gathering – this paragraph has the numinous shine of parable, especially if we know, as Bidart would have, that Bishop was forever falling and injuring herself during her drinking-bouts.

Her wit is drawn by the 'awful' – it's one of her favourite words, one of her most savoured critical terms – and in this paragraph she produces a perfect comic moment:

The Bard weekend was very successful on the whole, I think. Dr. [William Carlos] Williams read Friday night – talked, rather, in a completely scatterbrained but charming way. Afterwards there was a big & sort of awful party at which they served (I suppose they'd been counting on cold

weather) a kind of hot punch called GLUG full of raisins and almonds &
things and terrible. The room was so hot I felt faint & one enthusiastic
undergraduate spilled a cup of Glug all over me, to begin with. Finally Cal
& I just ran away and found the college cafeteria, where we drank some nice
cold milk and cooled off. He shared somebody's quarters with Eberhart.

Later in the same letter there is a hilarious account of 'a wild man
from California in a bright red shirt and yellow braces named
[Kenneth] Rexroth, who did his best to start a fight with everyone
and considered us all effete and snobbish Easterners'. As so often
there is an intense partying buzz of wit and fun that is continuously
winning and attractive to the point of complete ecstasy.

As Brett Millier shows in her biography, Bishop's most enjoyable
teaching experience was her course on letters which she found 'very
sociable'. In her unfolding, her fountaining correspondence, it is this
intense sociability, the wit and pizzazz of her sincerity, the giving of
herself fully to every correspondent, that builds a very powerful
sense of joy. Like a drop of water skipping on the hot plate of her
many miseries and problems, she dances in her prose like a writer
with that gift of being always twenty-two and eager for anything.

There are other, colder views of Bishop which as we're treading
the taut epistolary line between art and life need to be taken into
account. Though Millier mistakenly suggests that Bishop is not
included in *The Group*, it's clear that Lakey and the Baroness in the
novel are versions of Bishop and Lota. And when Bishop refused
McCarthy's request to visit her on holiday in North Haven in July
1977, she was expressing the hurt she felt at being portrayed as
coldly intelligent, 'inhuman like the moon', with a smile 'like a
lizard'. Nevertheless she is the authoritative, if mostly absent, centre
of that flawed novel. Bishop, Millier convincingly demonstrates,
was attracted to people of 'charismatic instability' – two of her
lovers committed suicide – and sought refuge in alcohol from her
own anxiety and suffering. This is information which admirers of
Bishop need, not in order to make moral judgements – in my view a
most improper exercise where artists are concerned – but to better
appreciate her writing. If Robert Giroux has been less than generous
with biographical detail this is because, as her friend and publisher,

he is naturally eager to present her at her sparkling best in this seminal selection. His annotation is unobtrusive, if rather too minimal, but this makes for undistracted reading. However, readers familiar with Kalstone, Millier and Goldensohn's work will find the contours of the selection rather too smooth and seamless – rather too party-best in its *tenue* – and there are some puzzling omissions.

One crucial omission I have already mentioned, but it is regrettable that Giroux did not include a letter which Bishop wrote to Lowell (30/7/64) where she launches into an exasperated critique of the London literary scene:

Oh so many poets – all the names at the bottoms of columns in those reviews, or at the bottoms of reviews – and most of whose poetry I can't tell apart. And all I'm afraid not terribly interesting – I'm afraid you're the only poet I find very interesting, to tell the truth! There is a deadness there – what is it – hopelessness . . . That kind of defiant English rottenness – too strong a word – but a sort of piggish-ness! – As if they've thrown off Victorianism, Georgianism, Radicalism of the '30s – and now let's all give up together. Even Larkin's poetry is a bit too easily resigned to grimness don't you think? – Oh I am all for grimness and horrors of every sort – but you can't have them, either, by shortcuts – by just saying it.

Kalstone quotes this passage in *Becoming a Poet* and it articulates the inspiration behind 'Crusoe in England', that masterpiece in which Bishop lovingly but critically recreates Larkin as Crusoe:

> I often gave way to self-pity.
> 'Do I deserve this? I suppose I must.
> I wouldn't be here otherwise. Was there
> a moment when I actually chose this?
> I don't remember, but there could have been.'
> What's wrong about self-pity, anyway?
> With my legs dangling down familiarly
> over a crater's edge, I told myself
> 'Pity should begin at home.' So the more
> pity I felt, the more I felt at home.

Larkin's witty, self-consciously dreary moaning-Minnie act (Crusoe dismisses the beer he brews as 'awful, fizzy, stinging stuff') is delicately parodied here. This is post-imperial England caught in an affectionate satire on its demoralized eccentricity that also draws in Bishop's Nova Scotian and New England, 'bluenoser' background. It's therefore unfortunate that Giroux didn't include this very interesting letter to Lowell.

More understandable are the reasons — cost presumably — which led to certain cuts being made after the first proof copies had been sent out for review, but I particularly regret the omission of an early letter to Stanford (1/12/33) in which Bishop laments that all the 'primary poetic sources have been made use of and we're in possession of a world made up of poetry, the natural world'. For people like herself, she says, the things to write poems about 'are in a way second-degree things — removed once more from this natural world. It's like Holland being built up out of the sea — and I think that I am attempting to put some further small structures on top of Holland.' From this startling letter — she was twenty-two when she wrote it — to a poem like 'Brazil, January 1, 1502' which saturates nature in art and which was written more than two decades later — there is a deep train of thought and imagining. And in the same letter to Stanford there is this perfectly framed paragraph:

T-wharf and vicinity has long been a favorite place of mine. I was interested to learn that people actually lived there — because all this year I have been elaborating a plan for living on a houseboat in Boston when I get through here. Have you seen any such around? A small chunky one, white perhaps. I think it would be so pleasant to drift down the Charles and simultaneously down the social classes, and tie up anywhere along the way. There used to be quite a colony of them where the Mystic and the Charles meet. I shall appoint you my Boston real estate agent.

In particular, the neatly inflected parabola of 'A small chunky one, white perhaps' has a most exquisite sentence-sound that is keyed by the *uh*-sound in 'such'. This is throwaway, witty Bishop, sounding every bit as wry and deadpan as Humphrey Bogart. A pity, then, that space could not have been found for this highly significant letter.

It is also slightly irksome to find a letter being described on its first publication as 'famous'. That adjective no doubt denotes how Giroux and other loyal and devoted friends of Bishop's passed some of her letters round within their coterie, but it blears the enjoyment of those who didn't have the good fortune to be initiates. It is – which Bishop never is – just a shade smug and self-regarding. Nevertheless, here is her response to a friend's request for information about home help and local stores in Boston:

I've talked to Mary (Whelan) who comes to me at about 8 Wednesday mornings. She seems quite willing to work for you, too – but I'm not sure how much time you would want her to spend. She has been at my apt. from 8 to 1 – at $3.50 an hour, that makes $18.00 – with 50¢ for carfare – I've told her she should get the 'Senior C's' card, and then she can ride for 10¢ a ride – she is *quite* senior, but keeps that a secret. I'm beginning to think this is a bit too much for me; also now that I'm home at last I don't need quite that much help. So – we talked about it and she said she'd be willing to work for me for 3 hours and for you for 2 – if that would be all right with you. She is not wonderful – except for her age, the 13 children, the hopeless, cranky 'Joe,' etc. – but she is by far the best cleaner I have had here. And she has the gift for making things *look* tidied up and dusted, at least. Well, you can tell me what you think and if you want to try her you could lend me a key and I'd escort her there next Wed. – also tell me what you want done especially.

A few addresses: My favorite drugstore is Tony Accaputo, Jr.'s – Commercial Wharf Pharmacy – the small one with an entrance across from the Rusty Scupper, also through on the next street – NOT the new, big pharmacy across Atlantic Ave. Tony – or both Tonys – are very nice and obliging – even drove off in a storm once to Mass. General to get me some drug or other – (2) You know about the Toscana Meat Market (their sausages are good). (3) Guiffre's Fish Market – on the end of Salem Street, or corner, before the expressway. They're very nice there, too. (4) Halfway down Parmenter St., on the left – between Hanover & Salem, is a nice vegetable store. On that corner of Salem St. is Polcari's Coffee Shop (not a café) – where you can get all kinds of things – teas, coffees, spices, etc. – jars of a wonderful Italian mixture of chocolate & hazelnuts, for desserts for friends with a sweet tooth, etc. – (5) Also on Salem St. – one of the Martignetti's – booze and groceries – their soda, Coke, etc., is the cheapest. (6) Drago's Bakery – 1st left off Fleet St. – North St. – the round breads aren't so good, but the long ones, *flutes*, etc., are the best – but they're apt to be all sold out by four o'clock. Between 12 & 1 they also sell freshly made pizza, by the square – good, but not as good as some others. (7) Fleet Market, to the right on North St. – go in the back door – is an old wholesale house that hasn't a retail store any more – but sells to ordinary customers. It's worth going to if you need quite a lot of things – usually very fresh – for one or two items the Parmenter St. shop is quicker & more agreeable. (8)

Off Hanover to the left – Prince St. – the first little bakery, on the left, is one of the best although it doesn't look it. (The one across the street is not good.) Their cannoli are good – ask them to give you the filling separate & put it in before serving. Also – they usually have *soft* macaroons. Down Hanover on the right – Trio's Ravioli Co. – make their own noodles, etc. – green noodles very good. Also Italian sauce – I sometimes buy it and just add meat or whatever – All kinds of spices there – and beans, etc.

This is one of her most outstanding poems in prose, another superreal masterpiece with a living passionate voice and hectic, heavenly detail. It's just a pity that it comes into the public light of day as already famous, already read and therefore robbed of our first pristine encounter with its living spirit.

Even so, *One Art* is a magnificent compilation, but let us also hope that a generous grant from the National Endowment for the Arts is now empowering a team of scholars to work on a collected edition of Bishop's letters and notebooks. And if – shocking thought – that work is still waiting to be commissioned, let it begin soon. Let it start tomorrow. There is also an urgent need for a complete edition of her prose writings which includes her reviews and the work she published while an undergraduate at Vassar (the reissue of her *Collected Prose* is welcome but it is not sufficient). A book which reproduces her paintings and discusses her very considerable knowledge of the visual arts would also be welcome. Robert Giroux drew his selection from over three thousand letters, and despite certain shortcomings he is to be congratulated for preparing the way towards a full, complete, properly annotated edition of Bishop's correspondence. Meanwhile let us celebrate the appearance of this extraordinary, this quite exceptional and wonderful work.

The Dean's Bellyful: Jonathan Swift

Swift was the founding father of the Anglo-Irish imagination. His prose initiates a form of obdurate and extremist irony which subverts the rational ethic on which it is apparently based. His stoic Roman republicanism and exasperated patriotism fascinated Yeats, who in that remarkable play 'The Words upon the Window-Pane' suggests that Swift was 'the chief representative of the intellect of his epoch, that arrogant intellect free at last from superstition'. For Yeats, Swift was an epic and heroic figure whose 'astringent eloquence' created the 'political nationality' of Ireland.

Swift was also a great prophet of the nightmare of European history. 'A Modest Proposal' and the account of Gulliver among the Houyhnhnms posit a reality where human beings can be processed into gloves and canoe-skins, and they also satirize that form of puritan economics which we now term monetarism. The cold hatred Swift felt for utilitarian values is expressed in a prose-style which has a hard, instrumental, rational clarity. His verse, however, is notable for its obsession with a fetid ordinariness, a mock-epic triviality:

> Sweepings from butchers' stalls, dung, guts, and blood,
> Drowned puppies, stinking sprats, all drenched in mud,
> Dead cats and turnip-tops come tumbling down the flood.

This apocalyptic vision of urban dreck is characteristic of the poems, and Swift frequently displays a mean-minded attraction to frowsty detail: 'Cracked lips, foul teeth and gummy eyes.' Essentially, he is an occasional poet who sings lightly about dandruff, drains, body odour, dirty underclothing and comic tarts. He seldom redeems or transforms these Manichaean details, and he is particularly obsessed by society ladies waking late in the morning:

Review of *Jonathan Swift: The Complete Poems*, edited by Pat Rogers.

She stretches, gapes, unglues her eyes,
And asks if it be time to rise;
Of headache, and the spleen complains;
And then to cool her heated brains,
(Her nightgown and her slippers brought her),
Takes a large dram of citron-water.
Then to her glass; and 'Betty, pray
Don't I look frightfully today?'

Swift's boyish curiosity is perhaps the most unattractive feature of his celibate intellect, and his preference for octosyllabics induces a kind of bored nausea, like travel sickness. Indeed, several poems stem from a particularly bad journey he made to Ireland in 1727, and his complaints about the 'muddy ale and mouldy bread' served at Holyhead strengthen that insistent vision of grot and fragments. Unfortunately, Swift's sense of the world's unlovable ugliness prevents him from cherishing poetic cadence as an end in itself, though there are some rare exceptions. The initial spondee in 'Small beer, a herring, and the Dean' helps to form a perfect and witty line. Swift's sparseness and lucid minimalism have a type of Dutch beauty, and his masterpiece, 'Cadenus and Vanessa', combines a baroque exuberance with a restrained and delicate chastity. It is a brilliant study in erotic platonism, a poem which both thinks and desires.

Although Swift argued in his prose for an ideal form of standard English which would exclude dialect words, his most powerful verse savours words like 'keck' (retch) and 'bonnyclabber' (sour clotted milk). And in 'An Epigram on Scolding' he delights in the kick of a non-standard accent:

Great folks are of a finer mould;
Lord! how politely they can scold;
While a coarse English tongue will itch,
For whore and rogue; and dog and bitch.

Swift valued the opportunity of 'vexing' his readers and this distinctive form of Anglo-Irish irony is deployed in 'Mad Mullinix and Timothy', a dialogue between a crazed Jacobite beggar and a Whig politician. It contains some marvellous passages of sustained invective or 'slegging':

> Thy peevish, and perpetual teasing,
> With plots; and Jacobites and treason;
> Thy busy never-meaning face;
> Thy screwed-up front; thy state grimace;
> Thy formal nods; important sneers;
> Thy whisperings foisted in all ears;
> (Which are, whatever you may think,
> But nonsense wrapped up in a stink)
> Have made thy presence in a true sense
> To thy own side so damned a nuisance,
> That when they have you in their eye,
> As if the devil drove, they fly.

Obsessively, Swift rhymes 'think' with 'stink', and this serves as shorthand for his vision of the intellect debased by the body politic. Although his verse can have the visceral authenticity of this anti-pastoral couplet – 'Dermot, how could you touch those nasty sluts! / I almost wish this spud [spade] were in your guts' – the poems are more remarkable for a gristly fussiness. Swift's verse-line lacks Dryden's sinewy plainness and it never rises to Pope's melody and precision. Nevertheless, the poems do possess a bleak, witty coherence, and they are well served by Pat Rogers's exemplary scholarship. With its skilful annotation and excellent biographical dictionary, this handsome volume has a magisterial and properly 'canonical' appearance. It represents an altogether nobler academic undertaking than any exercise in literary theory.

Billy's Victim: John Dryden

1988 sees the tercentenary of the Glorious Revolution in which William of Orange overturned James II's clumsy despotism and permanently changed the British political landscape. John Dryden was the major artistic victim of the Revolution, and it's therefore appropriate that James Anderson Winn's magnificent new biography of the Stuart Poet Laureate should celebrate the achievement of a writer who ended his life as an impoverished Catholic dissident in William's new Orange state.

It isn't necessary to share either Dryden's politics or his religion in order to admire his achievement as poet, dramatist, literary critic, propagandist and completely professional writer. It was his consistent refusal to allow aristocratic amateur writers to pull rank on him which makes his single-minded dedication to the craft of writing emblematic of an integrity many of his contemporaries denied him.

Aphra Behn's satire on 'Mr Dryden, Renegade' attacks his conversion to Catholicism during James's reign:

> Alas! how leering heretics will laugh
> To see a gray old hedge bird caught with chaff.
> A poet, too, from great heroic themes
> And inspiration, fallen to dreaming dreams.

Behn might justly have satirized Dryden's misogyny, but she focused her attack on his religious rather than his sexual politics, and predicted he would change faith again under a new regime. In fact, Dryden stayed loyal to Catholicism and suffered badly as a consequence. This principled sacrifice did not prevent Victorian scholars from labelling him a turncoat and time-server.

Macaulay maliciously misread a State document in order to

Review of James Anderson Winn, *John Dryden and his World*.

portray Dryden as a mercenary writer and this slur has had a powerful effect on both scholarly and popular views of his work. The writer who dedicated his imagination to the reconstruction of English culture after the failure of the Commonwealth has been subjected to the posthumous humiliation of being dismissed as a boring and arid writer who lacked both personal integrity and intellectual seriousness. His new biographer candidly acknowledges this slump, and offers a deeply researched account of the poet's life in order to allow us to hear 'his mighty music'.

Dryden was born in 1631, the eldest son of a Northamptonshire family of puritan gentry whose ancestors had benefited directly from Henry VIII's dissolution of the monasteries. Many of his relatives took the Parliamentary side during the Civil War and Dryden himself was ostensibly a Cromwellian. A civil servant under the Protectorate, he marched with Milton and Marvell at Cromwell's funeral, and published a cautious eulogy praising the Lord Protector's 'great example'. But Dryden was at heart a royalist and had moved away from his family's puritan values while a student at Westminster School under its famous headmaster Richard Busby.

Dryden became a dominant literary figure after the Restoration and enjoyed considerable financial success for a few years. A prolific political dramatist, who had five plays produced during 1667 alone, he was appointed Poet Laureate the following year on the strength of his brilliantly propagandist poem 'Annus Mirabilis'. At the height of the Exclusion Crisis in 1681, Dryden defended Charles II in *Absalom and Achitophel*, the greatest English political poem after *Paradise Lost*. Yet for all the witty, magisterial confidence of that mock-epic, Dryden appears to have been a cautious, taciturn man always uncertain where the next fee would come from and vulnerable to attack by hack writers, violent aristocrats and hired thugs. His enemies called his Catholic wife, Elizabeth, a 'whore', and like the popular press in Britain today they mounted vehement attacks on a writer whose talent should have commanded respect. Dryden would have recognized the punitive philistinism of the current attacks on Tony Harrison, Ian McEwan and other writers.

Although he was a skilled controversialist, Dryden showed

himself to be a conciliator and a loyal member of that invisible community of poets which can set differences of opinion aside in order to defend its own. Although he disagreed with Milton's republican politics, Dryden refused to say anything against the poet whose work he revered. When Charles Sackville sent him a copy of *Paradise Lost* in 1669, Dryden expressed his admiration by saying 'that Poet has cutt us all out'. There is something very humble and invisible about Dryden's personality which makes him a singularly impressive figure – his refusal to act a part, the paucity of anecdotes about him, the concerned spontaneity of his critical writings, all mark him out as a courageous professional.

Under the Williamite Revolution, Dryden was stripped of the Laureateship and the post of Historiographer Royal, and in a letter written during the last year of his life he expressed his anxieties about the persecution of Catholics by the new regime: 'We poor Catholiques daily expect a most Severe Proclamation to come out against us.' In a poem addressed to the painter Kneller, he offered a political history of painting which drew a coded analogy between the destruction of the Roman Empire and William's England:

> Goths and Vandals, a rude Northern Race,
> Did all the matchless Monuments deface.
> Then all the Muses in one ruine lye;
> And Rhyme began t'enervate Poetry.
> Thus in a stupid Military State,
> The Pen and Pencil find an equal fate.

Trapped in a 'stupid Military State', Dryden embarked on a magnificent piece of literary State-building – his translation of the *Aeneid*, which is a Jacobite riposte to the new regime and one of his finest achievements. Although the Jacobite cause was rotten and reactionary, Dryden's imagination has a sweet, consensual tolerance, and his legacy is that of a supremely deft cultural architect. He invented English literary criticism and refused to distinguish between what is now termed 'creative' and 'academic' writing.

An exemplary writer, Dryden managed to survive on the proceeds of his pen through forty years of vicious political violence. His new biographer brings that period of assassinations, pamphlet wars, rigged trials and legalized murder vividly to life and his fine study is a fitting monument to the figure who is, after Milton, England's most *engagé* writer.

Vernacular Verse

Some time back in the solid quiet of the 1950s, at primary school in Belfast, I came across this passage from *Huckleberry Finn* framed by the black official rubric of a comprehension exercise:

I made two mile and a half, and then struck out a quarter of a mile or more towards the middle of the river, because pretty soon I would be passing the ferry landing and people might see me and hail me. I got out amongst the drift-wood and then laid down in the bottom of the canoe and let her float. I laid there and had a good rest and a smoke out of my pipe, looking away into the sky, not a cloud in it. The sky looks ever so deep when you lay down on your back in the moonshine; I never knowed it before. And how far a body can hear on the water such nights! I heard people talking at the ferry landing. I heard what they said, too, every word of it. One man said it was getting towards the long days and the short nights, now. 'Tother one said *this* warn't one of the short ones, he reckoned – and then they laughed, and he said it over again and they laughed again; then they waked up another fellow and told him, and laughed, but he didn't laugh; he ripped out something brisk and said let him alone. The first fellow said he 'lowed to tell it to his old woman – she would think it was pretty good; but he said that warn't nothing to some things he had said in his time. I heard one man say it was nearly three o'clock, and he hoped daylight wouldn't wait more than about a week longer.

Huck's limber prose is a spoken prose, carefully worked to make it sound as natural and informal as the impromptu conversation he hears and reports. This is speech within speech, forming in a child's canny observant wonder, and on that first reading those voices crossing the still Mississippi in a resonant darkness had much more than a pointless banality. Like one of Wordsworth's time-spots, the prose has a visionary actuality I still can't fathom.

Many years later, I came across the last verse of St John's Gospel:

And there are also many other things which Jesus did, the which, if they should be written every one, I suppose that even the world itself could not contain the books that should be written.

The relaxed wonder and spontaneous innocence of that sentence come out from under the more formal rhetoric of the previous verses so that we seem to hear the voice of the translator, fresh and almost child-like now that the public statement has been made. Like Twain's prose, the biblical verse has a vernacular authenticity that bonds the reader in an immediate, personal manner.

Perhaps it's the official *gravitas* of public discourse, its chilling lack of kinship ties, that is the real target in

> Latin is a dead tongue
> dead as dead can be

Many vernacular poets might want to join in that kids' chant. Latin belongs to institutions, committees, public voices, print. Against that Parnassian official order, the springy, irreverent, chanting, quartzy, often tender and intimate, vernacular voice speaks for an alternative community that is mostly powerless and invisible. This oral community voices itself in a gestural tactile language – 'freedom a come oh!' – which printed texts with their editorial apparatus of punctuation and authoritative capitals can often deaden.

Reading these lines

> You shall have a fishy
> in a little dishy
> you shall have a fishy
> when the boät comes in

we need to hear 'boät' not as *bot*, but as the Northumbrian bisyllabic *bo-uht*. Often the editorial standardization of spelling flattens out vocal difference, and the same is true of the omission of the umlaut in Hopkins's 'black hoürs', where the two crucial dots foreground the Ulster-Elizabethan accent to create a dark, resonant pentameter line. That heavy guttural 'howers' appears in the singular in Faustus's final soliloquy, and at least to my ear has a much more interesting vocal tone than the standard, monosyllabic, very lightweight pronunciation *owrs* which has largely replaced it.

Such savoured cadences put us in touch with the passionate variety of regional speech, a speech whose often sensuous sound-patterns Whitman celebrates:

The smoke of my own breath,
Echoes, ripples, buzz'd whispers, love-root, silk-thread, crotch
    and vine . . .
The sound of the belch'd words of my voice loos'd to the eddies
    of the wind.

This is self-delighting speech, a stroking of the voice's buzzy plosive vibrations. And Whitman offers his definition of this vocal aesthetic when he praises the 'full abandon and veracity of the farm-fields' in Burns's Scots vernacular and asks:

Is there not often something in the very neglect, unfinished, careless nudity, slovenly hiatus, coming from intrinsic genius and not 'put on', that secretly pleases the soul more than the wrought and re-wrought polish of the most perfect verse?

With some reservations Whitman is here recognizing the gnarled, spiky qualities of verse formed by writers nurtured in an oral community.

Until recently, many of the poets I have included in this anthology would have been termed 'dialect' poets – a term which works to marginalize regional speech and privilege Standard English. *Vernacular* is a term used in sociolinguistics to refer to 'the indigenous language or dialect of a speech community, e.g. the vernacular of Liverpool, Berkshire, Jamaica etc.'. The problem with the term *dialect* is that it has a certain archaic, quaint, over-baked remoteness that really belongs in the dead fragrance of a folk museum. Yet those readers who dislike, say, Barnes's poetry might argue that his poems are merely the expressions of a self-conscious and parochial anti-quarianism. However, both Hopkins and Hardy admired and learnt from Barnes, and those three poets are kin with Whitman and Burns in a common family of vernacular writers. Such writers are linked by the way in which they employ language as speech process in their poems, not necessarily by their use of dialect words or regional accents – Christina Rossetti, for example, is one of the most significant members of this group of writers, yet she uses neither local accent nor *lexis* in her poems.

Hopkins admired Whitman's style for what he termed its 'savage' qualities, and in 'Inversnaid' he links this primitivist aesthetic to Scots:

> Degged with dew, dappled with dew
> Are the groins of the braes that the brook treads through,
> Wiry heathpacks, flitches of fern,
> And the beadbonny ash that sits over the burn.

The imagery of pubic hair echoes Whitman's 'silk-thread, crotch and vine', while the 'darksome burn' is a natural figure for Scottish speech, landscape, national poet. It's a wet wilderness which Hopkins imbues with mystery and violence – the liquid helter-skelter has a wild primitivist energy which 'treads' like a Highland clan loping down a brae into battle. Hopkins, like Whitman, aims to shock, and he makes calculated use of what would elsewhere be termed 'bad taste'. This in some ways camp aesthetic joins tenderness with violence, as in Whitman's 'Wheeze, cluck, swash of falling blood, short wild scream, and long, dull, tapering groan'. Such fascination with violence is common to children's rhymes – Davy Crockett is admired because he polished off his mother when he was only three, then polished off his father with DDT.

For Burns and Whitman these savage vernacular energies are essentially democratic and Protestant. They can be imaged in the figure Browning terms 'grand rough old Martin Luther'. But for Hopkins Luther is the 'beast of the waste wood' and is associated with Protestant nationhood and an aggressive individualism. Hopkins is therefore torn between his dedication to popular speech and a knowledge that the native alliteration of his verse – its Germanic consonantal density – expresses a cultural atavism which he as a Catholic ought to reject.

The Nordic is central to the imagination of British Protestantism, and it's celebrated in Hughes's 'Thistles', where the thistle-spikes thrust up like splintered weapons:

> From the underground stain of a decayed Viking.
> They are like pale hair and the gutturals of dialects.

The thistles are like 'Icelandic frost' and Hughes is here invoking ancestral energies similar to those Carlyle defines in *On Heroes, Hero-Worship and the Heroic in History*:

Frost the old Norse Seer discerns to be a monstrous hoary Jötum, the Giant *Thrym, Hrym*; or *Rime*, the old word now nearly obsolete here, but still used in Scotland to signify hoar-frost. *Rime* was not then as now a dead chemical thing, but a living Jötum or Devil . . .

Like John Thornton, the mill-owner in Gaskell's *North and South* who asserts 'I belong to Teutonic blood', Hughes is firmly on the side of an energetic Protestant individualism. His reaction against the civil decencies of Movement verse and identification with what he elsewhere terms 'the iron arteries of Calvin' make him a Thatcherite before Thatcher.

Hopkins observed the effects of the Industrial Revolution in northern England and was horrified by the poverty and suffering he saw, yet his poetic committed him to the Teutonic, the mill-building energies. He sought to subtilize the Anglo-Saxon inheritance through Celticism, Welsh vowel chimes, that Arthurian vision of Romano-Britain he invokes so desperately at the end of *The Wreck of the Deutschland*. He imagines a Celtic and Catholic, pre-imperial Britain, but he does so in a language still laced with a colonizing fire and stress.

Hopkins's term for the effect of spontaneous speech he seeks always in his verse was 'sprung rhythm'. He defined this rhythm as 'scanning by accents and syllables alone' – not counting up syllables – so that a foot could be 'one strong syllable' or 'many light and one strong'. He found hints of this rhythm in music, nursery rhymes, weather saws, popular jingles and in certain poets. Writing to R. W. Dixon, he said:

Here are instances – '*Díng, dóng, béll*; Pússy's ín the wéll; *Whó pút* her ín? Líttle Jóhnny Thín. *Whó púlled* her óut? Líttle Jóhnny Stóut.' For if each line has three stresses or three feet it follows that some of the feet are of one syllable only. So too 'Óne, twó, Búckle my shóe' *passim*. In Campbell you have 'Ánd their fléet alóng the *déep próudly* shóne' – 'Ít was tén of Ápril *mórn* bý the chíme' etc; in Shakspere 'Whý shd. *thís* désert bé?' corrected wrongly by the editors . . .

For Hopkins, sprung rhythm is a bridge between common speech and the verse of certain poets who employ what Hardy termed the 'Gothic' architectural principle of 'spontaneity' and 'cunning irregularity'. Such poets aim to give their verse a stressed texture rather than a regular syllabic veneer, for they associate a polished rhythm with betrayal and insincerity. These poets ride the currents of exclamatory demotic speech – like Peter in Hardy's 'In the Servants' Quarters', they voice syllables as if they are 'talking unawares'.

These natural cadences can also be found in ballad rhythm, a rhythm which belongs to oral culture and is enlisted by Coleridge when he argues that the metre of 'Christabel' is not properly 'irregular'. His metre may seem so, he suggests, because it is founded on a new principle of counting the accents, not the syllables, in each line. The syllables may vary line by line from seven to twelve, yet each line will be found to contain only four accents. Reminding Hopkins of this principle, Dixon notes that Coleridge read some of Tennyson's early volumes and remarked that Tennyson did not understand versification:

The meaning of that utterance must have been that Tennyson's verse is (very often at least) strictly quantitative, each verse having the same number & disposition of syllables as its fellow in the staff. The most remarkable example of this is Locksley Hall, which is without a flaw in this respect. I was reading it over the other day, & while it seemed a wonderfully ingenious piece of versification, wonderfully faithful to the rule which the writer had evidently put before him, yet I grew utterly satiate & weary with it, on this very account. It had the effect of being artificial & *light*: most unfit for intense passion, of which indeed there is nothing in it, but only a man making an unpleasant and rather ungentlemanly row. Tennyson is a great outsider.

Dixon did not realize that Hopkins admired the ungentlemanly or 'tykish', but his perception of the terrible hollow flaw in Tennyson's metric is exact and arresting, and it was shared by Hopkins. For most readers, though, Tennyson is the great insider, Hopkins the Victorian underdog who became a posthumous Modernist. But if Hopkins appears to exist underground in terms of nineteenth-century literary history, we should note that he belonged to that family of vernacular poets which includes Browning and Christina Rossetti – a poet badly neglected this century – as well as Burns, Whitman, Hardy.

Hopkins had a deep admiration for Rossetti, though he found Browning exasperating. And if Browning's vocal impersonations can often sound forced and ersatz, like hammy voices out of a costume drama, Rossetti's poems are always exactly keyed to the registers of the natural speaking voice:

> Her gleáming lócks shòwed nót òne thréad of gréy,
> Her bréath was swéet as Máy
> And light dánced in her éyes.
>
> Dáys, wéeks, mónths, yéars
> Áfterwárds, when bóth were wíves . . .

Throughout *Goblin Market*, Rossetti varies stress and syllable count so that her lines correspond to Hopkins's definition of verse as 'figure of spoken sound'. Where Hopkins looked to existing nursery rhymes and weather saws, Rossetti both drew on that traditional oral culture and composed her own nursery rhymes. Some celebrate pure sound and rhythm – 'Kookoorookoo! kookoorookoo!' – while others show that animism and identification with living creatures and plants which is such a feature of the vernacular imagination – 'Brown and furry / caterpillar in a hurry'. Others react characteristically against the respectable and the official – 'I caught a little lady wife / That is both staid and gay.'

Rossetti's critique of Victorian patriarchy is evident in *Goblin Market* and in the much less well-known 'The Iniquity of the Fathers upon the Children', where the alienated female voice wants to reject her conventional social destiny:

> Perhaps the rising grazier,
> Or temperance publican,

May claim my wifely duties.
Meanwhile I wait their leisure
And grace-bestowing pleasure,
I wait the happy man;
But if I hold my head
And pitch my expectations
Just higher than their level,
They must fall back on patience:
I may not mean to wed,
Yet I'll be civil.

Margaret doesn't want to surrender her autonomy and she is able to stand outside her society with an almost clinical radicalism:

Our one-street village stood
A long mile from the town,
A mile of windy down
And bleak one-sided wood,
With not a single house.
Our town itself was small,
With just the common shops,
And throve in its small way.
Our neighbouring gentry reared
The good old-fashioned crops,
And made old-fashioned boasts
Of what John Bull would do
If Frenchman Frog appeared,
And drank old-fashioned toasts,
And made old-fashioned bows
To my Lady at the Hall.

The shifting accents play against the observed cultural clichés so that we perceive the enormous gulf between the intimate speaking voice and the threatening masculine cheeriness of village society. Rossetti's criticism of patriarchal values is expressed as much by her deployment of this subtle voice and metric as by what the voice states.

Although Rossetti, like Clough, writes in Standard English, both poets share that rejection of an imposed, normative official voice which is such a common feature of vernacular poetry. They refuse to recognize the division between 'serious' and 'light' verse which the vogue for dialect verse in the Victorian period helped to enforce. Yet if Tennyson kept Lincolnshire speech and the vowelly language of his other poems strictly separate, 'The Spinster's Sweet-Arts' is more than a comic exercise. Like Margaret in 'The Iniquity of the Fathers', the female speaker refuses to succumb to male domination, while her reference to babies' 'bottles o' pap, an' their mucky bibs, an' the clats an' the clouts' allows Tennyson to write more frankly than he could in the standard language. And that full veracious abandon can be found in the anonymous 'A Pitman's Love-Song':

> Aw wish my lover was a ripe turd
> smoking doon in yon dyke seid
> an aw mysel was a shitten flee
> aw'd sook her allup before she was dreid

It's difficult to see how these lines could escape the often censoring effect of standard diction and accent.

Often regional English is charged with an erotic current – 'hold my bonnet hold my shawl / pray don't touch my waterfall', has to be voiced in black American English, while Whitman, like Dickinson, delights in the sensual nature of certain voices and sounds. Both poets, like Christopher Smart, like the anonymous voice of 'Oh trial!' or the equally anonymous Caribbean and communal 'Freedom A Come Oh!', witness to their experiences and beliefs in a distinctively Protestant, libertarian manner. Praising 'Nations, and languages, and every Creature, in which is the breath of Life', Smart aspires to a pure vernacular afflatus:

Let Anaiah bless with the Dragon-fly, who sails over the pond by the wood-side and feedeth on the cressies.

Like Burns's wee sleekit beastie or the animals and birds in Clare's poems, the dragon-fly and the cressies are not objects of empirical observation, but living, breathing parts of a more than personal vision. Lawrence draws marvellously on that close, sensitive, popular and native imagination in his depiction of Walter Morel in *Sons and Lovers* and in poems like 'Tortoise Shell' or 'Bare Almond-Trees'.

Sometimes the vernacular imagination confronts an aristocratic or public school voice directly:

> What I hated in those high soprano ranges
> was uplift beyond all reason and control

The particular voice Harrison hated was Hugh Gaitskell's, and the full patrician vowel can be irksome to those who prefer what Dryden termed 'our old Teuton monosyllables'. Yet in Clough's hexameters the range and limitations of that voice are beautifully dramatized when Claude says that Mrs Trevellyn

> Is – shall I call it fine? – herself she would tell you refined, and
> Greatly, I fear me, looks down on my bookish and maladroit
>   manners;
> Somewhat affecteth the blue; would talk to me often of poets;
> Quotes, which I hate, Childe Harold; but also appreciates
>   Wordsworth;
> Sometimes adventures on Schiller; and then to religion diverges;
> Questions me much about Oxford; and yet, in her loftiest
>   flights, still
> Grates the fastidious ear with the slightly mercantile accent.

Claude is precise, refined, a snobbish aesthete irked by Mrs Trevellyn's still slightly middle-class accent. His hexameters have a Hellenic spontaneity of consciousness which is challenged by the Trevellyns' bourgeois Protestantism, their embodiment of what Clough's friend, Arnold, termed the 'Hebraic'. Claude's voice is exquisitely modulated, it ripples and hesitates, preens and soars with an apparently perfect confidence. But it's also the accent of a frightened phoney, a highly cultivated young man who is unable to feel or to telegram real love and anger.

Clough is fascinated by the speaking voice's deft stops and starts:

Is it contemptible, Eustace, – I'm perfectly ready to think so, –
Is it, – the horrible pleasure of pleasing inferior people?

This is the grammar of speech, and its baroque suddenness erupts in
The Wreck of the Deutschland where Hopkins asks and exclaims

> But how shall I . . . make me room there:
> Reach me a . . . Fancy, come faster –
> Strike you the sight of it? look at it loom there,
> Thing that she . . . there then! the Master

These lines develop a technique initiated by Marlowe in Faustus's
final soliloquy: 'See see where Christs blood streames in the
firmament'.

Faustus's speech resonates in Donne's religious verse and is
echoed clumsily in Richard III's soliloquy before Bosworth. Marlowe's intense Protestant egotism enables a new poetry of consciousness, whose endlessly taut, swathing processes can be heard in the
naked thinking voice of Lawrence's free verse: 'I say untarnished,
but I mean opaque – .' Like Dickinson, Lawrence uses dashes to
denote the postures of the speaking voice, and though he didn't
share her puritan detestation of the codified formality of print, both
poets are joined by a common cultural root – dissenting Protestantism. They aim to communicate an overwhelming sense of the present
moment, the now of utterance:

> It's like the Light –
> A fashionless Delight –
> It's like the Bee –
> A dateless – Melody –

This is a language impatient of print, an orality that seeks to fly
through its authoritarian nets.

Similarly the Baptist witness of 'Oh trial!' breaks with Anglican
decorum to express a driven sense of mission and conviction:

> church light   church light
> church light till I die
> I been grown up in the church light side

an die under church light rule
oh trial!
great trevelation children ho!
trial!
we bound t'leave dis world

This voice, like the Rastafarian voice in 'Africa me wan fe go / Africa me wan fe go', rejects the official order and seeks an alternative and juster society. It's a communal speech which articulates the violent displacement of slavery and colonialism, the experience of losing language and homeland and having another language – or bits of other languages – imposed on you:

Come back to me
my language.
Come back,
cacao,
grigri,
solitaire,
ciseau
the scissor-bird

Implicitly, Derek Walcott rejects the idea of linguistic purity – a racist idea expressed in Spenser's praise of Chaucer as the 'well of English undefiled' – and imagines a language which carries and breaks free from history, a language which exults in its mixing of different races and cultures.

John Clare's oral writings issue from the experience of a kind of internal colonialism – Enclosure – which traumatized him and led him to reject Anglicanism and become a Ranter. Clare felt robbed of his language and complained that 'grammer in learning is like Tyranny in government'. His publisher, John Taylor, urged him to get rid of oral 'provincialisms' in his poetry – for example, to substitute 'gush'd' for 'gulsh'd' or drop 'himsen'. Taylor edited, reshaped and sometimes rewrote Clare's unpunctuated poems so that Clare felt robbed of his ties to the land and to his native speech-community. The restored texts of the poems embody an alternative social idea. With their lack of punctuation, freedom from standard spelling and charged demotic ripples, they become a form of Nation Language that rejects the polished urbanity of Official Standard. They are communal speech – the speech of the Northamptonshire peasantry – vulnerable before the all-powerful language of aristocratic politicians and the printed language of parliamentary statutes.

Clare's biblical Protestantism, his Ranter's sense of being trapped within an unjust society and an authoritarian language, show in this letter he wrote from Northampton General Lunatic Asylum:

this is the English Bastile a government Prison where harmless people are trapped & tortured till they die – English priestcraft & english bondage more severe then the slavery of Egypt & Affrica

In his anguished madness, Clare dramatizes his experience of the class system and its codified language as exile and imprisonment in Babylon. He, too, is crying out 'Zion me wan go home'.

The voice of Babylon speaks in this contemporary review of Clare's *The Shepherd's Calendar*:

We had not, however, perused many pages before we discovered that our self-suspicions were wholly groundless. Wretched taste, poverty of thought, and unintelligible phraseology, for some time appeared its only characteristics. There was nothing, perhaps, which more provoked our spleen than the want of a glossary; for, without such assistance, how could we perceive the fitness and beauty of such words as – *crizzling* – *sliveth* – *whinneys* – *greening* – *tootles* – *croodling* – *hings* – *progged* – *spindling* – *siling* – *struttles* – &c. &c.

The italicized words each have that unique, one-off, familial rareness Muldoon celebrates in 'Quoof', but here they enter the language only to be expelled by the uptight efficient voice of Official Standard. These are homeless, evicted words powerlessly falling through a social void. And in 'The Lament of Swordy Well' the common land protests against this type of violent social and linguistic engineering. Many of Clare's poems are pitched against the Lockean idea of individualism, personal property, the view that words are merely flat functional signs. It's as if Clare, like a native American, believes the land owns the people, instead of being owned by certain individuals.

From this point of view, printed language is alien, inauthentic and cruelly powerful. Print is a form of violence, its signs are like that 'curious T' which Pip's brain-damaged sister chalks on her slate in *Great Expectations*. In Dickens's novel, the letter *T*, a leg-iron and a hammer are identified – the *T* signifies Orlick who has felled Mrs Gargery with the leg-iron that clamped Magwitch's ankle. Dickens shows how the oral community which Mrs Gargery, Joe, Magwitch and initially Pip belong to is powerless before the force of print, the legal system, male violence and gentility.

Pip, like Clare, moves out of the oral community into the literate and hostile public world:

'mI dEEr JO i opE U r kr WitE wELl i opE i shAl soN B haBeLL 4 2 teeDge U JO aN theN wE shOrl b sO glOdd aN wEn i M preNgtD 2 u JO woT larX an blEvE ME inF xn PiP.'

Pip's inscribed speech is poignant because it contains the threat of future alienation – Pip will one day become a chill and educated gentleman who snobbishly looks down on the illiterate Joe. Now, in the moment of the hearth's warmth, Joe doesn't understand that Pip will write himself out of their Edenic oral world. The hearth is covered with all the letters of the alphabet – death's signs have infiltrated the house. And even though it's a statement of his bond of love with Joe, Pip's slate symbolizes the decomposition of paradisal speech, the beginning of the Fall.

I have no wish to sentimentalize orality, only to notice that the vernacular imagination distrusts print in the way that most of us dislike legal documents. That imagination expresses itself in speech and feels trammelled by the monolithic simplicities of print, by those formulaic monotonies which distort the spirit of the living language. When I consider this – consider the way in which print-culture overrides local differences of speech and vocabulary – I recall a moment when that imagination spoke directly to me. I was out in a boat, lazily fishing for mackerel with a man I was fond of, an old merchant seaman from Islandmagee in Co. Antrim. He nodded up at the rainwashed blue sky and said, 'D'you see thon wind-dog?' I looked up and saw a broken bit of rainbow and thought how rare and new 'wind-dog' seemed, how dull and beaten thin 'rainbow' was. It was MacDiarmid's 'chitterin' licht' of the watergaw just happening as he spoke.

It's from such moments that the inspiration for this anthology came. From an early age I became immersed in the wild dash and wit and loving playfulness of Northern Irish speech, a speech that is celebrated in Sally Belfrage's *The Crack*: 'You know what yer mon's like, like.' – 'Och aye. Not a titter of wit.' 'Did you get the sausingers but?' – 'I'm only after goin' til the shop so.'

In Robert Frost's terms, this is a speech packed with 'sentence sounds', sounds which writers gather 'by the ear from the vernacular'. Listening to a vocal phrase like 'Go you on back now' or 'I'll be with you in a minute but' or 'D'you see thon wind-dog?', I'm returned to Frost's aesthetic of the spoken word, to Huck's listening to those voices on the ferry landing, to these lines from a favourite Belfast street-song:

> my Aunt Jane has a bell on the door
> a white stone step and a clean swept floor
> candy apples   hard green pears
> conversation lozengers
> candy apples   hard green pears
> conversation lozengers

The lovely packed stresses – a whíte stóne stép and a cléan swépt flóor – have an ecstatic tribal innocence that suddenly breaks the surface-rhythm like a shoal of fry. And deep down I hear a phrase in another stanza – 'three black lumps' – as '*th-hee* black lumps'. For a moment, Belfast's Ormeau Road is the omphalos of the universe, then those doubts sóme navel-gazers are prone to intervene . . . might a poem by Betjeman not be having the same effect elsewhere?

But in that moment what I discover is an entrance to that wild and perfect garden which is celebrated in naïve or primitive art. That art was a powerful influence on Elizabeth Bishop's writing, and her cherishing vernacular affirms its value in 'Crusoe in England' when Crusoe exclaims, 'Home-made, home-made!', and then adds, 'But aren't we all?'

It hasn't been my intention to gather a series of homey, self-conscious accents, but to show something of the intoxication of speech, its variety and crack and hilarity. Many of the voices that speak here are disaffected and powerless. They know that out in the public world a polished speech issues orders and receives deference. It seeks to flatten out and obliterate all the varieties of spoken English and to substitute one accent for all the others. It may be the ruin of us yet.

Living Ginger: Jack B. Yeats

In a brief and scarcely known prose work, 'Homage to Jack B. Yeats', his friend Samuel Beckett celebrates this magnificent painter's 'desperately immediate images'. But the celebration is terse and curtailed, for Beckett refuses to expatiate on 'this great internal reality which incorporates into a single witness dead and living spirits, nature and void, everything that will cease and everything that will never be'. Calling Jack Yeats 'this supreme master', Beckett concludes that we simply have to bow before his work 'wonder-struck'.

Beckett's magisterial reverence is just, impressive, heartfelt, but we need to do more than bow helplessly before Jack Yeats's canvases – here is a major painter who has not been accorded the recognition he deserves.

Jack Yeats (1871–1957) had a long and fulfilled artistic life, but unlike his elder brother, W.B., he has yet to achieve international recognition. Revered in Ireland, his work has only been fitfully praised in Britain (notably by Herbert Read, Kenneth Clark and John Berger), though the exhibition of Yeats's late paintings at the Whitechapel Gallery last year did stimulate some interest. Like one of the travelling figures in his wildly dazzling canvases, this visionary painter is still moving down the road towards the promised land:

> Left, Left
> We Left Our Name
> On the Road
> On the Road
> On the Famous Road
> On the Famous Road

Review of Hilary Pyle, *Jack B. Yeats: A Catalogue Raisonné* (London: André Deutsch).

On the Famous Road
Of Fame.

Yeats devised this chanting ballad-refrain as the title for one of his finest paintings, and his tramping – tramping *not* marching – use of 'we' embraces all the tinkers, strolling players, ballad-singers, boxers, sailors and fairground crowds this republican democrat identified with. So pervasive is the sense of outdoor openness and travelling exposure in the paintings that they seem to be tragi-comic answers to the question his brother puts at the end of 'The Cold Heaven':

> Ah! when the ghost begins to quicken,
> Confusion of the death-bed over, is it sent
> Out naked on the roads, as the books say, and stricken
> By the injustice of the skies for punishment?

The homeless on-the-road quality in the paintings embodies Jack Yeats's intense love of popular culture and his gloriously deracinated communalism. It expresses many centuries of historical suffering, but it wears that experience lightly – like bright rags figured in raw oilpaint under a sky like 'a tinker's twisted withy tent'.

Yeats is the painter as ballad-singer. He often used snatches of ballads as titles for his paintings and he loved to collect sudden epiphanies like this:

> I married a tinker's daughter
> in the town of Skibbereen
> but at last one day she galloped away
> with me only shirt in a paper bag
> to the shores of Amerikay

Yeats is a deeply vernacular – even 'oral' – painter who is fascinated by singers and actors. He seems to be sketching in oils in order to catch the intensity of the vocal moment. This means that he is an insouciantly rootless, unplaceable painter whose work embodies the pervasively empty, the abandoned quality, of the Irish landscape. Implicit in his spontaneously cascading brushstrokes and the deliberately makeshift look of his paintings are the ruined cottages, the barren fields and aching emigrant atmosphere of what he termed in one of his prose works 'an only-just island'. They carry, too, the absence of a significant indigenous tradition in the visual arts. His figures come out of nowhere, carrying minimal baggage.

In another prose work, *The Amaranthers*, Yeats describes a ballad-singer walking home with a bundle of ballads 'flittering in his hands'. This flittering or 'whiffling' quality is essential to the profound surface excitement of the paintings. It is vividly expressed by Sickert in a letter to Yeats where he praised the movement of his figures within landscapes which have 'water, sky, houses ruffling like flags in support of them'. Yeats sought what he termed 'continuosity, impetuosity and exuberance'. He aimed at what in a lovely phrase he called 'the living ginger of Life', and this means that his paintings are always in process, always seeking a human absolute in 'the power of the moment'. He is therefore a highly theatrical painter who never falls into the trap of offering a premeditated staginess. Like the characters invoked in his friend Synge's *The Playboy of the Western World* – the 'pirates, preachers, poteen-makers, with the jobbing jockies; parching peelers,' – his figures are carefree, impoverished, exuberant travellers.

In one of his finest paintings, 'In Memory of Boucicault and Bianconi', he identifies a group of travelling players with a high tumbling waterfall, and this expresses his love of theatrical, especially melodramatic, excitement. The moist-bright pizzazz of Irish light, the experience of popular theatre and cinema, movement, emigration, singing, talking, thinking, all become identified. Even his interiors – the tragic *Nothing has Changed*, for example – have a sense of being open and exposed before an audience that is all buzz and hum or raptly present attention. No painter more favoured the present participle when devising titles for his works: *Rushing Waters*, *Man in a Room Thinking*, *Looking Forward*, *Looking Back*, *Tinker Whistling 'Donal Abu'*, *Going to Wolfe Tone's Grave*, *Something Happening in the Street*. There are many similarly active titles which point to what has been termed the 'quiveringly intensive vitality' of his brushstrokes or flicks of the palette knife.

If we seem to view many of his paintings through a proscenium arch, Yeats must also be seen as a highly literary painter. As Hilary Pyle shows, *On Through the Silent Lands* is based on the opening lines of Christina Rossetti's sonnet 'Remember':

> Remember me when I am gone away,
>   Gone far away into the silent land;
>   When you can no more hold me by the hand,
> Nor I half turn to go yet turning stay.

This late masterpiece shows an elderly bent man with what looks like a bowler hat pressed under his arm as he walks painfully down a hill towards a flimsy bridge over a swollen river. Beyond it are a lough and a strange cascading icy mountain. Yeats was nearly eighty when he painted this extraordinary picture. Like all his best work it powerfully communicates a sense of life bleak, joyous, eternal. It may be because this painting hangs in the Ulster Museum that I've come over the years to think of Yeats's figure as an Orangeman, perhaps one of the bowler-hatted Sligo Orangemen he knew as a child. His figure anticipates the tramps who also wear hats in *Waiting for Godot* and who may in some future production of the play be portrayed as wittily derelict Loyalists. By placing the hat under the old man's arm – he looks like an out-of-work actor or an impoverished auctioneer – Yeats signifies something of the enormous imaginative humility he brings to all his subjects. Rejecting any impulse towards the monumental and permanent, Yeats is able to make his paintings live in the moment, to exist as he titled one painting, *Now*.

It's this volatile, momentous sense of the present moment that makes Yeats such a paradoxical master – more, to adapt his brother's phrase, the master of the 'flaming door' than of the fixed, the 'still stars'. He approximates the painter to the strolling player or the faith healer – Friel is another dramatist with a kinned or cognate imagination – and though Yeats's paintings have that desperate immediacy Beckett discerns, they are also joyously immediate in a celebratory, rapt and ecstatic manner. The awe, the sense of loss and renewal, with which we contemplate them is rooted, I feel certain, in the experience of emigration. This is the experience which also produces and informs the pathos in some of the paintings – for example, *The Exile from Erin*, which shows an Irish businessman reading a newspaper in an office overlooking what must be Kilburn. This painting is the illustration which accompanies George Birmingham's witty essay on expatriate nationalism in *Irishmen All*. The sense of ontological displacement which is at the core of the emigrant experience is also the subject of *The Island Funeral*, which deploys the Blaskets-setting as a figure for the whole island – if that's the right adjective. The angular coffin, open boat, shawled women and the more distantly placed, anxious male figure pressed against the mast build an image of impoverished exposure which expresses that binary tension of island/mainland or island/other-island which is the essence of expatriation.

The sense of exile as process is often shown overcoming pathos and tragedy to vouchsafe the feeling of 'life endless' as Wordsworth terms it. This is not the pragmatist's or the realist's mental universe of ends, means, destinations and plain hard facts, but a spattery, complete vision of eternity. It's high time Jack Yeats's eternal travelling images were better known.

American Primitives

Perhaps primitive art holds more appeal for writers and the general public than it does for professional art historians? Dickens, Melville, Hardy, Lawrence, Hughes and Elizabeth Bishop – as her recently published letters copiously confirm – all draw on the naïve, the primitive, the magically and strangely untutored, as one of their richest imaginative resources. The mystical and devout Alfred Wallis is the inspiration behind Christopher Reid's subtle exercise in the naïve, 'Memres of Alfred Stoker', while Paul Muldoon in a very tender early poem celebrates that renowned Irish primitive painter James Dixon, who spent his entire life on windscoured Tory Island off the coast of Donegal:

> These representative lives
> Steered between the rocks of sea and land.
> And these other uncluttered journeys
> The Wild Goose leaving after
> A good dance in Tory Island hall,
>
> The Queen on her Royal Yacht Britannia
> Miss Rodgers driving the cattle home.
> The easy telling of these endings
> The Wasp wrecked on back of the lighthouse
> The Rothy Bay of Greenock
>
> The Fairholm on the rocks beside Alarin.
> Ninety people have been drowned
> Under the weight of this oil and canvas
> Though one survived by clinging to the brush.

Review of Deborah Chotner, *American Naïve Painters* (Washington, DC: National Gallery of Art, and Cambridge: Cambridge University Press).

Naïve painters love maritime subjects, often painting ships in glazed, static, exquisite detail so they appear more like tiny model ships preserved in bottles than wooden or metal craft straining against the elements. Such artists also set, as Muldoon implies, a delicate and very spiritual stress on survival, on the rescue of individual, local lives from oblivion. For them the provincial and the parochial is the land of milk and honey, immune to metropolitan sophistication. They have a salving delight in what Hardy termed 'the beauty of association' – the wear on a threshold, a beloved ancestor's old battered tankard are his examples – and they often infuse their work with what a native American might term the Great Spirit. These painters possess an animist vision – as small children's drawings do – of natural and man-made objects that gives their work a type of mute sanctity which at times is almost unbearably haunting.

American Naive Painting comprises the paintings in the great collection in the National Gallery in Washington – in Britain there is only the tiny but distinguished collection of English naïve art in Bath to represent what ought to be regarded as a major – indeed primal and essential – aesthetic category. British art historians with their aroma of country houses, pervasive snobbery and sporadic treachery tend to ignore such art, while in the USA they appear to suffer from a type of floundering embarrassment when confronted by Chipman's lovely, luxuriant still life *Melons and Grapes*, whose fruity profusion is admired even while the composition is being criticized for its 'skewed perspective' which creates the illusion that the fruit is 'slipping toward the viewer'. Worse, the vine's 'outsized' leaves are 'more appropriate' in size and scale to squash or melon leaves.

Again and again, the experts who have compiled this magnificent volume criticize the paintings for their 'awkward anatomy', 'simplified shading', incorrect drawing, stiff overdone poses, formulaic features and 'loose, clumsy' handling of paint. Thus a bold, stark, but at the same time delicate tapestry-like painting, *Mahantango Valley Farm* by 'Unknown', is criticized for its occasional 'crude passage' and deployment of 'a primitive perspective with no single vanishing point'. Such criticism is both tautological and entirely beside the point – a primitive painting *is* a primitive painting, and we can no more rebuke it for being one than we can dismiss a ballad for being a ballad. It lives by its own laws and follows its own rules.

What is lacking in both art and literary criticism is an autonomous category called the naïve, a category which rises effortlessly above the various negative connotations that term shares with 'primitive'. When this category is properly established – and also celebrated – then we can take the raucously favourite adjective employed by this volume's compilers, 'awkward', and recognize that a natural, instinctive, but also acquired deftness is only regarded as clumsiness from a conventional or limited or even perhaps over-educated point of view. Once we understand this, then perhaps art historians will begin to understand the sacral humanist aesthetic that has produced these paintings – paintings that have arisen like street songs and ballads out of the life of the American people. This is the visual equivalent of vernacular verse, a popular and democratic art form whose sometimes gawky figures turn their intense, direct gazes on the viewer and challenge us to patronize them.

From famous artists like Edward Hicks and Ammi Phillips to the Beardsley Limner, the Conant Limner and the fairly ubiquitous Unknown, these painters comprise a family which understands how to memorialize both the artist's contemporaries and the recent dead (there are some scary, intensely moving posthumous portraits of children) as well as knowing how to flatter, exaggerate, tantalize and introduce a pervasive tone of pure wonder. Hicks's 'painted sermons' are acknowledged masterpieces, but many other paintings express a religious sense far older than Christianity. It's this unified, perspectiveless, all-of-a-piece quality – a quality they share with cave paintings – that makes these works seem like tunnels that take us into a prehistorical lost world of light, wild profuse vegetation and gentle animals. They release us into Hicks's 'peaccable kingdom'.

How daring it was of Charles Bond to introduce a perched bird flapping its wings into his still life with fruit and dwarf pear tree. He wanted to redeem *nature morte*, unlike Horace Bundy who aimed to be naturalistic in his portrait of a Vermont lawyer, but succeeded in brilliantly evoking the claustrophobic oppressiveness of the Real in a dry, official office where a tight-lipped long-armed lawyer in a dark suit looks at us through mean, slightly narrowed eyes, behind him a pillar whose parched colour is matched by some heavy morocco volumes, a few leaning untidily in a manner that abets the powerful sense of threat that gongs out from this composition. Like oral tradition's view of the print world – all deadness and *écriture* – this painting confronts the punitively sterile and then overcomes it.

It's this atmosphere of the uncanny, the eerie or bizarre, that makes any criticism of a painter's failure to be fully and successfully naturalistic very wide of the mark. Here are pumped-up prize bulls, cheerful steam trains, triangulated geese formations, half-bitten sugar lumps, ear trumpets, Aphia Salisbury Rich and Baby Edward – here are meek lives and quietly proud lives, portraits with wild birds and cherished pets that concentrate the love and cherishing that make these works such permanently fascinating icons of the actually human. Their often highly precise draughtsmanship and elaborate detail builds an enchanted, estranged realism that can border on a Chirico-like metaphysical subject and dissolve the distinction between this world and the other world. Like fiddlers' reels, they summon the dead, and as Hardy recognizes in these subtly primitivist lines cast an ecstatic spell:

> Here is the ancient floor,
> Footworn and hollowed and thin,
> Here was the former door
> Where the dead feet walked in.
>
> She sat here in her chair,
> Smiling into the fire;
> He who played stood there,
> Bowing it higher and higher,

Childlike, I danced in a dream;
Blessings emblazoned that day;
Everything glowed with a gleam;
Yet we were looking away!

Yes, we have been looking away from these immortal works of art.

The Critic at the Breakfast Table

THE DISINTERESTED CRITIC

It is of the last importance that English criticism should clearly discern what rule for its course, in order to avail itself of the field now opening to it, and to produce fruit for the future, it ought to take. The rule may be summed up in one word, – *disinterestedness*. And how is criticism to show disinterestedness? By keeping aloof from what is called 'the practical view of things'; by resolutely following the law of its own nature, which is to be a free play of the mind on all subjects which it touches. By steadily refusing to lend itself to any of those ulterior, political, practical considerations about ideas, which plenty of people will be sure to attach to them. . . .

Matthew Arnold, 'The Function of Criticism' (1984)

Arnold remembered disinterestedness from his reading of Hazlitt and the eighteenth-century moralists. He liked the word, and proposed that English culture needed more of the principle – thinking about the word would lead to acting on the principle. He provides, in the course of the essay, a touchstone of disinterested thinking, and predictably enough it is from Burke. He singles out for praise Burke's 'return upon himself', and quotes the final turn of *Thoughts on French Affairs* in which Burke considers that a new system of things may have entered the world, and reflects that if this is so the record of his protests will matter little to posterity. Arnold does not allow for the dark-beyond-dark irony that many have felt in reading the passage; but he uses it very effectively, and it gives him a new meaning of disinterestedness: it is now the characteristic virtue, not of the member of the opposite party who still recognizes Burke's greatness, but of the member of no party at all. Culture stands apart from a world of passions, and returns upon itself.

David Bromwich, *Hazlitt: The Mind of a Critic* (1983)

David Bromwich's paragraph in the second chapter of his remarkable study of Hazlitt's critical writings picks up a famous remark which the young critic makes in an essay on Burke. It has always been a test with me of 'the sense and candour of any one belonging to the opposite party,' Hazlitt says, 'whether he allowed Burke to be a great man.'

By 'candour', Hazlitt means fairness, impartiality, justice, as well as its more limited modern meaning of unreserved openness and outspokenness. The term also carries meanings of kindness, sweetness of temper, freedom from malice, which he is arguing are qualities essential to the critic.

But this does not mean that the critic does not have a political position. To Hazlitt, who was fiercely attacked by those critics who constituted, he said, the invisible link between government and the police, this is impossible. What counts is to be able to admire Burke's style and arguments, even while you disagree with his savage gothic monarchism.

But Arnold thinks differently. He wants to take the critic out of the fray, so he seizes the term 'disinterestedness' and climbs into a tower.

In 'The Function of Criticism', which was delivered as a lecture in 1864 when Arnold was Professor of Poetry at Oxford, he explains that the disinterested critic must keep aloof from 'the practical view of things'. The critic must keep out of the region of 'immediate practice in the political, social, humanitarian sphere,' in order to make a beginning for a 'more free speculative treatment of things'. This is naturally the sort of thing which an academic audience would wish to hear, but it importantly asserts the idea that the critic as teacher should not stick a CND badge to their study window – or in the case of an Oxford don during the Falklands War hang a Union Jack from the window sill. But the critic as critic does not belong to an institution and must honestly admit to having an axe to grind. What counts is how finely the axe is ground, how fast and invisibly it is wielded. And the critic can admire a member of the opposition, as well as being inspired by their work – which is how Burke affected the republican Hazlitt.

But Arnold has a problem. He thinks the critic can float free into a realm of pure, weightless impartiality. Yet Arnold believes in a 'central authority representing high culture and sound judgement'. He wanted 'a recognised authority in matters of intellectual tone and taste'.

Intellectual tone and taste? Jasper and McMoon point the Arnoldian in the direction of a Bond Street tailor and laugh hilariously. You can't expect ideas to be as a Lancashire tailor once told Roy Fuller 'very toney'. Quite the opposite – ideas are dangerous and uncomfortable, as Burke knew when he praised the English for their sluggish dislike of them.

This is the problem when the critic mounts a pulpit and begins to talk in moralistic generalities. Or when the critic tries to explain what criticism as a cultural activity is all about. 'Sweetness and light' was Arnold's phrase for it. He stole it from that dangerous intellectual Jonathan Swift, and he repeats it like a mantra. This is not disinterested, rather it is to fall back upon the institutional, which in Arnold's case was the Anglican Church:

The pursuit of perfection, then, is the pursuit of sweetness and light. He who works for sweetness and light, works to make reason and the will of God prevail. He who works for machinery, he who works for hatred, works only for confusion. Culture looks beyond machinery, culture hates hatred; culture has one great passion, the passion for sweetness and light.

As Raymond Williams pointed out, this sounds like St Paul's description of Charity which suffereth long and is kind. It is the very reverse of objective or disinterested or impartial. It is merely an example of what William Empson scornfully termed 'neo-christianity'. Or as T. E. Hulme would say, it is 'spilt religion'.

Can 'disinterested' be redeemed and used in the sense in which it was employed by Hazlitt and the culture of rational dissent that formed his critical writing? Or must it be always condemned to carry the devious twist which Arnold gave it? Must we always minister to the self-esteem of those who carry institutional power and yet believe they are capable of impartiality? Who believe that as critics they are not always polemicists for a particular practical – i.e. ideological – attitude?

But hasn't the game moved on? No one any longer believes that the critic is like an old-style impartial civil servant. Still, is it generally agreed that one of the fundamental qualities that the critic needs to possess is a proper respect for one's opponents?

THEORY

Signifiance – A theoretical concept initially proposed and developed by Julia Kristeva (see *Semeiotiké: Recherches pour une sémanalyse*, Paris 1969; a brief account can be found in English in her 'The semiotic activity', *Screen* Vol. 14, No. 1/2, Spring/Summer 1973). *Signifiance* has sometimes been translated as 'significance', but this, with its assent to the stressed position of the sign, is exactly what it is not and it has here been left as *signifiance*. Barthes himself introduces *signifiance* as follows in a passage which gathers together a number of the terms that have been discussed in this present note: '. . . when the text is read (or written) as a moving play of signifiers, without any possible reference to one or some fixed signifieds, it becomes necessary to distinguish signification, which belongs to the plane of the product, of the enounced, of communication, and the work of the signifier, which belongs to the plane of the production, of the enunciation, of symbolization – this work being called *signifiance*. *Signifiance* is a *process* in the course of which the 'subject' of the text, escaping the logic of the *ego-cogito* and engaging in other logics (of the signifier, of contradiction), struggles with meaning and is deconstructed ('lost'), *signifiance* – and this is what immediately distinguishes it from signification – is thus precisely a work: not the work by which the (intact and exterior) subject might try to master the language (as, for example, by a work of style), but that radical work (leaving nothing intact) through which the subject explores — entering, not observing — how the language works and undoes him or her. *Signifiance* is 'the un-end of possible operations in a given field of a language'. Contrary to signification, *signifiance* cannot be reduced, therefore, to communication, representation, expression: it places the subject (of writer, reader) in the text not as a projection . . . but as a 'loss', a 'disappearance'. Hence its identification with the pleasure of *jouissance*: the text becomes erotic through *signifiance* . . .

Stephen Heath, introduction to *Roland Barthes: Image-Music-Text* (1977)

In the late 1970s, if my carbon dating is correct, the critical atmosphere in Britain began to change. Or at least it changed in the university seminar and lecture room. In those hotly contested *sites*, a new critical vocabulary began to take over — indeed the term 'site' seems to have anticipated its use by academic management culture in the 1980s as a replacement for the old-fashioned 'campus', with its benign idea of sanctuary.

Just as F. R. Leavis overthrew Sir Arthur Quiller-Couch, so Leavisite criticism was replaced by a new highly technical criticism which argued that *signifiance* is 'the un-end of possible operations in a given field of language'. Confident, empowered, armed with a stringent and often bizarre critical vocabulary, theorists began to ask radical questions about literary study. Maybe there was no such thing as literature? Perhaps that term was a *floating signifier* whose slipperiness ought to be *foregrounded* by referring to it always in inverted commas as 'literature'? The critic was now a powerful 'producer' who took 'literary' texts apart and explained their contradictions, those abysses of meaning into which they are forever receding.

As Stephen Heath remarks of *signifiance*, this activity cannot be reduced 'to communication, representation, expression: it places the subject (of writer, reader) in the text not as a projection . . . but as a "loss", a "disappearance".' Somehow this has something to do with erotic pleasure or *jouissance*, though it is difficult to see what erotic pleasure there is in Heath's arid prose, a prose so punitively earnest it reminds us that very few critics are forgiven for choosing to write in a rebarbative style. Mr Heath appears to have conceived his introduction to Barthes in a concrete underpass or in an idle moment during a management consultancy course in Leavis's old college.

For the reader of what an older Cambridge critic George Watson disdainfully termed 'our Sunday journalism' this may seem just a bit pointless and removed, but it has had a profound effect on the practice of criticism. From being traditionally regarded as the 'humble handmaiden' of literature, the new theoretical critic was regarded – at least during the 1980s – as the producer of certain critical works which aimed to rival various modernist literary texts. Freed from deference, elitism, the slavish worship of 'great' literature, students turned to paperbacks with titles like *A Theory of Literary Production* and breathed a collective sigh of relief. The world was divided into theorists and traditional critics. An enormous argument took place, battle positions were taken, friendships broken and chairs of literature wrested from the old guard. An entire television documentary, hosted by David Lodge and a filing cabinet, was devoted to a conference on theory at the University of Strathclyde.

Looking back, we can see – or, to use a John Bayleyish locution, it is possible to argue – that theory effected a sea change in criticism. It made the critical act important again by sowing a severe doubt in those who were used to exclaim how 'moving' or 'universally significant' or 'timelessly beautiful' a literary work was. It aimed to bring criticism closer to science and philosophy (though not to English empiricism which was treated as a huge joke). It aimed to strip away meaningless, subjective value judgements – they were hierarchical and elitist – and introduce instead a type of technical *discourse*. As Yeats said of the dying Synge, it chose 'the living world for text' and wrote about absolutely everything – menus, record albums, the semiotics of shoe laces, the male gaze and Edmund Spenser. And some theorists published books which sold in enormious quantities.

With the advent of theory, there returned that polemic and argument which real criticism thrives on, because the critic who is truly a critic is almost never consensual, never balanced or judicious, but always trying to break away from the orthodox and the generally accepted. Like Prometheus, the critic steals fire from heaven and brings it to humans on this earth. For this theft there is necessarily a price to pay – he or she is always breathlessly trying to stay ahead of the pack and is fearful of being devoured or, worse, left behind. The critic is eternally uneasy, restless, distinctly liverish, because – to quote Yeats again – in order to act as interpreter the critic has first to go down into the 'foul rag and bone shop of the heart', the place where the ladder of art starts from. Not the place where it should or ought to start from, but where it actually begins. Down among mixed, difficult, nasty or exhilarating emotions, the critic has to draw an idea from hunches and from the atmosphere of the social and cultural moment. The critic is condemned to ride the roller-coaster of the *Zeitgeist*, but in the front not the back coach.

The ride on the roller-coaster isn't as wildly plunging, nor as dispiriting, as it was in the late 1970s and early 80s; indeed it's difficult to know quite where criticism is at nowadays. Publishers are fighting shy of what are termed 'single author' studies in favour of brief student guides to contemporary novelists like Fowles and Rushdie, or reprints of established classics (Penguin have recently brought out two of Leavis's books again). The urge in the 1980s for new readings and rereadings of established authors seems to have passed. What the *signifiance* of all this is – or was – is hard to say, but the fairground is still open and, despite Heath's claggy technicalities, everyone is welcome to take a ride. Or to be taken for one.

SCHOLARSHIP

> Dark house, by which once more I stand
> Here in the long unlovely street,
>   Doors, where my heart was used to beat
> So quickly, waiting for a hand,

A hand that can be clasped no more –
Behold me, for I cannot sleep,
And like a guilty thing I creep
At earliest morning to the door.

He is not here; but far away
The noise of life begins again,
And ghastly through the drizzling rain
On the bald street breaks the blank day.

7. *And*] But *H.MS*. Cp. the ghost in *Hamlet* I i 148: 'And then it started like a guilty thing'. Also Wordsworth's *Immortality Ode* 148–51 (note the subject, and 'blank'): 'Blank misgivings of a Creature / Moving about in worlds not realised, / High instincts before which our mortal Nature / Did tremble like a guilty Thing surprised.'

9. J. D. Rosenberg, *JEGP* lviii (1959) 230, suggests an allusion to *Luke* xxiv 6, with the angel before the empty sepulchre: 'He is not here, but is risen'. Cp. Crabbe, *The School-Fellow* (published 1834), which begins 'Yes! I must leave thee, brother of my heart', and of which section II begins: 'He is not here: the Youth I loved so well / Dwells in some place where kindred spirits dwell: / But I shall learn. Oh! tell me of my Friend. / With whom I hoped life's evening-calm to spend'.

11. *drizzling*] dripping *H.MS*.

In Memoriam vii, *The Poems of Tennyson*, edited by Christopher Ricks (1969, 1987)

Before critics, editors with their judicial certainties and no-nonsense attitudes. Before interpretation, scholarship – the establishing of the best text, the list of variants, the suggested sources and analogues. Without such editions in our libraries – the Arden Shakespeare, Carey and Fowler's Milton, Howe's Hazlitt, Robinson and Powell's Clare, Kinsley's Burns, and many other scholarly monuments – how weightless and freefloating criticism would be. Editors come first, and sometimes like Herbert Grierson, who published his seminal edition of Donne's poetry in 1912, they decisively change criticism and writing – Grierson's Donne influenced Eliot and Yeats, and helped to shape modern poetry by offering an alternative, intensely *spoken* poetic to Tennyson's vowelly rhythms and eerie metrical smoothness. It also influenced that sour critic F. R. Leavis who stupidly thought he could use Donne as a weapon against Milton's style.

Editors have vast and exact knowledge. They have collated texts, held the watermarked paper of old manuscripts up to the light, deciphered scraggy handwriting, and they are deeply versed in the writer's biography. So when we read Tennyson's elegy to his dead friend Arthur Hallam, our appreciation of the poem – it's *In Memoriam*'s finest lyric – is immeasurably enhanced by knowing that it contains an allusion to *Hamlet* and to Wordsworth's Immortality Ode. The sense of desolation, guilt and a possible immortality is enriched by the allusions. Tennyson wants to see Hallam's spirit, but why does he compare himself to a ghostly guilty thing?

The answer – if there is an answer – is various. His religious doubts, perhaps the poem's homoerotic theme, underlie the phrase. And isn't there also the suggestion that he's like a fallen woman in a novel or melodrama returning to her lover's house? It's common in religious poetry for the soul to be imaged as female, God as a harsh male lover – Donne uses this traditional trope, and so does Hopkins when he compares his prayers to letters sent to 'dearest him that lives alas! away.' This is a type of bereaved cross-dressing – imagining his male grief and vulnerability as female – and it expresses the anger he feels towards his friend for dying.

It's then that Christopher Ricks's sifting of bibliographies and learned journals bears fruit – from the *Journal of English and Germanic Philology* he has gleaned that cunning allusion to the empty sepulchre in Luke, an almost invisible gesture which transforms Hallam into Christ. Now this exemplary editor enables us to see how all the massive contradictions in this brief lyric bear down on that apparently innocuous semicolon in line 9. Hearing the poem read aloud – for we must always divide listening from reading – the line becomes 'He is not here, but far away', not 'He is not here. But far away / The noise of life begins again.' It's a subliminally aural effect which introduces a kind of hope that is immediately cancelled by the last two lines. This is the Victorian view of the material world – dead, inert, spiritless, but with a faintly Wordsworthian pantheism still clinging to the word 'blank' for Tennyson. Or possibly clinging, for the last line is crushing.

In another note, Ricks points to the similarity of line four to the line 'But O for the touch of a vanished hand' in the lyric 'Break, break, break', and this enables us to see how the rhythm of both poems is torn between the three stresses in *break break break* and the anapaestic movement of:

But Ó / for thě toúch / ǒf ǎ vaň/išhed haňd (anapaest = *xx*/)

The same thing happens in *In Memoriam* vii which is written in regular iambic tetrameters:

Thě nóise / ǒf lífe / běgiňs / ǎgáin

before that rhythm is smashed by

Oň thě / baľd stréet / breáks thě / blánk dáy (spondee = //)

Here the hard alliterative rhythm comes fighting out of Old and Middle English poetry to wreck the elocutionary smoothness of the rest of the poem whose rhythm demands the fake velvety voice of Sir John Gielgud to render its full hollowness.

Critical judgement is out as to whether those two-ton spondees, as Clive James would term them, aren't a shade overdone. There are critics who regard Tennyson's poetry as ersatz, *voulu*, inauthentic, manufactured and stupid, like the awful moan of those doves in their immemorially heritage elms. And there are those for whom Tennyson is the supreme poet of the Victorian period. Ricks's magnificent edition places him squarely in the category of highly revered canonical poet, and all readers must be grateful for this editor's fine and exacting scholarship.

DOUBT

Do you know, a horrible thing has happened to me. I have begun to *doubt* Tennyson.

Gerard Manley Hopkins, letter to a friend, 10 September 1864

Tennyson had a brain (a large dull brain like a farmhouse clock) which saved him from triviality.

T. S. Eliot, 'Verse Pleasant and Unpleasant', 1918

Alfred Lawn Tennyson.

James Joyce, *Ulysses*, 1922

Criticism begins with doubt, begins with that sudden sinking feeling which is the critic realizing they've started to outgrow a style that used to appear entirely admirable. It is one thing to praise – this is the larksong of pure spontaneous joy everyone must give themselves to – but it is not enough to say over and over again *wonderful, marvellous, bellissima*! You have to be true to that lurking doubt, that uncomfortable voice which warns that it's time to abandon ship. So old styles sink away or are put reverently in museum cabinets, while new contemporary dangerous styles walk the streets and begin to be recognized.

Hopkins wrote his letter about Tennyson when he was just twenty years old. He'd been reading one of that season's new books, Tennyson's *Idylls of the Hearth*, and his youthful impatience with the Laureate's style – 'The slender coco's drooping crown of plumes' – had made him itchy to explain what was wrong with its yukky settled tameness.

The problem with Tennyson's style, he says, is that it is 'Parnassian' – by that he means it has a polished, marbled, obviously poetic quality that rolls its melodious vowels in an artificial elocutionary manner. The style is predictable, all on the same level, not inspired or generated by 'the stress and action of the brain'. It has a sort of mannered mediocrity about it which is unable to rise above its own flatness and sing without constraint. In one of the sonnets he was to write years later, Hopkins speaks of the rapture of inspiration – 'The roll, the rise, the carol, the creation' – and at the age of twenty he is anticipating that line by criticizing the droopy plume of Tennyson's style.

Though the word 'camp' wasn't available then, what he is

pointing to is the extraordinarily ersatz quality of Tennyson's verse. The way it is so often Tennysonian, self-parodying, sonorously hollow. So by doubting Tennyson, Hopkins is breaking out of the institution which his verse and public persona had become, and which it has remained. Hopkins's early doubt was the key which enabled him to escape the prison of that fake classical style, to smash his way out of what Matthew Arnold called the tradition of the 'full vowel'. Like Ted Hughes much later, Hopkins goes to Anglo-Saxon and Middle English, to alliterative metre, hard consonants and the rapid, savoured rhythms of vernacular speech.

We can tell with the benefit of hindsight that in 1864 Hopkins is beginning a new style and way of thinking that in the next century was called Modernism. James Joyce dismisses Tennyson as a gentleman poet, a gifted amateur who belongs at a tennis match in the Home Counties – Tennyson is Wimbledon, the summery status quo. Eliot similarly makes fun of him by imagining the slow bucolic tick of that melancholy, rather limited intellect. All three writers throw bricks at Tennyson – they radically *doubt* him – because they want to find and define their own styles against his. They want to resist his encroachment, his imperial rhetoric, his lack of any excitement.

Hopkins's term 'Parnassian' is worth holding onto and reactivating, because of the cluster of negative qualities which it defines (don't we all suffer from a lack of critical terms?). Subsequent critics can use it to discuss style – especially the type of style which scales too easily the slopes of that poetic Everest, Mount Parnassus. But we can also look at this interesting sentence from Hopkins's letter, where he says Parnassian is 'spoken *on and from the level* of a poet's mind', and wonder if that remark wasn't in his mind when, thirteen years later, he wrote the opening lines of 'The Windhover':

I CAUGHT this morning morning's minion, king-
    dom of daylight's dauphin, dapple-dawn-drawn Falcon, in his
      riding
    Of the rolling level underneath him steady air . . .

Criticism is also about searching out sources, moments of inspiration. So when in his letter Hopkins says that poets write Parnassian when they aren't 'inspired and in their flights', we can look at 'The Windhover' and see that this hovering and swooping kestrel is Hopkins's symbol for his own poetic style. That intense and unexpected moment – 'rolling level underneath him steady air' – is both a description of the kestrel hovering and of the level steady boredom of the Parnassian style that's repudiated as the kestrel hurls itself into the wind.

Out of Hopkins's doubt was born a critical term he never employed again but which he bequeathed to his future admirers. And out of it was born his fiercely anti-Parnassian verse. Reading Hopkins you are forever catching the tidal boom of a great world language and the storms and stresses of nineteenth-century history. English civilization is in large measure 'founded on wrecking', he says in another letter, and in his masterpiece, *The Wreck of the Deutschland*, he offers us a vision of that wrecking process. Perhaps *The Collected Poems of Alfred Lawn Tennyson* has been safely washed ashore? I rather doubt it.

BODY LANGUAGE

. . . in Indian art, whether in reference to poetry, painting or music, the operative word is rasa, or 'juice', and the person who responds to a work of art would inevitably taste its 'juice', or 'flavour'. Taste, in this context, has less relation to the upper-class British usage of the word, than to appetite; here, then, is a theory of aesthetics that admits of desire.

Amit Chaudhuri, unpublished thesis on D. H. Lawrence (1993)

Man of many snipes, – I will sup with thee, Deo volente et diabolo nolente, on Monday night the 5th of January, in the new year, and crush a cup to the infant century.

A word of my progress. Embark at six o'clock in the morning, with a fresh gale . . . land at St Mary's light-house, muffins and coffee upon table . . . snipes exactly at nine, punch to commence at ten with *argument*; difference of opinion is expected to take place about eleven: perfect unanimity, with some haziness and dimness, before twelve. – NB My single affection is not so singly wedded to snipes; but the curious and epicurean eye would also take a pleasure in beholding a delicate and well-chosen assortment of teals, ortolans, the unctuous and palate-soothing flesh of geese wild and tame, nightingales' brains, the sensorium of a young sucking pig, or any other Christmas dish . . .

Charles Lamb to Thomas Manning, 27 December 1800

Charles Lamb is looking forward to a wonderful dinner with lots of drink and talk, but he introduces a term – 'unctuous' – that was current among his friends and which they applied to works of art they admired. Nowadays, this word is wholly negative – anyone described as 'unctuous' or 'oleaginous' is clearly unpleasant, like Dickens's 'large, greasy, self-satisfied' Mr Chadband.

But for Lamb and his friends, a poem, painting, novel or play that was oily, unctuous, marrowy, juicy, was utterly admirable. They knew that the word traditionally carried the idea of deep spiritual meaning and also signified real enjoyment, acute pleasure. So they employed it as a term of the highest praise, just as kids now use 'safe' of someone they really like and admire.

Unfortunately, unctuousness has had its day. As Chaudhuri argues in his brilliant study of Lawrence, Western critics use a restricted language which excludes the physically immediate senses, touch and taste, or admits them only in order to express disgust – e.g. 'tacky'. Quoting Jacques Derrida, Chaudhuri shows that because we only talk about 'seeing' and 'learning' in criticism, we wall off 'sensation, collision, eroticism, and the surface': we are governed in our appreciation of art by 'distancing clarity, logic, perspective, and the ideal'. Thus we banish the body and exclude desire.

Is it possible to achieve a more integrated appreciation of art? Or must we be forever missing that 'erotics of art' which Susan Sontag recommends? Which is a way of asking if it's possible to make critical prose aspire to the grace and movement of the human body. When Hopkins discerned 'the naked thew and sinew' of the language in Dryden's verse, he was making this connection with the body. Yeats was always searching for a 'sinewy' style, and though it now seems dated, perhaps rather macho, 'muscular' used to be applied to prose. Before they were called 'clauses', sentences had 'members': 'articulate' is applied both to expression in words and to the body's joints. There is an idea of wholeness here which we find also in Walt Whitman, the genius who inspired much of Lawrence's best writing

Recently, the body has begun to be invoked by critical theorists, possibly as a reaction to the highly technical language which theory has – I won't say 'begotten' – which it has keyed into its restricted internet. Indeed, there is an academic critic who now concludes his lectures by stripping off in front of his audience. This is body language taken to a final absurdity, more an expression of disgust than of Whitmanesque exultation. The critic Hélène Cixous has written: 'Woman must write her body, must make up the unimpeded tongue that bursts partitions, classes, and rhetorics, orders and codes.' This is a cry against abstract or distanced language. A rejection of the idea of refined connoisseurship which accompanies the word 'taste' in Britain.

Praising the 'quiet flow of touch' in Etruscan wall paintings, Lawrence says: 'The sense of vigorous, strong-bodied liveliness is . . . somehow beyond art . . . as if this were the very life of the Etruscans, dancing in their coloured wraps with massive yet exuberant naked limbs, ruddy from the air and the sea-light, dancing and fluting along through the little olive-trees, out in the fresh day.'

Perhaps this is the dream of criticism – to go beyond art into the dance of life itself. Lamb invokes Rabelais in his letter because he wants to exaggerate pleasure, take it to extremes, so that it's orgiastic and uncontrolled. Though critics have said farewell to 'unctuous', the term 'carnivalesque' is now used to praise a wild, liberated, exultant style which celebrates by crushing as many cups as possible.

After carnival (the putting off of *carne*, the body) comes Lent, and that lean time isn't a good season for criticism, or for what Rabelais called 'fine and most juicy books'. So we're back to breakfast talk: big big breakfasts with sizzly rashers, sunny slippery fried eggs and champagne with orange juice.

SOLID SENTIMENTALITY

The matter of Raymond's style remained a mystery to me for many years. Why, for heaven's sake, could he not be clear? Or rather, why did he choose to write in a manner which could only be understood by other highly educated people, or by those already versed in the modish junk terminology of left-wing politics? Here was a man who believed that ideas should belong to the whole population, whose own best work had sprung out of his time as an adult education tutor, yet who persisted in ploughing through the English language as through a field of dry bones ... How could this highly sophisticated man not see that unless he laid his thoughts out clearly and simply in everyday language, he had no chance of reaching the very people whose interests he sought to advance?

David Hare, 'Cycles of Hope: A Memoir of Raymond Williams' (1989)

David Hare's memoir of Raymond Williams was delivered as a lecture at a literary festival in Hay-on-Wye in 1989, published in the *Guardian*, then reprinted in a collection called *Writing Left-Handed*. This is the perfect genesis for a critical essay – the drama of a performance in front of an audience, then the journalistic intervention, then the reminder two years later in book form. All critical writing aspires to an ideal spoken form that must always have bounce and topicality, like live theatre. And David Hare is a distinguished dramatist, so he knows what he's about. The critical spirit is alive and well in his buoyantly intelligent prose – it's in exasperated conflict with the claggy dreariness of Williams's writing.

Hare was the first left-wing writer to express his frustration with Williams's criticism and the huge respect it has been accorded. Noting that Williams was 'the intellectual leader of the academic left', Hare points to two major weaknesses: the indifference to prose style, and the belief that a literary work cannot be good unless 'it has a morally good aim'. Reading his books, Hare says, is like finding 'the world's most exciting ideas somehow trapped under the ice'.

In this memoir of Williams, Hare parts company with a whole culture of piety, romantic notions about the working class, and worship of Clause Four. With these old-style values goes a basically utilitarian attitude to art. This comes through – in a blurred and clumsy manner – at the end of Williams's brief study of George Orwell. Conceding that *Nineteen Eighty-Four* has 'a certain bleak honesty', he asserts that it is full of political contradictions which combine with the lack of what he terms 'any independent social identity'.

This language is so abstract you wonder what he is maundering on about. What is an independent social identity? What is the 'genuine terror' which the lack of that vague identity produced? Is this not a displaced religious language which simply says that Orwell was not worthy?

Williams goes on to preach Orwell quietly into the ground:

But what in Orwell was a last desperate throw became for many others, absurdly, a way of life. His radical pessimism was combined with an accommodation to capitalism and with an illusion of the imminence of social democracy. What in Orwell broke down in terror became a comfortable and persistent world view (in an older generation even lasting beyond Vietnam).

The only useful thing, now, is to understand how it happened. In a confused and mobile history, his kind of loss of identity has continued to occur. The affiliation he tried to make, that he was ready to die for, was prevented by the political contradictions of those years and was lost, finally, in illusion and terror. The writer had to be split from the political militant.

The weasel word is 'useful'.

With this insidiously inclusive and banal term, Williams exhorts us to put our shoulders to the wheel. The flaws he detects in Orwell's novel are merely sign-posts on the way towards a social goal, towards the holy city of a genuinely socialist society (Williams had been disillusioned with Harold Wilson's Labour government).

In the closing sentence of his extended essay he introduces a faintly elegiac cadence – it's too feeble to quote – and suggests that we have to 'move on'. History did move on. Williams's study was published in 1971; eight years later, the old-style labourism at the work's emotional centre was swept away by Thatcherism. Williams is like a character in a Chekhov play who speaks in anxious clichés in a society sleepwalking towards revolution – Hare cleverly compares him to the self-important professor in *Uncle Vanya*.

Though he was socially comatose in this work, Williams did insist on placing literary texts in society, and Edward Said and other critics from the Arab world have praised his achievement. But I have never read a page of his prose without being filled with boredom and itchy rage – how dreary! how decent! how morally self-righteous that unemphatic, uninflected manner is. It has no kick and no skip. None at all.

Opening *The Country and the City*, one of Williams's major works, I find a few dreadfully dull paragraphs on Joyce's *Ulysses*. That epic work doesn't fit the moral canon which Leavis, Williams and other Cambridge critics designed years back – it rejects that terrible puritanism at the heart of the criticism still written by those who slavishly follow Williams.

Williams was an anti-tank captain in the last war, became an adult education tutor and helped create that brave old world that was Attlee's Britain. For all the reverence we may feel for that heroic social moment, there's no point in trying to hold on to a static version of the values which inspired it. Let us take Clause Four and the collected criticism of Raymond Williams and gently place them in some heritage museum, then appoint Raphael Samuel curator and lock the door. Piety be damned!

THE CRITIC AT THE BREAKFAST TABLE

POLEMIC

In a novel called *Left of Centre* which is now safely out of print, Paul Johnson wrote what is generally agreed to be the most embarrassing spanking scene ever penned.

The eclipse of that otherwise unreadable novel did nothing to dim the memory of the cringe-making episode which was continually recalled to mind by Johnson's public and social behaviour. This often involved drunken and boorish conduct towards women, including his wife. On a famous occasion in a Greek restaurant in 1973 he struck her across the face for disagreeing with him in public and, when rebuked for this by a colleague of mine, threatened to put him through a plate-glass window. At a lunch given for the Israeli ambassador to Britain in the boardroom of the old *New Statesman* I watched Johnson bully and barrack Corinna Adam, then the foreign editor, as she attempted to engage Gideon Raphael in conversation. 'Don't listen to her. She's a communist!' he kept bellowing, his face twisted and puce with drink. 'Fascist bitch!' he finally managed, before retiring to a sofa on the other side of the room and farting his way through a fitful doze for the rest of the meal. The combination of his choleric, lobsterlike complexion and his angry mane of ginger hair used to excite comment. 'He looks,' said Jonathan Miller after witnessing one of his many exhibitions of dementia, 'he looks – like an explosion in a pubic hair factory.'

Christopher Hitchens reviewing Paul Johnson's *The Intellectuals* in *Critical Quarterly* (1989)

Polemics are rarely sighted these days. In the late 1980s Chatto and Windus published a series called *Counterblasts* which aimed to revive the lost art of political pamphleteering. Looking at counterblast number three – John Lloyd's *A Rational Advance for the Labour Party* – I find a crease at the bottom of page four. I never got to the next page and I never will. Lloyd's polemic didn't work. Why?

The reason *A Rational Advance* didn't work is because it was worthy, decent, essentially tame. Though its title echoes one of the most famous pamphlets ever published – Jonathan Swift's *A Modest Proposal* – it has nothing of the cool insinuating irony of that master of angry compassion. Nor has it any of the ferocity of that other great Irish polemicist, Edmund Burke.

Here is Burke in 1796 attacking a fabulously wealthy English aristocrat who had benefited from enormous land grants made to his ancestors by Henry VIII and who supported the democratic principles of the French Revolution.

The Duke of Bedford is the Leviathan among all the creatures of the Crown. He tumbles about his unwieldy bulk; he plays and frolicks in the ocean of the Royal bounty. Huge as he is, and whilst 'he lies floating many a rood' he is still a creature. His ribs, his fins, his whalebone, his blubber, the very spiracles through which he spouts a torrent of brine against his origin, and covers me all over with the spray – everything of him and about him is from the Throne. Is it for *him* to question the dispensation of the Royal favour?

These sentences from *Letter to a Noble Lord* form one of the most famous passages in all polemical writing in English. The ducal leviathan takes us right to the heart of this kind of critical writing – to its visceral, primitivist urgency, its imaginative over-the-top extremity, its almost cherishing playfulness. Burke has found a magnificent symbol for the noble duke and he refuses to let it go. He even throws in a quotation from *Paradise Lost* about the whale-like Satan floating many a rood to develop the theme of magnitude and – in his supremely unfair terms – evil.

The link between Hitchens's onslaught on Johnson and Burke's famous attack on the Duke of Bedford is important, because the polemicist is always an isolated and irascible figure motivated by what Yeats terms 'passionate intensity' – a writer who goes into battle by invoking the tiny band of fellow polemicists who practised this difficult art. George Orwell was one of them, and he's an inspiration for Hitchens. Like Swift, Orwell observes the sheer awfulness of power, its lies, its tacky language, and he writes angrily – he wants to destroy something. So does Hitchens.

Here, we have the belief that the critical writing matters and can alter by its intensity the poise of forces and shift the huge weight of the status quo. If this sounds deadly serious it both is and isn't, because there is always a line from polemic to social comedy, to the group of wits who sit in the coffee house and smile over the latest pamphlet. So Hitchens moves from his angry opening to a scene where the apoplectic Johnson complains of the seating arrangements at some dinner and exits, shouting: 'I won't have it. I'm going to my club.' His customary difficulty in fighting his way across a room was compounded on this occasion, Hitchens says, by his wife who tried to persuade him to stay and then pointed out sweetly, 'Paul dear, you don't *belong* to a club.'

If this all seems a bit personal, it's because the book under review – Johnson's *The Intellectuals* – seeks to discredit the ideas of important figures like Marx and Rousseau by examining their private lives. Johnson is therefore fair game, and with uproarious delight we learn that he once kicked the family dog, Parker, at a cricket match (nice touch, the cricket match).

The whole point about polemic is that it throws fairness, decency, balance, objectivity, the rules of cricket, to the winds – there must be something wild about it. It's the intellectual equivalent of boxing. But there's something deeper. Polemic is the articulation of conscience – it's about bearing witness to injustice and folly. At its heart, there is a tragic cry which receives no answer. Hitchens talks tough, but behind his celebrated writing you sense a terrible tragic disgust. It's the cry of Lear on the heath attacking all 'servile ministers'.

Beyond the sport of admiring Hitchens's contempt for Paul Johnson, Bernard Ingham, George Bush and Bill Clinton, we catch the damp reek of something anguished and desperate that's altogether other than his sometimes raspy adjectives and studied put-downs. It is the voice of true pity, something inseparable from anger. Yes, the polemical critic knows when to lose his temper. And how.

TIMING PRAISE

The freedom of Chaucer is heightened, in Burns, by a fiery, reckless energy; the benignity of Chaucer deepens, in Burns, into an overwhelming sense of the pathos of things; – of the pathos of

human nature, the pathos, also, of non-human nature. Instead of the fluidity of Chaucer's manner, the manner of Burns has spring, bounding swiftness. Burns is by far the greater force, though he has perhaps less charm. The world of Chaucer is fairer, richer, more significant than that of Burns; but when the largeness and freedom of Burns get full sweep, as in *Tam o'Shanter*, or still more in that puissant and splendid production, *The Jolly Beggars*, his world may be what it will, his poetic genius triumphs over it. In the world of *The Jolly Beggars* there is more than hideousness and squalor, there is bestiality; yet the piece is a superb poetic success. It has a breadth, truth and power which make the famous scene in Auerbach's Cellar, of Goethe's *Faust*, seem artificial and tame beside it, and which are only matched by Shakespeare and Aristophanes.

Here, where his largeness and freedom serve him so admirably, and also in those poems and songs, where to shrewdness he adds infinite archness and wit, and to benignity infinite pathos, where his manner is flawless, and a perfect poetic whole is the result, – in things like the address to the mouse whose home he had ruined, in things like *Duncan Gray, Tam Glen, Whistle and I'll come to you, my lad, Auld lang syne* (the list might be made much longer), – here we have the genuine Burns, of whom the real estimate must be high indeed. Not a classic, nor with the excellent σπουδαιότης of the great classics, nor with a verse rising to a criticism of life and a virtue like theirs; but a poet with thorough truth of substance and an answering truth of style, giving us a poetry sound to the core.

Matthew Arnold: 'The Study of Poetry' (1880)

Never begin with immediate undiluted praise of a subject. All you can do, when the first rapture ends, is hesitate, qualify, and inevitably go down from the high note you struck at the start.

Matthew Arnold knew this, because he realized that the critic is out there in front of an audience and has to hold its attention. His audience is confident, patriotic, almost entirely English, and so he begins the section on Burns with a passage which appears to dismiss him as a poet who deals 'perpetually with Scotch drink, Scotch religion, and Scotch manners'.

In the course of a few sentences he uses the word 'Scotch' fourteen times – his audience relaxes, takes his side, even titters a bit in conscious superiority. It enjoys the knockabout critical comedy in which Arnold says that Burns appeals to his 'partial' fellow Scots. But those readers who aren't Scottish, how can they like a poet who portrays not a beautiful, but 'a harsh, a sordid, a repulsive world'?

Next, Arnold finds that Burns 'comes short of the high seriousness of the great classics'. He is not Dante, and neither is Chaucer. Arnold's audience, though it would prefer Chaucer to equal Dante, is comfortable with this judgement, because Arnold has just praised his poetry in terms which sound rather like the march of the British Empire: 'His poetry transcends and effaces, easily and without effort, all the romance-poetry of Catholic Christendom; it transcends and effaces all the English poetry contemporary with it, it transcends and effaces all the English poetry subsequent to it down to the age of Elizabeth.'

This is Chaucer dominant, and Arnold's almost martial sense of his poetic power is meant to be compensation for a lack of high seriousness. Wilde thought the term was fatuous, and in 1895, fifteen years after 'The Study of Poetry', he mocked it in the subtitle to *The Importance of Being Earnest*: 'A Trivial Comedy for Serious People'. But in 1880 Arnold is sitting pretty. That big blank phrase *high seriousness* settles everything.

It's then that he begins to shift his ground and aim at that strain of passionate eulogy which must underpin all criticism, however often it may pick and qualify and hesitate and find fault. His account becomes a competition between Burns and Chaucer which gives precedence to the founder of English poetry and yet focuses attention on Burns. Here, Arnold has a spontaneity, a spoken directness and concentrated enthusiasm of manner which makes the 'Scotch' and earlier passages mere disposable stages towards critical lift-off. A criticism that is incapable of this larkrise, this unpremeditated song, is bound to be barren. Belle-lettrism be damned, we as audience demand to be surprised by joy, inspired and uplifted. The critic must have a vision of the artist's work as a unique whole: here Arnold celebrates Burns's Promethean energy that invisibly pits him as a national force against the Union and the imperial identity which this rather suave critic otherwise held dear.

Looking, more coldly, over Arnold's performance, those unenthused slouchy spectators Jasper and McMoon are troubled:

'*Puissant!*' says Jasper, 'a vile word, *puissant.*'

'For the Norman barons,' says McMoon. '*Powerful* is just about OK, but yon other critical term is dire and dead.'

'Like *splendid*,' says Jasper. 'Pure Derek Nimmo. Twee. Anglican. Pathetic.'

Other readers may doubt the idea of a poetry which is 'sound to the core'. It reeks of bible classes or public school. OTC stuff.

So beware such ways of praising a literary text. Jasper and McMoon will laugh at you.

On the other hand, look how Arnold pushes Goethe to one side (a bash at Bismarck, that?), and sets Burns high up with Shakespeare and Aristophanes. This is praise which is all the stronger for seeming to be won against the grain of Arnold's own prejudices about Scottish culture, Presbyterianism and the erotic wildness of Burns's poetry.

We admire in Arnold what he praised in Greek classical culture – a quick and flexible intelligence. Prissy and mannered and safe as Arnold can so often be, he is a critic who soars on occasion. This is one of the high spots in his much mythologized, much maligned criticism.

'Would this be a balanced verdict you're offering?' asks McMoon.

Perish the notion – but I'm glad you raised it.

GOING TO LAW, OR THE WEIGHT OF A MAN'S BALLS

Richard Hoggart recalled
Examined by Mr Hutchinson

Q: Mr Hoggart, yesterday afternoon you expressed the view that in this book D. H. Lawrence was expressing a view which was virtuous and puritanical in some aspects. Do you remember?

A: Yes, I do.

Q: I want to ask you first of all, is that view of yours an original view?

A: I do not believe it is original, I do not remember where I have seen it. I think perhaps I arrived at it myself, and I'm sure other people have too.

Q: I wonder whether you could just enlarge on the reasons why you take that view of this book?

A: Yes. I am thinking, first of all, of the whole movement of the book, and the enormous insistence which Lawrence makes on arriving at relationships of integrity with whomever you are related, not only the women with whom you are in love. This seems to me – it is my own background too – to be one of the characteristics of the English Nonconformist Puritan tradition, and to be in striking contrast with the much more permissive attitude which one finds in most novels, very often good ones. If one looks at *Lady Chatterley* one is struck markedly again – it is almost as though he is saying 'I will be responsible for my own conscience right to the last end'. This I take to be one element in the British Puritan conscience. It seems to me strikingly in evidence in this book.

The *Lady Chatterley's Lover* Trial, 1960

Critics are always on oath, but they're seldom asked to step into the witness box and offer an opinion to a judge and a jury. But in October 1960, a number of distinguished literary critics – Noël Annan, Helen Gardner, Graham Hough, Richard Hoggart – stood up in the Old Bailey and expressed enthusiasm for the unexpurgated version of D. H. Lawrence's *Lady Chatterley's Lover*.

This piece of high comedy has gone down in cultural folklore. The prosecuting barrister's question to the jury – 'Is it a book that you would even wish your wife and your servants to read?' – was the most hilarious moment of the trial. But there were many others, like this exchange between Hoggart and the same barrister, Mervyn Griffith-Jones:

Griffith-Jones: 'The life within life, the sheer warm, potent loveliness. And the strange weight of the balls between his legs! What a mystery!' . . . Perhaps that is enough. That again, I assume, you say is Puritanical?

Hoggart: It is Puritanical in its reverence.

Griffith-Jones: What! Reverence to the balls? Reverence for the weight of a man's balls?

Hoggart: Indeed yes.

Silly Griffith-Jones. What an enemy of freedom. This benighted lawyer was trying to hold back the 1960s! Why, he even suggested that Lawrence's novel was badly written. But as Germaine Greer was to point out much later, in *Lady Chatterley* are enunciated 'all the great phoney lies of sexual liberation'.

Lady Chatterley is a dire novel, one that reeks with a special nastiness. Lawrence hates Jews, blacks, lesbians and the Irish. There's no love in this novel, not a trace of it. Only a cold factitious sexual lyricism. And a lot of race hatred which, oddly, Greer ignored.

But what of Hoggart's contribution to the case? Is this an example of a critic making a disastrously mistaken aesthetic judgement because he wanted to assist the cause of free speech?

The first point is that Hoggart is accurate in his cultural placing of Lawrence. The second is that his answers embody one of the weaknesses of nonconformism – that relentless stream of compulsive autobiography which takes everything personally and cries *me, me me!* without ceasing.

The critic ought not to draw attention to his or her personal experience. The readers out there do not care what the critic had for breakfast or what social class he or she belongs to. Hoggart was seeking street cred and once more demonstrating how the English class system warps the spirit. This is the critic as a sort of unconscious Norman Wisdom. It may still go down well in Albania, but for the rest of us it's eejit talk. Background ought never to be asserted. The critic who says, 'Look at me, I'm from Ballymena,' is going to find only ballymeanings in texts that have become mere mirrors of the self. As James Joyce shows, there are nets of class, race, language, gender that must be struggled through, not embraced. It's fine to glimpse your own navel now and then, but don't ever gaze at it.

What a pity, though, that a huge, almost invisible subject – English nonconformist culture – was raised in the Old Bailey in a way that sounded pompous and egotistical. Apart from Val Cunningham's study of nineteenth-century novels, *Everywhere Spoken Against*, and a short book by Donald Davie, *A Gathered Church*, there is silence on this matter.

Should the critic therefore adopt a formal and impersonal style?

Yes – the critic should be cold and distant as the stars. Rigorous, without a shred of personality. The critic should have nothing for breakfast but a starvation diet of shadows and ambition. T. S. Eliot is one of the masters of this classical style of literary criticism. What he says of the artist in 'Tradition and the Individual Talent' is also true of the critic, whose progress must be 'a continual self-sacrifice, a continual extinction of personality'.

But after a while we're bound to find this impersonality arid, even sinister. Then along comes Lawrence, who cries out in his essay on Benjamin Franklin: 'Anyhow, I defy you. I defy you, oh society, to educate me or to suppress me, according to your dummy standards.' Direct, emphatic, spontaneous, honest – this is the dissenting style of criticism and no one is better at it than Lawrence. Its purpose is to set people arguing, to chase critical judgement in the sheer crack of people talking vehemently, hilariously, passionately. *Lady Chatterley* is grim, but Lawrence is a risk-taker who always demands a relationship with his readers. Like Greer, he forces you to take a position. For all his overweening egotism, he lacks the steely authoritarianism of Eliot. He's more like Captain Ahab – many admirers have helplessly followed him to the bottom of the ocean, but others rise like Ishmael and live to tell the tale.

What we see in Hoggart's ill-judged witness is the bubble trail of an admirer being pulled down in the huge suck of Lawrence's personality. Resist that dominance. And never seek to be ratified by any institution, either, ought to be the critic's motto.

LINGO JINGO

As by the cultivation of various sciences, a language is amplified, it will be more furnished with words deflected from original sense; the geometrician will talk of a courtier's zenith, or the excentrick virtue of a wild hero, and the physician of sanguine expectations and phlegmatick delays. . . . The tropes of poetry will make hourly encroachments, and the metaphorical will become the current sense; pronunciation will be varied by levity or ignorance, and the pen must at length comply with the tongue; illiterate writers will . . . by publick infatuation rise into renown, who, not knowing the original import of words, will use them with colloquial licentiousness, confound distinction, and forget propriety.

Samuel Johnson, 'Preface to The Dictionary' (1755)

The political nature of Johnson's remark is evident in his choice of words which by their resonance associate an ignorance of the classical languages with sexual immorality and the breaking down of class division: 'public infatuation', 'colloquial licentiousness', and 'confound distinction'. As the compiler of the *Dictionary*, founder of literary criticism, and author of a prose style that was avidly read and imitated, Johnson was a uniquely important populariser of ideas which emphasised the distinction between refined and vulgar English. His rhetorical sweep brought vividness and range to concepts which might otherwise have had neither. No other writer concerned with language . . . had such an extensive and tenacious appeal . . .

Olivia Smith, *The Politics of Language* (1984)

Olivia Smith is an American scholar whose ideas about language were prompted by the effects of the Black and women's movements in the United States. As the balance of power shifted, Black-American began to be understood as a language with its own grammar and syntax, instead of being regarded as sub-standard and incorrect.

Applying this experience to language in England during three troubled decades, she discovered a massive argument about English which reverberates to this day. Smith's spirited study drew a lot of attention and influenced critics and researchers. They understood that only those critics who feel passionately about the history of the English language can have a vision of its hurtling creativity, its chariot of fire. As the psalmist, or more properly his translator, puts it:

When Israel went out of Egypt, the house of Jacob from a people of strange language; Judah was his sanctuary, and Israel his dominion.
The sea saw it, and fled: Jordan was driven back.

The language we write and speak has an atavistic memory of the grip which that 'strange language', Norman French, used to have on it. The Normans tried to crush it, but English fought its way out of internal exile. Like an echo of the Big Bang on the far fringes of the universe, that victory is still present in the language we use now. There is a libertarian exultation in the very sinews of English which rejoices in its early success and which is always trying to escape from experts who want to make it respectable.

Samuel Johnson famously toasted the next insurrection of black slaves in the West Indies, but he was no liberator. He forced the language so successfully into a straitjacket that the culture has yet to shake it off. The influence of this much mythologized, often endearing Tory anarchist still broods over us. Gloomy, vulnerable, bullying, anxious and authoritarian, he successfully froze the active energies of the language and forced it to sound like a translation from Latin. Monotonous, singsong, full of polysyllabic phrases and obvious balances, he writes a kind of rhyming prose which sounds boring and phoney. Like a man holding his breath to stop himself from boking, his style has a heavy, almost velvety conservative gloom which hangs over those polished periods like the atmosphere in some neo-classical mausoleum.

In the extract Smith criticizes, Johnson means by 'illiterate' those writers who are ignorant of Latin and Greek. Though he was an epic conversationalist – great crack altogether – he wants to repress the vernacular and fix the language forever as a second-rate version of Latin. He wants it to be eternally toasting a king over the water and never to recover its native confidence. *Out upon it sir*, as conversational Johnson would most uncivilly interrupt, *you're talking like a damned Whig*. But as Jasper was telling McMoon only the other day, now that the inglorious Union is fading, it's about time that criticism took an Orange tinge.

Recently, Johnson has become popular among literary theorists, really because his Tory scepticism and contradictions suit a critical approach which stresses indeterminacy and the way texts 'turn against themselves'. Olivia Smith's study is passionately different from this cosy sinking feeling of nothing really mattering much. She examines how a series of neglected figures like John Fell and John Horne Tooke associated spoken English with liberty and used the speed or 'despatch' of speech to challenge the cumbersome, hierarchical view of the language Johnson encouraged. Like the children of Israel they seek to break out of his 'intolerable' Latinity, as that gritty lexicographer Noah Webster called it. William Cobbett protested against the 'passive obedience' inculcated by the rules of grammar in popular textbooks, and he published his own grammar book to affirm the values of what Smith terms 'an intellectual vernacular'.

Who remembers Cobbett's grammar now? Like almost all his works, it's out of print and can only be found in cheap Victorian editions in second-hand shops. Can Britain ever become, in the Australian poet Les Murray's phrase, a 'vernacular republic'? How do we free up our prose and make it sassier, wilder, more direct and fluid?

These are tricky questions, but they point to the inescapable fact that critical prose must carry a memory of the battles fought in previous generations and beware of the nets that are cast for it – in Britain it's the net of class and deference, coupled with a forgetfulness about the languages English has suppressed, which entangles so many writers. So the critic has to try to get near the raw edge of the language and stay with it. Which means that critical prose must follow Cromwell and choose the free way, not the formal.

Bring me my bow of burning gold – bring me my arrows of desire.

WHO COMES FIRST?

Gilbert: But, surely, Criticism is itself an art. And just as artistic creation implies the working of the critical faculty, and, indeed, without it cannot be said to exist at all, so Criticism is really creative in the highest sense of the word. Criticism is, in fact, both creative and independent.
Ernest: Independent?
Gilbert: Yes; independent. Criticism is no more to be judged by any low standard of imitation or resemblance than is the work of poet or sculptor. The critic occupies the same relation to the work of art that he criticises as the artist does to the visible world of form and colour, or the unseen world of passion and of thought. He does not even require for the perfection of his art the finest materials. Anything will serve his purpose.

Oscar Wilde, 'The Critic as Artist' (1890)

Who comes first, the artist or the critic?

Until relatively recently there was no doubt about the answer to that question: artists had precedence, critics were followers and latecomers, the humble if sometimes pretentious servants of the work of art. Writers created beautiful poems, fictions, plays, while critics extracted a few of their favourite quotations, added some prose commentary and called the result, say, *Early Modernism* or *James Hogg: The Last Phase*. So critics were merely opinionated and belated shadows, totally dependent on the works they discussed.

Oscar Wilde disagreed, and in a witty dialogue essay, 'The Critic as Artist', he allows Gilbert free rein in a long conversation with his morally serious friend Ernest, who represents the Victorian middle class's dedication to the gravid and responsible side of Matthew

Arnold's critical writings. Ernest follows Arnold in believing that it is the function of the critic to make us see the work of art 'as in itself it really is'. Gilbert thinks this is boring and foolish – the purpose of the critic is to have fun, to make things up, to invent.

Criticism is about enjoying yourself. The great critics communicate the pleasure of art. They do so by becoming the equivalent of actors or musicians, who perform and at the same time interpret a work in performance.

Ernest is worried by Gilbert's stance, and wonders whether criticism really is a creative art. Oh yes, says Gilbert. It works with materials, and puts them into a form that is 'at once new and delightful'. And then, pushing his argument to extremes, as the true critic has to on occasion, he argues that the highest criticism is, in its own way, 'more creative than creation'. And – with a wink at one section of his audience – Gilbert remarks that criticism, 'as the Greeks would put it', is an end in itself.

James Joyce agreed – criticism comes first, is truly and originally creative and classical. This is the inspiration behind Joyce's anti-novel, *A Portrait of the Artist as a Young Man*, where his pitiless double Stephen Dedalus cleaves his way through a Dublin childhood and adolescence to find his vocation as an artist. But before he can realize that ambition, he has first to become a critic.

At his boarding school, one summer evening, Stephen Dedalus becomes obsessed with a rhythmic pattern of words – *soft grey sky, soft grey air* – and with a different pattern of sound that is made by cricket bats hitting cricket balls. He keeps playing with the sounds, repeating them, until the first section of the novel closes with a reprise of the sounds:

The fellows were practising long shies and bowling lobs and slow twisters. In the soft grey silence he could hear the bump of the balls: and from here and from there through the quiet air the sound of the cricket bats: pick, pack, pock, puck: like drops of water in a fountain falling softly in the brimming bowl.

This is a critical moment of vision, an epiphany, for what the young Stephen is realizing is that he is enveloped in a style and language that is mannered, precious, dead, second-hand and second-rate. It is, as we now would say, a 'discourse' shaped by the prose of Walter Pater and Cardinal Newman, and by Wilde's prose as well.

But how to break out of it into a different form, rhythm, style? Joyce later describes Stephen passing Dublin shop-signs and feeling imaginatively shrivelled as he walks among 'heaps of dead language'. How can he get out of this staleness? By learning Irish and writing in that language, perhaps? No, that wasn't the road he wanted to take. He must instead revitalize the English language, make Irish-English stretch and sing and fly out at the stars.

This is where the sound of the cricket balls comes in. Their consonantal chunkiness, the playful form and elaborate rules they imply, the subtly accurate recognition that they sound exactly like plucked violin strings or water-drops hitting the tight, still surface of a bowl of water — these sounds signal the classical spirit which breaks down soppy, kitsch, self-regarding phrases like 'falling softly in the brimming bowl'.

This critical perception was equivalent for Joyce to the difference between classicism and romanticism. Romanticism, he wrote, is an insecure, unsatisfied, impatient temper' whose wild figures 'lack the gravity of solid bodies'. Classicism is a temper of 'security and satisfaction and patience'. It has a 'quick intelligence' and is always aware of limitations.

Hearing the sound of an almost invisible cricket match, Stephen recognizes the gravity of solid bodies and the contrasting flimsiness of routine, sentimental, facile rhythm — 'and from here and from here through the quiet air'. *Pick pack pock puck* — the critic seizes on these sounds and prepares the ground for art to grow.

After you, says the artist to the critic.

AMBIGUITY

That time of year thou mayst in me behold,
When yellow leaves, or none, or few do hang
Upon those boughs which shake against the cold,
Bare ruin'd choirs, where late the sweet birds sang.

In me thou seest the twilight of such day,
As after sunset fadeth in the West,
Which by and by black night doth take away,
Death's second self that seals up all in rest.
In me thou seest the glowing of such fire,
That on the ashes of his youth doth lie,
As the death-bed, whereon it must expire,
Consum'd with that which it was nourish'd by.
  This thou perceiv'st, which makes thy love more strong,
  To love that well, which thou must leave ere long.

William Shakespeare, Sonnet 73

To take a famous example, there is no pun, double syntax, or dubiety of feeling in 'Bare ruined choirs, where late the sweet birds sang', but the comparison holds for many reasons; because ruined monastery choirs are places in which to sing, because they involve sitting in a row, because they are made of wood, are carved into knots and so forth, because they used to be surrounded by a sheltering building crystallized out of the likeness of a forest, and coloured with stained glass and painting like flowers and leaves, because they are now abandoned by all but the grey walls coloured like the skies of winter, because the cold and Narcissistic charm suggested by choir-boys suits well with Shakespeare's feeling for the object of the Sonnets, and for various sociological and historical reasons (the Protestant destruction of monasteries; fear of Puritanism), which it would be hard now to trace out in their proportions; these reasons, and many more relating the simile to its place in the Sonnet, must all combine to give the line its beauty, and there is a sort of ambiguity in not knowing which of them to hold most clearly in mind. Clearly this is involved in all such richness and heightening of effect, and the machinations of ambiguity are among the very roots of poetry.

William Empson, *Seven Types of Ambiguity* (1930)

Empson's response – a quick critical aside – to Sonnet 73 is probably the most famous moment in modern literary criticism. *Seven Types of Ambiguity* was drafted in two weeks when Empson was an undergraduate at Cambridge and published in 1930. It is at once the rock and the shifting sand on which a mass of critical commentary is founded.

An ambiguity, Empson states, means something 'very pronounced, and as a rule witty or deceitful'. He uses the term in an extended sense and concentrates on any verbal nuance, however slight, which 'gives room for alternative reactions to the same piece of language'.

The joy of ambiguity as a critical concept is that it allows the reader to find subtleties in the text which open out like a secret labyrinth below the printed words. To adapt Eliot's lines on the Treaty of Versailles, poems are revealed to have 'many cunning passages, contrived corridors / And issues'. Tracing what Empson terms 'the machinations of ambiguity', we enter the intricate, devious world of the imagination with its multiple ironies, its trembling light and fluid playfulness. Here we find 'the very roots of poetry'.

Many of the critics Empson influenced took this concept to mean that what counted above all was 'close reading' or 'practical criticism' – the minute, painstaking analysis and dissection of image and phrase. Empson's teacher, I. A. Richards, published a famous and influential critical handbook called *Practical Criticism* in 1929, and for several generations critics minutely dissected poems and plays, sometimes even novels. Marvell's lovely, witty, estranging couplet in 'The Garden' – 'Annihilating all that's made / To a Green Thought in a green shade' – drew armies of close readers to discover whole universes in its grain of sand. Hostile to biography, historical experience and ideology, this critical practice eventually became so imploded and self-serving that it collapsed. Texts ceased to be richly ambiguous and were now deconstructed into abysses of contradictions where nothing added up. Everything was decentred, ideologically produced, somehow routinely manufactured and dead or random and botched. Literature became a scrap-heap of cultural artefacts, authors became 'producers', and the world turned into a series of discourses shaped by innumerable concerted conspiracies. Everywhere voices were raised against the 'hegemony of canonical texts' and against those critics who still persisted in trying to tease out their hidden meanings.

Yet in Empson's application of the concept of ambiguity and his brilliant, helter-skelter interpretation of Shakespeare's line, the parenthesis '(the Protestant destruction of monasteries; fear of Puritanism)' compresses a powerful historical sense. Until he threw in that reference to Henry VIII's destruction of the monasteries how many readers understood the specifically Catholic sense of desecration that the line carries? This is an image of the crucifixion which expresses a tragic sense of loss, abandonment and violent destruction. His flesh hangs on his skeleton like dead leaves or like Christ's body on the cross – how perfectly Shakespeare fuses the images of body/tree, body/cross, body/church. And how strangely the agony of being hopelessly in love becomes a cry out of the English Catholic experience of martyrdom and persecution. Shakespeare is writing in code because the state is Protestant: this hard historical fact, Empson is suggesting, is the reason why his language and imagery are so multilayered, Ovidian, shifting, and involve so many complex machinations. The term 'machinations' insists that imaginative language is inescapably political, however hard subsequent critics tried to remove art from the real world of human struggle and suffering.

Empson also published poetry, and he succeeded in making several generations of students into poets of the text who knew how densely charged literary language can be. Among the poets he influenced, the present Poet Laureate, who also studied English at Cambridge, worked for ten years on an enormous study of Shakespeare which insists that his Catholicism was deep, committed, tragic and heroic. In *Shakespeare and the Goddess of Complete Being* Ted Hughes argues that Shakespeare in his plays and poems witnesses the 'prolonged savage persecution and threatened extermination of the old catholic tribe'. If we ignore the tribal texture of feeling in Shakespeare's bare ruined choirs, we are left with a lyric which reduces emotion to the merely private and personal, and so denies that solidarity or identification with historical experience which is such a crucial part of our existence as social beings. There is such a thing as society, Shakespeare, Empson and Hughes tell us, and this is what it feels like when an oppressive state in the name of reform starts to tear things apart.

GETTING IT WRONG

Herman Melville is describing his fall into the sea from the yard-arm of the U.S. frigate *Neversink* . . . as he floats under water in an almost trancelike state:

'I wondered whether I was yet dead or still dying. But of a sudden some fashionless form brushed my side – some inert, soiled fish of the sea; the thrill of being alive again tingled in my nerves, and the strong shunning of death shocked me through.'

Commenting on these lines F. O. Matthiessen writes:

'But then this second trance is shattered by a twist of imagery of the sort that was to become peculiarly Melville's. He is startled back into the sense of being alive by grazing an inert form; hardly anyone but Melville could have created the shudder that results from calling his frightening vagueness some "soiled fish of the sea." The *discordia concors*, the unexpected linking of the medium of cleanliness with filth, could only have sprung from an imagination that had apprehended the terrors of the deep, of the immaterial deep as well as the physical.'

The only difficulty with this critical frisson about Melville's imagination, and undemonstrable generalisations such as 'nobody but Melville could have created the shudder', and so on, is the cruel fact that an unimaginative typesetter inadvertently created it, not Melville; for what Melville wrote, as is demonstrated in both the English and American first versions, was coiled fish of the sea. It is disheartening to find the enthusiasm of critics so easily betrayed . . .

Fredson Bowers, 'Textual and Literary Criticism' (1959)

F. O. Matthiessen – a distinguished American critic of the 1930s and '40s – is fascinated by that strange, suggestive phrase 'soiled fish of the sea' in Herman Melville's novel *White-Jacket*. He is so taken with the phrase that he cannot follow his intuition and hear a sceptical inner voice telling him that the Pacific Ocean wasn't polluted in those days and that therefore there must be some mistake. After all, Melville, the epic novelist and prophetic chronicler of the soul of the new American republic, deserves this kind of enthusiastic interpretation. And perhaps there was something in Matthiessen which felt that nature and the body were somehow filthy. He wrote an early study of T. S. Eliot, who looked on ordinary life as 'dung and death'.

The craggy textual scholar Fredson Bowers was dismayed by the vulnerability of Matthiessen's judgement, though in fairness he includes a remark by one John W. Nichol, who said that the 'change' – 'mistake' he means – does not invalidate Matthiessen's general critical position: 'It merely weakens his specific example.' Nevertheless, Nichol adds that such a 'textual slip' could in the proper context have offered 'an entirely false conception'.

Is Nichol trying to argue that textual accuracy doesn't matter too much? Bowers insists that it matters absolutely, and he goes on to call William Empson a 'frequent offender' because of his 'careless use of imperfect texts, complicated by a more than ordinary inaccuracy of quotation'. Empson, for example, mispunctuates an Eliot poem in order to praise its syntactic ambiguity, when he should have checked his quotation before hazarding an interpretation.

For the critic who went, or would go, to school with Empson, this is a salutary criticism. To adapt Baden-Powell on personal hygiene, the good critic checks his or her references and quotations not once, but several times. And the critic, like a true swell, stays in the best hotels where the finest editions are available from room service.

But supposing time and money are short? Or supposing you are stranded, like the revered German scholar Erich Auerbach in a foreign country in wartime with only a few books and an inadequate library? The possibilities for special pleading are endless, so perhaps the only thing to do is to admit it's a fair cop, guv, to whatever forensic Bowersite convicts you of error, and then try to do better. The history of criticism is littered with tiny errors, huge *faux pas* and comic misquotations. What critic worth their salt has a clear conscience on this matter?

There is another argument, which wasn't available to John W. Nichol back in 1949 when he commented on Matthiessen's boo-boo, and that is to argue for the *ludic* or what has been termed 'the free play of critical discourse'. This displaces Bowers's judicial authority (well, let's pretend it does) and allows for what another American critic, Harold Bloom, terms 'creative misprision'. It's a slightly daunting, pseudo-technical term which states that all readings of literary texts − especially those made by other creative writers − are always misreadings or acts of 'creative correction' which empower new works of art. Thus D. H. Lawrence, writing an essay on Melville, is really following a spoor that will lead him to a new poem, novel or story, maybe even a play (Lawrence's paintings, too, are linked to his admiration for that great primitivist).

The problem for the critic is that there is no work of art which lies beyond their critical argument − Matthiessen wasn't preparing the ground for his own novel, he was simply writing criticism. But Harold Bloom isn't impressed by this, arguing that most so-called accurate readings are worse than mistakes, and that 'perhaps there are only more or less creative or interesting misreadings'. He makes this suggestion because he wants to restore the link between creative and critical writing.

It wasn't until early in the last century that a major critic emerged who wasn't also a major writer. Until William Hazlitt began to publish his essays and reviews, the significant critics had also been important writers. Dryden and Samuel Johnson wrote poems and plays as well as literary criticism, and so did Coleridge. And although Bloom has published a novel, he made his reputation as a critic and will always be regarded as one *tout court*. But he very properly insists that the act of interpretation is creative. What he is saying is: don't play safe as a critic. Don't be obvious, don't be boring, don't offer plodding descriptive explications of whatever text you happen to be trying to interest your audience in. Launch yourself out into space and don't heed the consequences. As the wise butterfly collector Stein tells another seafaring character – Conrad's Lord Jim – 'to the destructive element submit yourself and with the exertions of your hands and feet in the water make the deep, deep sea keep you up'. The critic is a daredevil, an existentialist, a risk-taker, a header. If the artist in Joyce's famous symbol is Daedalus, the patient craftsman, the critic is Icarus, the impatient son who condemns himself to fly eternally into the sun and fall back among the soiled fish of the sea.

CAMP

Many things in the world have not been named; and many things, even if they have been named, have never been described. One of these is the sensibility – unmistakably modern, a variant of sophisti-cation but hardly identical with it – that goes by the cult name of 'Camp'.

A sensibility (as distinct from an idea) is one of the hardest things to talk about; but there are special reasons why Camp, in particular, has never been discussed. It is not a natural mode of sensibility, if there be any such. Indeed the essence of Camp is its love of the unnatural: of artifice and exaggeration. And Camp is esoteric – something of a private code, a badge of identity even, among small urban cliques.

Apart from a lazy two-page sketch in Christopher Isherwood's *The World in the Evening* (1954), it has hardly broken into print. To talk about Camp is therefore to betray it. If the betrayal can be defended, it will be for the edification it provides, or the dignity of the conflict it resolves. For myself, I plead the goal of self-edification, and the goad of a sharp conflict in my own sensibility. I am strongly drawn to Camp, and almost as strongly offended by it. That is why I want to talk about it, and why I can. For no one who wholeheartedly shares in a given sensibility can analyse it; he can only, whatever his intention, exhibit it. To name a sensibility, to draw its contours and to recount its history, requires a deep sympathy modified by revulsion.

Susan Sontag, 'Notes on Camp' (1964)

This is one of the most celebrated essays in modern critical history. To read it is to watch a plenary consciousness at work.

Sontag's notes are for Oscar Wilde, and are interspersed with quotations from that camp genius. Sontag defines camp as, among other things:

> one way of seeing the world as an aesthetic phenomenon
> disengaged, depoliticized – or at least apolitical
> androgynous
> reeking of self-love
> effacing nature

Old Flash Gordon comics, 1920s women's clothes belong to the 'canon of camp'; Greta Garbo and Jayne Mansfield are camp, and so are the cast-iron orchid stalks that frame the entrances to the Paris metro. Camp is often bad or decorative art, and is best defined through lists of often very amusing examples – the speeches of Charles de Gaulle, certain turn-of-the-century postcards.

This essay deluges the reader with things that are 'old-fashioned, out-of-date, *démodé*'. Old bakelite phones, the sort you get in black and white movies, would be one example, feather boas another. There is a junky eeriness about camp. It comes back at us like those movies with the phones in them, and those smooth, sculpted black cars driven by smokers in suits.

Camp lets us glimpse the terrible void at the heart of style. Maybe it's self-protective and a form of revenge? Down with romantic authenticity, it says. Nature and earnestness, Wilde's twin targets, are frauds. Camp is self-consciously self-conscious: like listening to dialogue that is all monologue. It could, as non-campers like Jasper and McMoon would say, get severely on your tits. Which is perhaps why Sontag writes her essay in numbered notes. In this way, she both reins her subject in and suggests its plenitude.

For Sontag, the 'great serious idol' of camp taste is Greta Garbo. Her 'incompetence' as an actress enhances her beauty. She is 'always herself'. This recalls a remark of Jean Cocteau's which haunted Sartre: 'Victor Hugo was a madman who believed he was Victor Hugo.' Perhaps camp is a form of alienation? A type of passive existentialism?

Sontag's point number 36 is that there are other creative sensibilities beside the seriousness – both tragic and comic – of high culture and of the 'high style of evaluating people'. One cheats oneself as a human being if one only has respect for the style of high culture, 'whatever else one may do or feel on the sly'.

To define camp more closely, Sontag discusses the kind of sensibility whose trademark is 'anguish, cruelty, derangement' – Bosch, Sade, Rimbaud, Jarry, Kafka, Artaud are her examples. Camp, she says, is third among the 'great creative sensibilities': the sensibility of 'failed seriousness, of the theatricalisation of experience'. It incarnates a victory of style over content, aesthetics over morality, irony over tragedy. It puts the world in quotation marks, and is strangely philosophical because it saturates everything with thought and irony. Auden's question in 'Mountains': 'Am I / To see in the Lake District then, / Another bourgeois invention like the piano?' is a brilliant piece of camp. It comes out of his early Marxism and out of Wilde's habit of seeing nature as culture. Ever since Turner and the Impressionists, Wilde remarks, London's sunsets have improved remarkably. And there is a poem by Elizabeth Bishop in which fireflies are seen rising 'like the bubbles in champagne'.

Which tells us that camp has a lot to do with leisure and consumption. Watching an old movie on a wet afternoon, we are watching ourselves watch *an old movie on a wet afternoon*, and we know that we have entered the dusty hell – or is it heaven? – of past consumption. But all is not lost: Sontag's point is that camp taste 'transcends the nausea of the replica'.

This is the critic as poet: what wit, what sensuous intelligence! How we love being told that camp is the answer to the problem of how to be 'a dandy in the age of mass culture'. The new-style dandy 'appreciates vulgarity' and understands that this sensibility is 'the good taste of bad taste'. Which is a way of theorizing about why we watch *Blind Date* and why Dame Edna is so subversive and popular. Is the concept of celebrity part of the rhetoric of a camp sensibility? Where are the lengthy critical studies called *Camp and Shopping in the Age of Mass Culture*, *The Semiotics of Camp*, *Late Bourgeois Camp*?

Maybe we also need a word of warning. I recall an article in a gay journal some years back which argued that camp is in practice highly conservative, that it accepts the status quo in a passive fashion by sanctifying things-as-they-are. So is there such a thing as Radical Camp? Elizabeth Bishop, at moments in her poetry – the way she links colonialism and consumerism, for example – is one answer to that. So is the presiding genius of Sontag's essay, Oscar Wilde. When the cultural history of republican radicalism in these islands is written, dear Oscar will be there, garlanded with lilies.

Yes, lilies belong in the list, and so – at least among men – does the word 'dear'. As in 'Time for a drink, dear boy.'

DEEP CULTURE

'No, Emma, your amiable young man can be amiable only in French, not in English. He may be very *aimable*, have very good manners, and be very agreeable; but he can have no English delicacy towards the feelings of other people – nothing really amiable about him.'

'You seem determined to think ill of him.'

'Me! not at all,' replied Mr Knightley, rather displeased: 'I do not want to think ill of him. I should be as ready to acknowledge his merits as any other man; but I hear of none, except what are merely personal; that he is well grown and good-looking, with smooth, plausible manners.'

Jane Austen, *Emma* (1816)

The generally successful careers of the Austen brothers – in the Navy, the law, the Church – illustrate the relative mobility of the English class system, and the steady tide of prosperity which made it relatively common at the end of the 18th century for young men to better themselves. Had times been less prosperous for the gentry, Jane Austen might have written less sanguinely about the role of the individual within society. Had they been more prosperous for her, she might not have seen so clearly the effect on her class of its increasing wealth.

She is the gentry's greatest artist, and she arises at a time when they seem to be still at the height of their power, influence and prestige . . . In England, the gentry had steadily over the centuries acquired complete legal ownership of the land . . . England had no peasantry: only tenant-farmers and agricultural labourers, who had the civic advantage of not being legally directly subordinate to the gentleman, and the disadvantage of having no rights whatever to the Land. On his own estate and in his village the English gentleman enjoyed a position of unique autonomy.

Marilyn Butler, *Romantics, Rebels and Reactionaries: English Literature and its Background 1760–1830* (1981)

Jane Austen is the only English writer whose admirers regularly used to refer to her by her first name. Rather like Margaret Thatcher, who tiresomely spoke of Churchill as 'Winston', readers who talked about 'Jane' fondly believed they were supping on the ambrosial essence of English culture. That type of *cultural essentialism* (as it is now known) disappeared a couple of decades back, and we're now much more interested in the historical and ideological forces which shape works of art. But the cultic status of 'Jane' still holds in certain quarters, and when Edward Said linked *Mansfield Park* with the West Indian slave-trade in his *Culture and Imperialism*, some reviewers were enraged. The *Independent*'s Geoffrey Wheatcroft, on a trip to Antigua, felt the need to defend Austen's use of that island as merely a plot device. There are certain writers you criticize at your peril. As a Labour MEP fatuously remarked of Clause Four, they are at the 'deep roots' of the culture.

In *Emma*, the *aimable* but unamiable Frank Churchill is the type of figure who was attacked by the reactionary *Anti-Jacobin Review*. They wrote, in 1798, that the 'regicides of France and the traitors of Ireland find ready advocates in the heart of our metropolis, and in the seats of our universities'. Frank Churchill has a first name which suggests he is French and therefore not, frankly, English, while his surname (significantly, it's adopted) links him with the brilliant Whig general – Winston's ancestor – who betrayed James II and ushered in the Glorious Revolution with a foreign king at its head.

But Knightley, the perfect gentleman, is named for St George, the patron saint of England. And, as if the patriotic point isn't clear enough, his home is called Donwell Abbey – so he represents the Church of England, tradition, heritage, or what Austen calls 'true gentility, untainted in blood and understanding'. Describing his estate, she praises 'English verdure, English culture, English comfort, seen under a sun bright, without being oppressive'.

Now look at what Butler has to say about the gentry – and at how subtly Austen's last adjective naturalizes what was in fact an extremely oppressive political system. 1816, the year of *Emma*'s publication, was a time of depression and discontent, with a major riot in London's Spa Fields in December. I can't help thinking that Emma's tedious, sweet old selfish dad is a benign portrait of the mad and reactionary George III. The novel is dedicated to the Prince Regent, whom Austen privately detested, a contradiction no amount of secret irony can explain.

'But Jane Austen is a great, timeless, transcendent novelist,' comes the cry from the wheatfields. 'You can't drag her down into the mud like this.'

Neither Butler nor Said deny that Austen is a great writer, but neither is prepared to fall down and blindly worship a (in some ways) polemical text that has been ripped out of its social context: the dismal year which followed Wellington's victory at Waterloo. Butler challenges ahistorical readings of a period which is still known as 'Romantic' – although it wasn't until the 1860s that the term was posthumously clamped on to a very mixed body of writers. Writers do not exist in isolation, she says – writing and publishing are social activities. Texts are living things that are collectively produced, not fossils we rescue from dried-up river beds after the flood of history has subsided.

Take William Blake. Butler wants to argue that we shouldn't read his work as though he was 'singlehandedly the author of his own text'. We need to recognize the 'corporate author', the urban sub-class linked to the vast body of Dissenters who tried to uphold the principles of the Glorious Revolution – and who often supported the American and French Revolutions. Early reviewers of Wordsworth and Coleridge's *Lyrical Ballads* linked that work with Tom Paine's *The Rights of Man* and attacked the poems which used 'mean' (that is, non-genteel) language.

For some critics, it's a straightforward choice between admiring writers whose political opinions they share and disliking those writers they disagree with. But although *Emma* might be simply – crudely – anti-Jacobin, it is also a subtle psychological portrait of a young woman growing up in a very limited society from which there is no romantic possibility of escape.

The novels, therefore, are also critiques of the new individualism, built on an ethic of social responsibility and duty. Faced with competition and a society that felt increasingly atomized, Austen is no more complacent than is a very different writer like John Clare, England's most gifted nature poet.

So Jane Austen's fabled two inches of ivory had a social message etched on them. Think of all those rural post offices the government recently tried to close – where would 'Jane' have stood on that issue?